# THE MEDIEVAL JEWISH MIND

לזכרון
נשמות הורי היקרים
אבי מורי ר' אליהו בר' אברהם מרדכי
ואמי מורתי מ' רבקה בת ר' זליג

*In loving memory
of my dear parents*
*ALEXANDER and REBECCA PEARL*

# THE MEDIEVAL JEWISH MIND

*The Religious Philosophy of Isaac Arama*

*by*

CHAIM PEARL

VALLENTINE, MITCHELL—LONDON

BY THE SAME AUTHOR
A Guide to Jewish Knowledge
A Guide to Shavuoth
The Minor Jewish Festivals and Fasts
Rashi: Commentaries on the Pentateuch

First published in Great Britain 1971
by Vallentine, Mitchell & Co. Ltd.,
18 Cursitor Street
London, E.C.4.

ISBN: 0 853 03043 X

Copyright © CHAIM PEARL 1971

All rights reserved. No part of this publication may be reproduced, stored in a retrievel system, or transmitted, in any form or by any means, electronic, mechanical, photocopying, recording or otherwise, without the prior permission in writing of Vallentine, Mitchell & Co. Ltd.

Printed and bound in Great Britain by
Tonbridge Printers Ltd., Tonbridge, Kent.

# CONTENTS

| | | |
|---|---|---|
| | Preface | Page vii |
| | Introduction and Biographical Note | 1 |
| 1 | Philosophy and Religion | 6 |
| 2 | The Conception of God | 18 |
| 3 | The Creation of the World | 27 |
| 4 | The Soul | 56 |
| 5 | Free Will | 70 |
| 6 | Reward and Punishment | 88 |
| 7 | The Purpose of Divine Law | 104 |
| 8 | Prophecy | 129 |
| 9 | Summary | 151 |
| | Epilogue | 164 |
| | Notes | 169 |
| | Abbreviations | 197 |
| | Selected Bibliography | 198 |
| | General Index | 203 |

# PREFACE

This book was commenced some years ago at the suggestion of the late Dr. Isidore Epstein, a distinguished principal of Jews' College, London. At the outset, the works of Isaac Arama seemed of great interest and value because they provided voluminous source material for the preacher. Indeed, the *Akedah Yitzhak* had been used for centuries for precisely this purpose. But it soon became clear that Arama's writings were philosophical rather than homiletic and that they contained a searching examination and exposition of all doctrines in the wide range of Jewish beliefs. The chief problem for the reader interested in Jewish theology however is that Arama's treatment is not structured and that his teachings on any one subject are widely scattered throughout his bulky commentaries on the Bible. It was therefore considered advisable to systematise his philosophy by arranging his expositions under several categories so that the reader can more easily understand his approach to a particular subject without having to search through his entire work. The categories included in this book represent the list of subjects which were the chief concern of all medieval Jewish theologians.

A highly significant aspect of Arama's work is that it shows his eclectic treatment of his subject. He knew the writings of his predecessors and contemporaries and is well acquainted also with Arab theologians and the Greek philosophy which they popularised. Arama sifts their writings, he rejects what is unacceptable and embraces into his own philosophy what he regards as consistent with Jewish teaching. This eclecticism is both a weakness and a strength.

It is a weakness in that he shows little originality—beyond his presentation and homiletic insights. It is a strength in that he is able to gather together the vast corpus of Jewish religious teaching and evaluate it all in the light of the normative Jewish doctrine of his time. From this point of view Arama becomes an ideal representative medieval Jewish philosopher and his writings become an authentic expression of the medieval Jewish mind.

For technical reasons, very short Hebrew phrases have been

## PREFACE

transliterated in the body of the text as well as in the notes. The method of transliteration here adopted is simplified and, I hope, avoids all unnecessary academic small points which often obscure rather than help.

I am happy to acknowledge my gratitude to the publishers, Vallentine, Mitchell, and their executive and technical staff for their work in seeing the manuscript through the Press. The value of a book of this kind is necessarily enhanced by an index and I was relieved to be able to put this arduous task in the capable hands of my students Daniel Bradburd, Stephen Leon and Alan Mintz.

New York, 1970

# INTRODUCTION AND BIOGRAPHICAL NOTE

## I

Among the Jewish teachers of the Middle Ages, Isaac Arama has been regarded as a great master of homiletics and his writings have been sources for Jewish preachers even till this day. Despite Arama's popularity as a homiletic source, however, scant attention has been paid to him as a religious philosopher, although his long sermons contain abundant material covering such a vast scope that hardly a subject of Jewish philosophical interest is omitted. It is true, of course, that Arama shows, on the whole, very little originality in his philosophical dissertations, yet neither does he slavishly follow the teachings of any of his great predecessors. He is, for example, keenly aware of the magnificent stature of Maimonides, frequently referring with admiration to his views, yet not infrequently will he claim the right of disagreeing with the great master.

Arama's philosophy is rather eclectic and he casts his net wide over the whole range of medieval Jewish philosophy, including the writings of Arab philosophers and the Arab translations of classical Greek thinkers. His chief ambition was to present to the people an exposition of Judaism which could be accepted on a philosophical basis always emphasising that religion is the master over philosophy and not the reverse. Arama felt consstrained to make his attempt at a reasoned explanation of Judaism because he lived in an age when Greek and Arab philosophy were widespread among the intelligent, and many Jews felt the necessity to enquire into the traditions and doctrines of their ancestral faith. Further, in Arama's day Jews were often compelled to attend churches and listen to Christian sermons, many of which were well ordered and rational expositions in support of Christian doctrines. In the face of this dangerous threat to the religious loyalties of his people, he regarded it as his strict responsibility to explain Judaism by argument and dissertation as learned and as philosophically expounded as were the efforts of the non-Jewish theologians on behalf of their doctrines.

In order to equip himself for this task, Isaac Arama read widely and studied deeply the learned works of his Jewish contemporaries and predecessors. He also made himself familiar with Arab and Greek thought. He quotes freely not only from Talmud and Midrash but from the classical exegetes, such as Rashi, Ibn Ezra and Nahmanides; from the grammatical works of Ibn Janah and David Kimhi; from the philosophical works of Isaac Israeli, Judah Halevi, Bedaresi, Abraham bar Hiyyah, Abraham Bibago, Gersonides, Crescas and Albo. In addition, he keeps Maimonides as his central guide in most of his discussions. Among his non-Jewish references he frequently comments on Aristotle's Ethics and Metaphysics and on Aristotle's commentators, Averroes and Ibn Sina. Algazali is also drawn upon. It is this vast treasury of scholarship ranging from biblical literature to the Talmud, Midrash, Jewish commentators and philosophers, Greek philosophy and Arab learning that gives Arama's writings depth as well as authority.

Arama's chief work is the *Akedath Yitzhak* and is the one which made his name both as a philosopher and as a master preacher. The whole work is made up of one hundred and seventeen long essay sermons contained in one hundred and five chapters, written in the order of the weekly readings from the Pentateuch. While among German Jews the main emphasis in sermons was didactic, particularly on ritual matters, and among the Spanish Jews the stress was on philosophical points of interest, Arama harmonised both aspects of the old sermon and interspersed them with moralisings of interest to his hearers. Each sermon is divided into two component parts, the investigation and the exposition. The investigation takes the form of an analysis of the broad philosophical idea underlying the scriptural text and it is here that Arama shows his ability as a philosopher of Judaism attempting to explain the transmitted teachings of his faith to his people.

In the second part the author examines the scriptural text and illumines it with reference to the conclusions he has arrived at in the investigation. It might be thought that this division creates an artificial dichotomy in each sermon. The fact is, however, that investigation and subsequent exposition are joined harmoniously together so that there is no sense of artificiality or disjointedness. On the contrary, each sermon with its two parts is presented as a whole. For indeed, while Arama's intention in the investigation is to present the ideas and beliefs of Judaism in a cogent and attractive form which would be acceptable to a generation trained and accustomed to philosophical enquiry, he yet offers this presentation through the instrument of the biblical and rabbinic texts. Again, while in the second part, the exposition, his chief purpose is to explain the scriptural passages, he does so chiefly with reference to the philosophical standpoint arrived at in the investigation.

In the investigation Arama covers most of the theological questions which exercised the minds of the thinkers of his day ; the nature of God, creation, angelology, the soul, death and immortality, free will and God's foreknowledge, sin and repentance, the Messiah, the place and role of Israel in the world, the character of the Law, the purpose of ritual prayer, the relation of philosophy to religion, the nature of prophecy—all these and many other questions are examined. To the extent that he finds the ultimate truth always in Judaism of tradition and does not follow an independent line of enquiry, irrespective of where it may lead him, Arama is no philosopher in the technical sense but rather the philosopher of Judaism. He examines the current non-Jewish beliefs and practices as well as the opinions and behaviour patterns of his co-religionists and weighs them all up in the scale of his critical faculty which is securely pinned down to Jewish teaching. Each opinion is critically examined in the light of what he considers to be true Jewish doctrine. He thus relinquishes none of his religious heritage and while feeling himself free to explore other avenues, he does so only to return to the greater truths which he finds in Judaism.

Arama wrote his *Akedath Yitzhak* over many years and before completing it in its present form he wrote and finished a smaller work, *Hazuth Kashah*, which was published after the larger work and which contains a summary of his main theological position. In addition to the above, Arama is also the author of a commentary on the Five Megillot and of a small volume, *Yad Avshalom*—a commentary on Proverbs which was written in memory of a beloved son-in-law who died shortly after his marriage.

The edition of 1849, with commentary by H. J. Pollack, contains in one collection the *Akedath Yitzhak, Hazuth Kashah* and the commentary on the Megillot. It is this edition of Arama's writings which has been used in preparation of this work.

## II

Of Arama's life story we know comparatively little and what outline we possess is indicated chiefly in his own writings and particularly in his Introduction to the *Akedah Yitzhak*. H. J. Pollack's edition contains a brief biography of Arama. Pollack's source is almost entirely our author's Introduction to the *Akedah* though he also acknowledges the following, *Sefer Yuhasin* (Abraham Zacuto), *Shalshelet Hakabalah* (Ibn Yahyah), *Zemah David* (David Ganz), *Siftei Yeshenim* (Shabtai Bass), *Koreh Hadorot* (David Conforte), *Seder Hadorot* (Yechiel *Heilprin*) and German Jewish historians of whom he makes a direct mention of the historian Jost. Israel Bettan, in his *Studies in Jewish Preaching*, writes briefly on Arama's life story and in his interesting essay on our author he makes use of Pollack's biography and of Arama's own Introduction to the *Akedah*. From the above all too scanty sources the following main biographical points become clear.

Isaac ben Moshe ben Meir Arama was born in northern Spain about 1420. The exact year is not known nor is the town of his birth. He lived, as a youth, in the town of Zamora in the province of Leon, where he received a thorough talmudic education at the feet of eminent scholars who lived in Zamora and in nearby France. In due course he became teacher to numerous students who flocked to him to study Talmud under his expert guidance.

His fame as a scholar soon spread and he was appointed rabbi of Tarragona, a city on the Mediterranean coast, and which was some considerable distance from Zamora. This fact he places to the credit of the Jews of Tarragona who were zealous enough for Jewish scholarship to import a rabbi and teacher from afar. It would appear that while in Tarragona he ministered also to the Jewish community in Fraga which, although described by Arama in his Introduction, as being near Tarragona, was nevertheless about sixty miles distant from it. Arama's desire to set up a talmudical college similar to the one he headed in Zamora received a set-back when it became clear that his new community could not support even the few students who accompanied him from Zamora. They accordingly left him and he turned his efforts into other directions.

His great contribution towards the philosophical explanation of Judaism was developed in his Sabbath sermons and he worked on the entire collection during his stay in Tarragona.

Later on he moved to the more important rabbinate of Calatayud, in western Aragona, and it was there that he thoroughly revised his material for publication. In Calatayud he also wrote his other commentaries on the Five Megillot and on *Proverbs*. Moreover, he had the opportunity at last of turning again to his chief delight in teaching young students and he was enabled to set up a college to which the young came for guidance and instruction.

The date and place of Arama's death are somewhat obscure. Most authorities agree that he joined the exiles from Spain in 1492. Abraham Zacuto thinks that he finally went with his son, Meir, to Salonica where he died. So, too, Jost in his history, writes that Isaac Arama died in Salonica. David Conforte, the author of *Koreh Hadorot*, thought that only Meir made his way to Salonica and if Isaac left Spain he would have died in Naples. This is the opinion of Israel Bettan, who writes that Isaac Arama died in Naples in 1495. H. J. Pollack is alone in assuming that Isaac Arama died in Spain a short while before the expulsion.

# 1 PHILOSOPHY AND RELIGION

## I

Jewish writers in the Middle Ages invariably recognised the importance of two sources of religious knowledge or truth. The first was revelation and the second was reason. The first arose out of the authority of the Scriptures, while the second found its texts in the Aristotelian and neo-Platonic philosophies which were widely known and discussed by the theologians of Judaism, Christianity and Mohammedanism. It was not always a question of reconciling a conflict between revelation and reason, between religion and philosophy; sometimes it was a problem of explaining Scripture and the Talmud philosophically. The Bible does not contain a systematic presentation of theology nor can the Talmud and Midrash be regarded as scientific or lucid expositions of basic questions of Jewish belief.

Until the main impact of medieval Greek and Arab thought was felt by the Jews, it could be said that little if any concern was shown at the absence of an independent and consistent philosophy. The homiletic interpretations of the rabbis may have been inconsistent and contradictory but Judaism rested not so much on an acceptable or consistent philosophy as on the authority of the Law. In general, a large amount of freedom was allowed in the field of theological or philosophical speculation, although strict conformity and consistency was expected in the field of practical religious law. It has been pointed out often enough how the Bible itself contains confusing and contradictory references on doctrinal subjects that are generally regarded as fundamental and passages can be found for and against a particular teaching. Thus, in the matter of the freedom of the will, for example, one can find in the Bible passages which seem to make clear the teaching that man is perfectly free to choose his path in life, for good or bad[1] while it is a simple thing again to refer to texts which seem to suggest that the reverse is true and that man's conduct is determined by God.[2]

In other matters, too, the Bible is either vague or silent. The first chapter of Genesis gives an account of the creation but so many aspects of the subject are omitted for the satisfaction of the enquiring mind. How did God create the Universe? Was there an external existing hylic matter or was the Universe created *ex nihilo*? What of man's soul? Is it form or matter, pre-existent or created with man, destructible or immortal? What of God himself? What is the nature of his unity? Can we speak of God's essence or his attributes?

Of course, as has been intimated already, the rabbis of Talmud and Midrash were not entirely without their concern for philosophical truth and theological doctrine but their efforts in this field must be regarded as mainly homiletic than scientific since their attempts at philosophical speculation were undertaken not so much to evolve a theological truth as to illustrate a moral teaching. This is the rabbinic Aggada, or non-legal part of their writing; it is the poetry of Judaism, its lore and its spiritual beauty. But when it is isolated and objectively examined it can hardly be recognised as a clear systematic and unambiguous statement on Jewish religious philosophy. Maimonides is thus not at all hesitant in repudiating some of the statements of the rabbis as being completely unphilosophic.[3]

The fact is that the rabbis of the talmudic period were themselves not serious philosophers nor did they consider it harmful that Judaism had no set of theological doctrines which were universally accepted. Schechter has pointed out that the majority of modern Jewish theologians have accepted the belief that Judaism has no dogmas. This is the only dogmatic belief that Judaism possesses (after the basic dogma of God's unity).[4] He himself goes on to show how wrong this view is, but there is no smoke without fire and in so far as it gained credence it must stem from this basic fact that Bible and Talmud are not concerned with theology or a systematic presentation of a set of beliefs. They reveal the Divine law and teaching interpreted as a way of life. There is truth in the well-known cliché that the emphasis is on deed rather than on creed. That is not to say that correct belief was unimportant, but rather that correct belief was implied and assumed to be already in possession of the individual. Indeed, correct deed could only spring from correct belief.

But there was no need to overstress the importance of correct belief since the people in any case never questioned the validity of the basic assertions about God, Torah, or reward and punishment. Still less was it necessary to analyse or systemise the details of such beliefs into a formal theology. Consequently the rabbinic writings abound in various assertions which, while they imply a belief in the One God, in a Creator, in revealed Torah or in reward and punishment, nevertheless show a curious partiality for a wide individual freedom in the description and explanation of many of such beliefs.[5]

## II

It was not until the tenth century when Jews in Spain and elsewhere came face to face with the impact of Christian and Mohammedan theology that it became necessary to restate philosophically the beliefs of Judaism. Moreover, about the same time the Jews were beginning for the first time to read and consider the writings of Aristotle and neo-Platonism. By then the Arabs had learned well from the Syrian Christians and in turn were able to influence Jewish thought through their Arabic translations and commentaries. A new world of ideas was opening up for the Jewish scholars in which for the first time they read about the Greek philosophical theories of creation, of form and matter, of substance and motion, of the theories of time and place, of the spheres and their movers. Aristotle too had something to say on the soul, on immortality, on the law and on the virtues. In fact there was hardly a subject in which they were interested religiously which was not illumined for them by Aristotle or what they thought was written by Aristotle.[6]

Then there was inaugurated a period of intense philosophical activity on the part of the Jewish scholars. At times it was undertaken in order to combat the claim of other religions: often it was undertaken to cater for the enquiring mind already trained in philosophical speculation but which needed satisfactoy proof for the validity of Judaism. Thus, Maimonides wrote in his Introduction to his celebrated philosophical work that it was his object 'to afford a guide for the perplexed,' i.e., 'to thinkers whose studies have brought them into collision with religion, who have studied philosophy and have acquired sound knowledge and who, while firm in religious matters, are perplexed and bewildered on account of the ambiguous and figurative expressions employed in the Holy Writings.'[7] For Maimonides religion was true and reason was valid. It was only necessary to apply the latter to explain the former and his *Guide* endeavours to do that, i.e., to explain Judaism scientifically.

Without compromising with the essential beliefs of Judaism

the method of critical analysis is brought to bear on the beliefs of Judaism which he then attempts to prove are true by a process of reasoning and to show that their truth is demonstrable according to reason. For some scholars of his day and afterwards Maimonides laid too much emphasis on the importance of reason and too little on pure faith when there arose a question that could not be entirely explained by the process of reason. Thus it was felt that Maimonides compromised with the biblical view of prophecy and miracles, to mention just two, while his views on the educative purpose of sacrifices raised a storm of protest all around. At the same time, there were others who went further than Maimonides in their rationalisations.

But, it may be argued, this was bound to happen as soon as Judaism was treated philosophically. Religion rests on faith, on the supernatural revelation of the Divine word and will; philosophy is a science resting on reason. Is it proper to expect the two to meet and for one not to give way to the other? In so far as the accepted traditions of Judaism, born out of the Bible, were apparently modified to suit the demands of reason, Maimonides and the others were philosophers while those who were not prepared to adapt their biblical viewpoint may not deserve that title, being still restricted from accepting a truth demonstrated by reason when it is contrary to traditional teaching. Maimonides was a philosopher because he was a rationalist, but can we say the same of the others who recognised final truth only in the accepted religious tenets of their people?

This touches on the whole problem of medieval philosophy and raises the basic question—not restricted by any means to Jewish philosophy of the age—as to whether the religious scholasticism of the Middle Ages can be properly called philosophy at all. The historians of philosophy would undoubtedly admit that Thomas Aquinas constructed a philosophy, but only because he was a rationalist. So, too, as we have already said, Maimonides, as a rationalist, enters the ranks of the philosophers.

But there were others like Judah Halevi in the eleventh century and Isaac Arama in the fifteenth who, far from taking reason as the source of truth, found that reason was often inadequate to reach truth and that we must find final truth in a more ultimate source. For them that source is revelation. So we are entitled for one moment to consider whether such a system as can be built up on that initial faith is really philosophy.

The answer, for a thinker like Halevi, would be that for the

Jew revelation is philosophically true. God exists and he is the Creator—this he will prove by philosophical argument. This being true then, it is logically demonstrable that God is omnipotent, that he can intercede in the affairs of the world and man, and that man was created by him for a purpose. That purpose is no secret since God revealed his will through Moses and the Torah. Revelation is then the final measuring instrument by which we can test the validity of our reasoning. Revelation is the other side of the truth of God's existence and we can accept it as the starting point in our philosophical system. We do not understand the whole of revelation; rather we do not easily understand it. Therefore we turn to philosophy in order to draw out the content of our faith and the nature of revelation.

Only the Greeks and the rationalists can reason without the help of religion and to that extent they fall into many errors. It is possible then to use religion as the starting point of philosophy; to turn to philosophy in order to *explain and illumine* the truths of religion. The Jewish religious philosopher would accept Lessing's remark 'The great religious truths were not rational when they were revealed, but they were revealed so that they might become so.'[8] Here, too, we get an indication of the meaning of the idea of philosophy as the handmaid of religion. It is in this first sense then that we can speak of a Jewish religious philosophy, i.e., a philosophy which the religious Jew used *to explain the content* of his religious faith.

But in a second sense also, religion can be philosophically supported since the religionist can attempt to demonstrate that true human happiness lies in obedience to God's law. The Ethics of Aristotle are certainly part of his philosophy, but no more than the ethics of the Torah are part of Jewish philosophy. What the Jewish philosopher will do is to arrange the ethics of Judaism into an ordered and reasoned system and to prove that greatest happiness is found in obedience to such a law. It will be shown by this that reason alone can never satisfy reason and that without God's law there can be no satisfaction.

What were the main topics discussed in medieval Jewish philosophy? Generally speaking there was nothing relating to human life and thought which was regarded as outside the legitimate area of their scholarly enquiry. 'Nihil humani alienum a me puto est.' Terence's dictum would adequately summarise their attitude, as it is indeed true also of Judaism generally. Nevertheless, it is possible to recognise the chief subjects of concern under the following headings. God, his unity and attributes, the creation, the revelation and the phenomena of prophecy and miracles, the apparent conflict between God's omniscience and man's freedom, the concept of reward and punishment, the purpose of the Divine commandments and the origin and destiny of the soul. In addition to these there were many matters relating to medieval cosmological ideas touching upon the heavenly spheres, their number, composition and motions. But those are no more than of purely academic interest to the modern reader while the questions mentioned first are still of considerable importance to the modern discussion.

After these introductory remarks we can come to our own author.

## III

It can be repeated that when it became a question of conflict between religious faith and the theories of philosophers then Arama invariably sides with religious faith. For him philosophy is a help in understanding religion and if it cannot do that, or if it seems that philosophical argument is against religious tradition then it is philosophy which is wrong and religion which is right. That is his credo briefly put and in which he shows himself quite consistent. For this reason it has been suggested that Arama is no philosopher; he has nothing new, nothing original to offer.[9] Worse, he fails to follow the line of philosophical enquiry to a conclusion irrespective of where it will lead him. But this criticism is not altogether valid. Arama's philosophy contains religious faith as its first reasonable plank. To believe in God the Creator who exercises his control over the individual man he holds to be the most reasonable of all philosophies, attested by the word of God himself.

Like Judah Halevi before him, with whose attitude Arama has very much in common, he insists that reason and philosophy are quite inadequate to supply the answers to many problems affecting religion. It is only revelation that can help us to understand the truth about God's nature and his dealings with man. In so far as the philosophers do not possess revelation then they must fail because their methods are wrong and only the boastful fool will think that his own mind can lead him to the truth.[10] The Jews, however, are in a very unique position because they are all the people of revelation. Abraham was chosen by God because of his goodness and through him the

Hebrew tribe was singled out by providence. Later, the entire nation of Israel received the Torah and it is through the instrument of Torah, not through philosophical speculation, that we can approach an understanding of religious truth.

This attitude need not affect Arama's approach to every subject. He goes far, hand in hand with Maimonides, in his treatment of cosmological matters and parts company with him only on what appears to him to be a matter touching on religious faith. He makes a valuable philosophical contribution in his treatment of the nature of the soul while there is some originality in his theological position touching such subjects like prophecy and the purpose of Divine law. He concedes that descriptions of God in the Scriptures are metaphorical and hide a deep philosophical truth beneath a layer of simple language. Even when he submits as the only valid beliefs the traditional doctrines of Judaism he does so only after a critical examination of the other theories popular with the philosophers of his day.[11]

Arama's attitude towards the supremacy of religious tradition over Greek philosophy shows itself throughout the whole of the *Akedah*. But he wrote a little work called *Hazut Kashah*— 'A Burdensome Vision,'[12] in which he devotes himself almost exclusively to stressing this point. At the same time he uses the opportunity to castigate those other Jewish philosophers who, in their enthusiasm for Greek teaching, relegate the Torah to a position of subservience. Thus, the prefatory note of the first publisher gives as the purpose of the book . . . 'to stir up our zeal and raise an old-new complaint against those Jewish philosophers who deal shamefully with the Torah.'[13]

The relationship between religion and philosophy is illustrated by the relationship of a mistress to her handmaid.[14] The mistress is the authority over the other whose proper function is to help the mistress whenever needed. How strange it is when the positions are reversed and the mistress becomes subservient to her servant. But that is an illustration of the situation when religion has to be distorted to fit in with philosophical theory. This is the cause of the 'Grievous' or 'Burdensome Vision'— that the mistress is being supplanted by her handmaid.[15]

Arama, of course, recognises the usefulness of philosophy and he acknowledges that the Gentile philosophers merited the description *haside umot ha-olam* 'the pious of the nations,'[15] but it was not until Abraham came that God was recognised as the great author of life who concerns himself with

individual man. אברהם אבינו גברה ידו בכח פילוסופותו ובעוצם
חקירתו על כל חכמי דורו ונודעה לו מעלה יתירה על כלם בהגעת האמיתות
'Abraham our forefather was superior to all the wise men
of his generation in the power of his philosophy and the
strength of his reasoning, so in his attainment of the truth he
knew a greater excellence.'[17]

But this greater understanding was given to Abraham only
through his recognition of the truth about God. He showed his
superiority over all the others by his complete faith in God.
Indeed, the Divine command to Abraham to slay his son Isaac
is an illustration of this important point, that although the
command was beyond all reason yet Abraham was willing and
anxious to obey the voice of God since faith in God is far above
all consideration of the rationality of God's command.[18]
Abraham becomes then the prototype of those faithful Jews
who put religious faith above reason or who bend reason to the
service of Torah. 'There are those, however, who under the
disguise of innocence and piety repudiate the Torah and deny
its very principles, changing its meaning in order to make it
fit in with their fanciful philosophical theories which are a
source of extreme danger to the health of Judaism and the
Jewish people. These pseudo-philosophers pretend to be partial
to the Torah, or at least claim to be fair interpreters who wished
to effect a reconciliation between religion and philosophy. But
what happens in the result? Philosophy becomes too precious
a prize for them and rather than compromise with their theories
they change the meaning of the Torah.'[19]

Arama interestingly refers to the conduct of Christian theologians who are faced with a similar conflict between religious
beliefs and certain current philosophical teachings. These
Christians and even Mohammedans are more loyal to their
religious and traditional beliefs than are the Jews. 'For indeed,
Edom and Ishmael have acted more righteously than the rebels
of Judah. For although the others received their religion later
than the Jews they chose to be faithful and maintained their
religion so that nothing was conceded to philosophy. Particularly the Christians[20] maintained the veracity of their Scripture
and the account of the miracles, to demolish entirely the theories
of the philosophers, however illustrious and strong they were.
On the other hand, our own wise philosophers who were first
with Divine Torah which was given to them as an inheritance
and who had no share or portion in speculative philosophy
which was strange to them, they are the very ones who have

reversed the order and have now fallen in love with philosophy.'[21]

This is not to imply that Christian scholars have repudiated philosophy; not at all. They have simply taken the correct view that philosophy is the servant of religion and not its master. 'The Christians acknowledged the validity of philosophy and chose its ways and demonstrations, they built its walls and set fast its doors. But on any point where it is against their religion, whether in root or branch, they ascribe the deficiency to philosophy and to its inability to comprehend the wonderfully miraculous words of God on which prophecy is based. For Divine religion is high above philosophical research.'[22] This is as clear a general statement as we can expect to find in Arama on the relationship between these two sources of knowledge. Reason and philosophy are good but their scope is distinctly limited. They can help us to understand and explain much in religion but they cannot explain everything since they stop at the prophetic, at the miraculous, at the point where God intervenes in the life of the individual or nation. This is not the fault of reason and philosophy, it is just that their usefulness ends where religion continues. In this respect religion is on a higher level than philosophy.

So long as knowledge of religious truth is not compared say, with mathematics or physics, then all could be well. Philosophy can help us to understand the facts and the laws of science while revelation will open the doors to our understanding of religion. It is, however, because Jewish thinkers have failed to recognise the legitimate area of philosophy that Judaism has become impoverished. So Arama complains 'And with regard to our faith we have indeed become a proverb and a byeword to all the world. For while many have retained their steadfastness in Divine Torah, believing in the creation, in miracles, in prophecy and in reward and punishment, we remain in our iniquity, and are robbed and bereaved of it.'[23]

## IV

Now what were the special religious-philosophical problems which gave Arama and his age so much concern? In an interesting passage[24] Arama gives a list of ten questions which seem to have been the debating points of his age and puts the query 'Why did God not reveal the truth about these things in the same way as he revealed the commandments from Sinai? His answer is that such a revelation could cause only confusion since ordinary men would never understand the truth about these things. The only safeguard we have is in faith and so long as we believe that there is a Creator who is a personal God then all else will follow. Arama's query and reply are, however, of less importance in our present context than his list of points which were the popular theological problems of his day. They are as follows:

1. How can the many emanate from the One God who is a simple unity?
2. How can the first material sphere be moved by its intelligence which is pure spirit?
3. Does God move the spheres himself without any intermediary?
4. How does God know future contingencies and the things which change when his own knowledge is unchangeable?
5. How can God's knowledge of future events be connected with things which do not yet exist?
6. How can God's foreknowledge of man's choice still leave man free to choose?
7. What are God's attributes, and how can he be said to have attributes at all?
8. Are the spheres spiritual beings for which reason they move in a circular direction as against material bodies which fall rectilineally?
9. Why do some spheres move from east to west; others from west to east?
10. What is the exact number of the spheres?

This list is by no means exhaustive since Arama deals with many other matters not mentioned above. Yet they give a useful indication of some at least of the problems of his time. As can be seen, several of the above questions are cosmological and the list may indicate where lay a chief centre of interest in medieval philosophical discussion. In his polemic against the Jewish philosophers Arama shows more concern however for safeguarding the traditional attitude towards Divine providence and knowledge, prophecy and the truth of miracles. He refers to Divine knowledge and providence, to the literal truth of the miracles and to reward and punishment as the *sh'losha pinot ha-bayit* 'three corner-stones of the house.'[25]

In another place he explains that his task is to provide an adequate answer to those false philosophers who bring their dangerous opinions to bear אם בעגיגי האותות והמופתים ואם באופני הידיעה וההשגחה והנבואה 'whether in matters relating to the signs and miracles or with reference to God's knowledge and providence, or to the phenomenon of prophecy.'[26] The trouble with the philosophers is that their rationalisations about God and creation have established him as the first cause of all existence without any power of intervention in natural law. Having become slaves to the Greek concept of natural law and cause and effect there is no room at all for the supernatural; miracles, prophecy and providence are ruled out. As with the Greeks, so with these false philosophers, God has become the insensitive impersonal first cause and nothing else. שמו בעיונם את הבורא ית' כעמוד זה החזק והאמיץ שכל העולם בנוי עליו לא רואה ולא שומע גם לא מרגיש גם לא יודע רק את עצמו אלו ישוער נעדר, יעדר המציאות כלו ואלו כל המציאות יעדר ישאר הוא, בקיומו וזהו תכלית שלמותו אצלם. 'In their speculations they have made the Creator, blessed be he, as a mighty strong pillar on which all the world is built. He does not see or hear, neither can he feel. Nor does he know anything other than himself. If it could be imagined that he did not exist then all other existences could be missing. While even if all other existences should be missing he would remain in existence. This they hold to be the limit of his perfection.'[27]

This heresy comes about, continues Arama, through overmuch philosophising about God. By removing from him all corporeality, plurality and sensory knowledge we take away all concept of knowledge and activity which are usually associated with such normal attributes and so people fall into the error of believing that God does not see or hear, know or feel love, or show anger. Such a cold scientific concept of God would naturally exclude the possibility of miracles or even of creation.[28] Arama does not require us to associate with God any corporeality, emotion or change but only that we are to believe that all physical and spiritual existences are comprehended by God. The Bible puts things simply since it 'speaks in the language of men' and therefore has to ascribe to God ordinary actions and emotions otherwise no one would be able to understand the way of God at all. But in trying to interpret anthropomorphic expressions we must beware against removing from God all knowledge or emotion of any kind to such an extreme extent that God is entirely removed from any form of contact with the world of men who are his creatures. It were better, says Arama, to embrace the simple statement that God is angry, or sees, or hears, and understand all this unphilosophically but meaningfully, rather than to interpret them philosophically and come to a denial of God's knowledge and providence.

## THE MEDIEVAL JEWISH MIND

ואין ספק שההישרה האלהית לא תקפיד אל תעות ההמון בצד מצדדי
הגשמות כשהקפדתה אל תעותיה בהעדר הידיעה ומיעוט ההשגחה וסילוק
היכולת שזה מביע אל שבוש הדעת לבד וזה מביע אל כפירה גמורה.

'There is no doubt that the Divine discipline would not be as offended at the error of the masses in ascribing corporeality in any sense to God as in the errors involved in removing knowledge, providence or ability from him. For the first leads only to faulty knowledge while the second error would bring one to absolute atheism.'[29] Whatever Maimonides said on this point is thus contradicted and the criticism of Rabbi Abraham ben David of Posquieres at Maimonides' inclusion in the list of heretics one who ascribes corporeality to God is mentioned with apparent agreement by Arama.[30]

The above reference from Arama's own exposition is extremely important for the insight it gives into his true mind. Rather than fall into sin through philosophising about the difficult passages of the Bible, it were better, he maintains, to accept them simply and even in their literal meaning. It must not however be thought that Arama was a literalist in his approach to the Bible. Not at all. He frequently points out that the literal meaning gives only half the fruit of a text. The other half of its produce can be extracted by understanding its hidden allegorical meaning. Indeed, as a master of homiletics it could hardly be otherwise and the employment of allegorical interpretation is one of his regular methods of expounding the scriptural text. Nevertheless, the literal meaning is real enough and quite valid. Further, for the masses of the simple folk who could not follow the deeper mysteries hidden below the surface of the text it were better for them to be satisfied with the obvious and literal meaning of the plain words of the Bible. For to retain a meaningful religious faith is of greater importance than to aspire to sophisticated philosophical views.[31]

# 2 THE CONCEPTION OF GOD

## I

Despite the fact that Arama often attempts to concentrate his exposition of an important subject in one, or more often, in a group of sermons there is no systematically ordered presentation of a Jewish religious philosophy in his writings since his views on all important questions are dispersed over the whole work and immersed in layers of extraneous homiletic material. The interested student is therefore constrained to piece together many widely scattered views and to mould them all into something of a whole. This is particularly the case when we examine his concept of God, for with the exception of a single section on the attributes of God, he has not found it necessary to treat the subject formally at all and the most we can recognise is an indication in several places of an attitude which substantially represents the views of his predecessors. He has nothing new to offer in his doctrine of God and even what he has to say is not treated by him in any extensive way. This apparent slightness of treatment is rather unusual for Arama and is contrasted with his treatment of other important religious philosophical subjects.

It may be thought, particularly in view of the fundamental importance of a doctrine of God in any religious philosophy, that Arama's treatment is therefore unequal. Yet this very reticence on his part may be due to his recognition that the existence of God is a matter for pure faith alone and that one cannot reason to a belief in the existence of God. So, we do not find in Arama any attempt to prove the existence of God beyond the general statement that since the world was created we must believe that a Creator exists. Together with other medieval Jewish thinkers he recognises the existence of God from the belief in a created world since nothing can create itself. This places the whole emphasis on his treatment of the creation—a subject which he deals with most extensively and which we shall examine in detail in the next chapter. In the meantime it is necessary here to say one or two things further about his concept of God.

Believing that God exists, Arama then goes on to say that we cannot really know much about him. Jewish teaching can only declare that God *is*, but not *what* he is and his essence and positive attributes are altogether impossible for the human intellect to comprehend. Arama quotes in a spirit of complete agreement the statement of Bederasi *taklit mah sheneda shelo nedaeka*. 'The summit of our knowledge is that we cannot know Thee,'[1] and he further elaborates on the point in the following manner, 'It is clear that the summit of man's potential wisdom of the Divine Being is that he cannot know him. This is the difference between one wise man and another...' for the wiser a man becomes the more he will realise the incomprehensibility of God.[2] In this respect he quotes with agreement[3] the saying of Albo *ilu y'dativ heyitiv* 'If I knew him I would be him,'[4] since only God can know himself.

Interpreting the text 'Neither make thyself over wise, why shouldest thou destroy thyself?'[5] he suggests that this has meaning for the man who would try to search out knowledge about God's essence more than he can possibly comprehend who would fall into the pit of destruction which is atheism as a result of his fruitless examinations into something which can never be known.[6] Arama uses the well-known rabbinic comparison of the essence of God to the soul[7] to make several postulates about God. These are (1) that he exists; (2) that he is incorporeal; (3) that he is external; (4) that he is incomprehensible. It is the last of these points which touches on our present theme that the essence of God is unknowable כמו שעם פרסום מציאות נפשך עמך מהותה מדעתך בחדרי חדרים כן תחוייב אליך לדעת שהאל ית' עם עוצם פרסומו הנה עצמותו ומהותו נעלם ונסתר מכל ההסגות האנושיות 'Although the existence of the soul is evident to you,[11] nevertheless its essence is hidden from your knowledge in the innermost recesses. So you must know that despite his evident manifestation, God's essence is hidden and withheld from any human comprehension.'[8]

Nevertheless, we do from time to time attempt descriptions of God. We describe his works, we describe his power and his mercy. The Bible frequently points to such Divine characteristics as will and knowledge, while the Talmud and rabbinic writings generally abound in descriptions of God's qualities and character. How are we now to understand all this? If God is unknowable then how can he be described at all? In the first place it should be said that medieval Jewish writers frequently made a distinction between the essence *mahut* of God, and his attributes *toarim.*[9] It is the essence of God which is unknowable and which cannot be defined in any way: the attributes, however, may sometimes be used as convenient terms with which to describe certain aspects of God's activity. But straight away it must be said that there are different categories of attributes and it is clear that many philosophers rejected the idea of ascribing to God attributes of any kind. This problem formed a separate part of the discussion which was widespread among Arab and Jewish philosophers of the Middle Ages.

II

Those who did ascribe to God various attributes clearly accepted authority from the Scriptures where Divine attributes are explicit. Those, however, who argued against the concept of Divine attributes took up their position on the grounds that the Divine attribute must be either identical with the essence of God or is a quality which is added to it. In the first case the attribute is nothing more than a tautological expression, while in the second case it offends against the doctrine of God's simple unity by making it composed of different parts or even destroys the idea of God's unity by adding something to the nature of God. Among the Jewish thinkers who rejected the idea of the attributes Maimonides is the most definite and uncompromising.

The belief in God's unity and incorporeality necessitates that 'God had no essential attribute in any sense whatever.'[10] We must believe this since ordinary attributes are accidents, i.e., super-added to essence which would destroy the concept of God's unity. If the attributes were not additions but God's essence then, as we have already said, they are tautologies.[11] Even when we say that God exists it is doubtful whether in so ascribing the attribute of existence to God we do not imply that existence is an accident, i.e., super-added to God's essence.[12] Hence it was carefully pointed out that God's existence, *metsiut*, is the same as his essence *mahut*. But this term, essence, is really unknowable and Jewish teaching does not describe the essence of God. We are taught that God *is*; not *what* he is. 'We comprehend only the fact that he exists, not his essence.'[13] In this way we speak of the existence of God meaning with the same expression to imply his unknowable essence. There were those, again, who rejecting the idea of the attributes yet could not find it possible to conceive of God without at least four or five so called essential attributes, viz., existence, life, power, wisdom and will.[14]

Maimonides will not compromise to that extent and for him 'God exists without the attribute of existence. Similarly he lives without possessing the attribute of life; knows without possessing the attribute of knowledge; is omnipotent without possessing the attribute of omnipotence; is wise without possessing the attribute of wisdom, all this reduces itself to one and the same entity.'[15] Only thus, thought Maimonides, can we safeguard the concept of God's simple unity. For all that, it is possible, says Maimonides, to ascribe a certain kind of attribute to God. This is the kind that describes God's different actions, as Creator, it being understood, of course, that all such attributes of action derive not from a multiplicity of attributes but from God's simple unity.

The key passage to Arama's characteristic attitude on the problem of Divine attributes is worth quoting in full. לכן אנחנו הנמשכים אחר משה רבינו ע"ה שהוא אמת ותורתו אמת הנתונה מאל אמת מק"ו שאנחנו נקיים מכל הבלבולים האלו שכיון שידענו נאמנה שהוא יתע' חדש העולם אחר שלא היה ברצונו המוחלט א"א שלא נתארהו בתוארים צרופיים אל פעולותיו כי איך אפשר שברא העולם ולא יהיה בורא או שעשאו ולא יהיה עושה ושיעמידהו ושיקיימהו ויסדרהו תמיד ושלא יתואר במעמיד ומקיי' ומסדר והנה כשנמשכו עוד עניני הנמצאים בעלי הבחיר' אי אפשר שלא נתארהו בכל התארים הנמשכי' מן הרצון והכעס והחסד והחנינה והקנאה והנקמ' ובכלל כל התארים המורגלים תוארי הפעולות. Therefore, we who follow Moses our teacher, peace upon him, believing him to be true, and his Torah received from the Lord, blessed be he, how much more so should we[16] be free of all these misconceptions. For since we know that God, blessed be he, created the world *ex nihilo* by his absolute will, it is impossible not to describe him with attributes associated with his actions. For how could he create the world and not be the Creator ; how could be have made it and not be the Maker ; set it up, establish it and order it continuously and not be described as One who sets up, establishes and orders. . . . Further, it is impossible that we should not describe him with all those attributes derived from his will, anger, kindness, compassion, jealousy, vengeance and in general, all those attributes which are frequent in the Torah and which Maimonides calls the attributes of action.'[17] If we understand this to be Arama's central teaching on the subject of the attributes then it appears that he agrees with Maimonides allowing that we may speak of God as the Creator, the all knowing and powerful, being careful at the same time never to suggest that these attributes are elements in God's essence since such an error would destroy the concept of God's true unity. On the other hand we may legitimately distinguish between attributes of essence which impinge upon the idea of God's unity and the attributes of action by which alone we can properly describe God's relation to the Universe and to man.

This distinction between the essential and active attributes had already been made, before Maimonides, by Bahya Ibn Pakuda.[18] Perhaps, Arama, by including such attributes as will, anger, mercy, compassion and vengeance comes closer still to Halevi who includes all these attributes of 'emotion' within the category of the active attributes.[19] With regard to all attributes associated with the name of God, Arama insists, in the same way as Maimonides,[20] that they are in no way to be considered as involving a plurality in God but must be considered only in relation to his simple unity. אמנם יושפעו מעצ־ מותו הפשוט כל אלו הדברים מבלי שיתרבו לו תוארים מקריים מוסיפים על עצמותו 'But they [the attributes] emanate from his simple essence; not a plurality of attributes added on to his essence.'[21]

Further, there is a sense in which we might even speak of attributes of God and understand from them not their positive but their negative implications. This was a well-known medieval Jewish approach to the question which finds its most thorough-going representative in Maimonides.[22] Since we cannot know the essence of God and it is incorrect to ascribe any positive attributes to him, the most we can postulate is what he is *not*; but not what he *is*. Thus, when we say that God is living, since the attribute of life cannot be part of, or added to, the Divine essence, the idea can have meaning for us only through its negative implications, that is, that by the statement 'God is living' we can only understand that God is not dead. Similarly with all other positive attributes, e.g., God knows, God is one, God is the first, all that we may understand from this is that God is not ignorant, that there is no plurality in him and that he is uncreated. Maimonides sums up the general theory when he says 'Know that the negative attributes of God are the true attributes; they do not include any incorrect notions or any deficiencies whatever in reference to God, while positive attributes imply polytheism and are inadequate.'[23]

With all this, Arama is again in perfect agreement 'For when we say that he is one we do not intend the positive unity which is an accident of the concept One—i.e., it distinguishes quantity —but we know that he is not more than one. Similarly when we say that he is, first all we wish to say is that God is without a cause. So with the attribute of existence, and with all of them. This is the meaning of what God said to Moses at Sinai "And I will take away mine hand, and thou shalt see my back; but my face shall not be seen." For the term "face" undoubtedly is the peculiar expression for positive knowledge, while the term "back" is the peculiar expression for negative knowledge which is its reverse.' Arama then goes on to explain that even this negative kind of knowledge is of value for by learning what a thing is not, one can still understand something of its character. So he is in general agreement with many of his predecessors when he says ויותר יצדק שהוא זולת מה שישיג ממה שהוא דבר שישיג 'For it is more correct to say that God is not what man comprehends than to say that God is what man comprehends.'[24] On a more original level, in which Arama shows his characteristic genius for exegesis, he enquires into the rabbinic homily that the angels pronounce God's name after three words, viz., *Kadosh, Kadosh, Kadosh* while we pronounce it after two words only, viz., *sh'ma Yisrael*.[25] There are, he says in explanation, three degrees of existence, the existence of the material, which is the world of matter, the existence of the heavenly spheres and the existence of the angels. The angels, therefore, can praise God threefold knowing that he is not material, he has no comparison with the spheres and he is no spirit like the angels. Israel, however, has knowledge of only the two lower forms of existence. Hence, for the third grade they have to insert the name of God.[26]

## III

We have already referred to the question of anthropomorphisms in the Bible but as the subject forms an essential part of the medieval conception of God it is necessary to say something further on the matter here before we lead up to a statement of Arama's own attitude.

Sometimes, the Bible in its simple phrasing ascribes human characteristics to God. Thus, the Bible refers to the hand of God, his foot, mouth, eye, ear, his throne, footstool, walking, speaking and many other expressions which are appropriate only to the body and personality of man. This problem was seen by the early *Sopherim* or scribes, the successors of Ezra, who tried to overcome some of the more glaring anthropomorphisms by textual emendation. Later, the Aramaic translators of the

Bible (Targum) made efforts to redeem the text from anthropomorphic expressions by substituting the idea of the *memra* or the word of God which carried the action instead of God himself. To it, not to God, were ascribed the deeds appropriate only to human nature. Later on, the rabbis tried to overcome the same difficulty in a variety of ways. Sometimes they would preface an apparent humanisation of God with the word *K'ilu* or *K'vayakol* i.e., 'it is as if God were to do such and such.' Sometimes they would ascribe actions to angels rather than to God himself. Further, the general principle was laid down that the Torah often speaks in simple language so that it could be better understood. However, later rabbinic literature in the Gaonic period (eighth to tenth centuries) under the influence of mystical teachings, often went to great lengths in the crudest anthropomorphic expressions and ideas.[27] This led to a resurgence of the rationalist criticisms against anthropomorphisms voiced by Saadia, and carried, with a few exceptions, right through the line of medieval Jewish philosophers.[28]

Viewing the period as a whole it would seem that with most Jewish philosophers it was a question of reconciling two apparent irreconcilables. On the one hand they maintained the strongest beliefs in the incorporeality of God who is removed from all human limitations of body and feeling; on the other hand he is a God who is closely related to the world and man which he created and who therefore has direct contact with the material world. To satisfy the first point, they agreed that God could not properly be described with positive attributes, but they had to avoid conceiving of God as a cold metaphysical idea, a mere philosophical abstraction distinctly removed from his creatures. For some Jewish philosophers then, God had to be thought of in warm human terms, but carefully, so as not to offend against the first philosophical principle of the incorporeality of God. Hence the inconsistency of Saadia, or more particularly, of Judah Halevi—a philosopher whose thinking is so clearly based on Jewish tradition, history and revelation.

Perhaps only Maimonides followed his philosophical route to its logical conclusion with a fearless consistency. God is incorporeal, hence any notion which attaches to God human properties, physical or emotional, is against Judaism, and one who believes in such false ideas is not only wrong in his theory about God, but is an heretic who has forfeited his portion in the world to come.[29] But this uncompromising dogmatism found its opponents even among the noted scholars of the age, for Abraham ben David of Posquieres complains against the extreme view of Maimonides and adds 'Many greater and better men have held this opinion for which they believe they found authority in the Scriptures, or more particularly in a confusing view of the Aggada.'[30] The inference from the last phrase may be that this severe critic of Maimonides was not himself perfectly certain about the true meaning of rabbinic texts touching upon the subject, but was nevertheless against any attempt to raise the principle of anti-anthropomorphisms to such a dogma that pronounces all anthropomorphisms to be heresies.

In assessing the position of Arama on this question we may conclude that he is, like so many others, strongly opposed to anthropomorphic ideas. But again, like many others, his opposition is theoretic, like Halevi's, certainly not dogmatic like Maimonides.

His anti-anthropomorphism stands out in many places. Thus, for example, he opens his exposition of the Tabernacle sections of the Pentateuch[31] by enquiring into the purpose of a physical abode for one who is without bodily form. Why should God require a dwelling place? Why should the Torah speak about the Lord of the Universe as though he were one of the kings of the earth requiring a lodging? Support for anti-anthropomorphism is found explicit in the scriptural warning against believing that at the time of revelation the Israelites saw any image[32] and from the rabbinic appelation of God as *Ha-makom* i.e., 'The Presence.' This term Arama understands to mean to imply that God is the source of all things present or existent. Not only the subject of the Tabernacle but many other passages in the Bible present difficulties. Thus it is hard to understand the text 'And I will come down and speak there with you...'[33] since everything that moves must be corporeal and 'God forbid that we should ascribe to the Supreme Being any corporeality, division or composition.'[34]

As will be readily apparent, Arama's starting point is that anthropomorphic descriptions of God are absolutely wrong in principle. Why, then, does the Bible contain such expressions? Simply, says our author, so that we should be more clearly aware of God's nearness and the Divine providence which exercises its care over the individual. If God were kept isolated as a pure philosophical conception then there is danger that he becomes impersonal, removed altogether from the material universe. This is the belief which the Torah must contest and it does so by describing God in human terms of a kind that enable

us to understand his nearness. Speaking of the errors which often follow a too philosophical concept of God, Arama writes
ולזה היה כל דבריהם אלו לפוקה ולמכשול באזני עם הארץ לומר כי אחר שאין לו חושים כחושינו וכוחות ככוחותינו שאינו משיג ויודע דבר לפי שלא צוייר אצלם הרגש באופן אחר וגם יאמרו כי מי שאינו יושב ושוכן בקרב העם המונהגים ממנו אי אפשר שיוכל להשיגם ולכוון בעניני הנהגתם ופעליהם.
'Consequently all their words were a trap and an obstacle for the simple minded since because God has no sense like our sense, or power like our human power, then he cannot comprehend or know anything because they cannot imagine any other kind of perception. Furthermore, they say that if God does not dwell or abide among the people who are led through him then it is impossible for him to control and concern himself with their affairs and deeds.'[35] In this way, Arama understands the purpose of God's command to Israel to make a Tabernacle 'that I may dwell in their midst.' So, too, all anthropomorphisms and anthropathisms do not really tell us about God's nature, but only help us to understand the very nearness of God in all human affairs. We have already taken note of this attitude but it it one that recurs again and again throughout the pages of Arama's work. God is personal. This, for Arama, comes next to the belief in God's existence. Explaining the Ten Commandments[36] he sees the very first commandment as a command to believe in God's existence *hiyuv metsiut* and in his providence *mashgiah*. These are the twin truths about God which we must grasp *Emet metsiut Eloha, mashgiah ... v'yakol* 'God's existence is a truth; so, too, it is true that he watches, wills and is all-powerful.[37]

This, then, is Arama's credo which is a main theme in all periods of Jewish religious thought and represents the basis of any meaningful faith. God is above the world, incomprehensible, unknowable, without positive attributes and yet he is within the world as a living and a guiding force, close to the world and man who are his creatures. It is not always easy to reconcile these two concepts of the transcendent and immanent God. But it is not impossible even on philosophical terms, so long as we postulate a God whose essence is unknown and incomprehensible to man, and to whose powers there are no limits.

# 3 THE CREATION OF THE WORLD

## I

Among the problems which exercised the minds of medieval Jewish thinkers the questions arising out of the biblical account of the creation were perhaps the most difficult of all. Greek philosophy was in many ways acceptable to the Jewish thinkers of the age, yet it could never propound a theory of creation which implied that God created the Universe *ex nihilo*—from nothing.[1] On the other hand, the Jewish scholars were unwilling to limit God's omnipotence by submitting to any theory which so limited God's power and most of them rejected all beliefs which did not accept the idea of creation *ex nihilo*.[2]

Even Maimonides, the greatest Jewish Aristotelian, who travels with the Greek philosopher along so many roads leaves his master's side on this issue. The central problem in the entire discussion was this point, whether God created the existing Universe out of nothing or whether it was eternal. Around this central question, several subsidiary ones were discussed. If the world was created in time, does this imply a change in God's will, from a state of non-creativeness to a state of wilful creativity? Can a world of impure matter emanate from a God who is pure spirit? Can a God who is absolute unity create a world manifestly composed of different parts? Was time created or was it eternal? What is matter? How do the heavenly spheres move? These and several other questions form part of the comprehensive discussion on the creation and we shall need to include a consideration of some of them in our examination of Arama's treatment of the subject. But as we shall see, they fall from the central question which is—creation or eternity of the world.

Before proceeding to our investigation of Arama's standpoint it will be useful to refer briefly to the various views held in his day.

In the main, there are three principal theories to be noticed. In his *Moreh Nevukim* (Guide to the Perplexed) Maimonides lists them as follows. First, the theory that God brought the

Universe into existence out of a state of non-existence. At first nothing existed except God. Then God brought forth, *ex nihilo*, all things by his will. 'This is the first theory, and it is undoubtedly a fundamental principle of the Law of our teacher Moses; it is next in importance to the principle of God's unity.'[3]

The second belief, and one which is generally known as the Platonic theory, is based on the assumption that nothing can be formed from nothing and it does not necessarily limit God's powers by taking away from him the ability to do the impossible[4] since 'the nature of that which is impossible is constant . . . and there is no defect in the greatness of God when he is unable to produce a thing from nothing, because they consider this as one of the impossibilities.'[5] The theory is then developed that prime matter existed all the time by the side of God and so long as there was God there was the prime matter. One did not exist without the other. Out of this prime matter the Universe was fashioned. This does not mean, of course, that the prime matter is equal to God, for the relationship between the two is as the clay to the potter, or the iron to the smith: the creator can fashion what he wills out of the substance. The third theory of the origin of the world is that of Aristotle, who claimed that since God is eternal and can never change his will to create the Universe at a particular point in time, the process of creation is eternal, the motion of the spheres is eternal, and consequently the Universe is uncreated; it always existed and always will exist since that which had no beginning can have no end.

Maimonides makes little or no difference in his final estimation of the second and third theories. To him they are both untenable since even the second, or Platonic view, in positing the belief in an eternal prime matter would place beside God something else which is eternal. This initial enumeration by Maimonides of the three chief theories is undoubtedly too simple and avoids the various cross-currents and later influences that disturbed and confused our understanding of the real meaning of Plato and Aristotle. Nevertheless, it is important to know that whatever be the original teachings of the Greek philosophers on the subject, the above outline was thought by medieval scholars to be their authentic teaching and we are therefore justified in taking these three main views as our starting points in examining the doctrine of the creation in the Middle Ages.

Jewish philosophers rejected the Aristotelian theory of the

eternity of the Universe,[6] although some like Gersonides postulated a theory of eternal matter, while others like Ibn Gabirol developed a theory of creation *ex nihilo* in combination with a system of emanation.

The several Jewish views may therefore likewise be set down under three headings: (1) Creation *ex nihilo*; (2) Eternity of Matter; (3) Emanation. Views 2 and 3 in Jewish thought are really divisions of the theory of emanation. The former can be called emergent emanation and the latter volitional. The first hypothesis is reproduced in most Jewish philosophies from Saadia[7] and postulates the theory that God directly created matter out of which the world was fashioned. The second hypothesis follows Alfarabi's explanation of the theory of emanation. God thinks himself and emanates the first intelligence. The intelligence thinks of God and itself and so emanates the spheres[8] and the range of the translunary and sublunary world. The third view is represented by Ibn Gabirol[9] who introduces God's will as a factor in the process of emanation. Will is here a Divine attribute, and God is able to produce several different effects by will and design.[10]

## II

Arama regarded creation *ex nihilo* as dogmatic and essentially at the foundation of Judaism. His treatment of the subject is found mainly in his first five long sermons in the Book of Genesis. In these chapters he deals not only with the central problem, viz., creation or eternity, but he writes also on the attendant subjects such as the beginning of time, the composition of the heavenly spheres and their motion, the order of creation and several other matters all arising out of his treatment of the text. Interspersed with all this, Arama in his usual broad style, includes several lengthy exegetical expositions of biblical texts with which he illumines his subject. In our present examination of Arama's views it will be necessary from the outset to exclude any analysis of his exegetical sections except those that are important for understanding his philosophical position.

Arama begins his first sermon by referring to Aristotle's well-known enumeration of four kinds of causes for any existence[11] —the material, the formal, the efficient and the final. Because in many cases the cause of particular phenomena may not be known, he says that some people have argued that there is no cause for them but that their existence is due to chance and Arama submits a three-fold argument to prove that natural phenomena could not be the result of chance.[12] First, that which is not caused, being a mere chance happening, is rare; secondly, an accidental or chance happening has no ordered form or shape; and thirdly, it has no final end. But in the world of nature, says Arama, the number of existences whose causes are unknown to us is very numerous; they are all of perfect order and design and they certainly have a final end in the scheme of the Universe.[13] Arama finds support for his arguments against chance from several exegetical treatments of the biblical text. One such support he obtains from his exposition of Psalm 19. 'The heavens declare the glory of God and the firmament showeth his handiwork.' The exegesis is very clever and he proceeds to expound the Psalm as a description of the order of Nature. The homiletic skill is, as nearly always, quite remarkable, and a good example of Arama's forte. What, however, is equally remarkable is the fact that Arama really believed that the text must hold a proper science and philosophy of Nature. He does not seem to regard the Psalm as a piece of poetry or as a religious song. It may be that, but just as important to him is the belief that the words contain scientific truth and he sees this truth inherent in the text to coincide with his own theories of the natural world. אמנם ספורי התורה האלוהית עם היות שהם רומזים אל ענינים נפלאים עמוקים מכל מקום הספורים ההם כפשטן הן בתכלית האמת. 'For while it is true that the stories of the Divine Torah point to deep and wonderful matters, nevertheless the narrative must be taken simply as an expression of the exact truth.'[14] It is in this spirit that Arama finds support for scientific theory from the actual text of the Psalm. In itself it is a splendid piece of exegesis and Arama keeps his main points before him all the time, for however much he gets involved in the complications of textual explanations he is here intent on illustrating two sets of proposals. The first is that little exists by chance because, as we have seen, the chance happening or existence is rare, it is without proper place or design in itself and it has no purpose. Secondly, all existence has, as Aristotle made clear, four causes, material formal, efficient and final. These two sets of propositions are illustrated by the Psalm.

Arama is quick to point out however that this does not mean that Aristotle believed that the Universe was created since all that the Greek philosopher holds is that the Universe has a necessary cause. For everything in existence there must be a necessary cause; for this preceding cause there is another cause before it and so on. But all this leads to a prime cause since there cannot be an infinite number of causes. This prime cause is not a creator but is jointed eternally to the Universe as the *intellectus* to the *intellectum*. The former necessarily implies the existence of the latter and exists in eternal duration with the latter. 'Like the *intellectus* to the *intellectum* . . . which is eternal like its eternity, but was not created after they had not been.'[15] In this way, Arama touches at this early stage on Aristotle's view of the eternity of the Universe, and agrees with the refutation of the theory of eternity by Maimonides in his *Guide*.[16] Here Maimonides clearly states the difference between the Aristotelian theory that the Universe is the necessary result of the first cause and his view that the Universe was created by a deliberate act of God's will. 'According to Aristotle everything besides that Being (first cause) is the necessary result of the latter . . . while according to our opinion, that Being created the whole Universe with design and will, so that the Universe which had not been in existence before, has by his will come into existence.'[17] This is the main point in the first sermon. Granted that the Universe does not exist by chance, the question remains—was it created or is it the eternal necessary result of a first cause?

Arama now takes the above three arguments against existence through chance and uses them as a support for his view of creation by God as a definite act of his will and finds some help for his attitude from Psalm 104 which he treats with his customary skill. The verse *Mah rabu ma'aseka* ' How manifold are Thy works, O Lord,' signifies the abundancy of phenomena in the natural world and represents the first objection to their existence through chance or without cause. *Kulam b'kokmah asita* ' In wisdom Thou hast made all of them' is related to the second argument against chance since all existences portray the wisdom and artistry of a Creator. While the word *asita* ' Thou hast made' points to a definite act of will. He quotes in this connection the view found in Ibn Gabirol's *Keter Malkuth*.[18] Finally, the phrase *mal'ah ha-arets kinyaneka* ' The earth is full of Thy possessions' touches upon the third argument against chance, namely, that all existences have a purpose and here the purpose is the propagation of their own species by a power which is implanted into every living creature.[19] Now when all this is harnessed to the view that God created everything by his will we cannot ask why anything was made in one particular shape or form rather than in another, for the answer is that he made everything according to his will, to which there can be no further question.[20]

We now come to one of the great arguments against any theory of creation. To assume that the world was created in a point in time must imply that the Creator allowed a state of non-existence to precede his act of creation. This would mean that the Creator was deficient in power until such time as he brought the Universe into existence, or that he was without something he needed, on account of which need he created the world. In either case God becomes deficient. Further, in whichever of the above two ways it be regarded, it at least seems that by creating the world *de novo* God effected a change in his will since before the creation he allowed a state of non-existence. Arama does not face the problem at this stage and the most he says is that he is in agreement with Maimonides who explains in his *Guide* that creation *ex nihilo* in no way implies a change in God or in his will.[21]

Arama agrees that it may not be at all possible for us to grasp all the details of creation and that there will be many problems remaining unanswered, so we must recognise the limits of the human intellect and grant that there are things outside the bounds of our knowledge. But the greater part of the truth is nevertheless there for all to see, since a study of things before us in the world, their design, their function and their purpose will lead us to appreciate that it is all the work of a masterplanner. Further, however difficult some of the details of the study may be, it is still possible for all to understand the core of the truth about creation which is that God is not merely the first cause, as is maintained by the Aristotelians, but he is also the active Creator of the Universe. והוא לבד יתברך לא לבד סבת הסבות כלם כי אם היותו פועל הדברים כלם אחר שלא היו בכוונה ורצון גמור 'And he, blessed be he, is not only the prime cause, but also the Creator, who, by his definite intention and will created all things after they were not.'[22]

The terms *sibah*, cause and *poel*, Agens or Creator, form the subject of a chapter in the *Guide to the Perplexed*. The great controversy between the Mutakallemim and the Philosophers was that the former refused to call God the cause and used the term *Agens* since they said 'If we say that God is the cause ... this would involve the belief that the Universe was eternal, and that it was inseparable from God.'[23] To exist, means to be willed by God and it is not enough to say that existence comes from God since that would imply that it necessarily derives from him ' as the shadow is caused by the body, or heat by fire, or light by the sun.'[24] Hence the Arab theologians refused to call God the first cause. But Maimonides insists on the validity of the term first cause since God is ultimately the efficient, formal and final cause of all existence. This Aristotelian conclusion is also enunciated by Arama who, while he insists, as we saw above, that God is the *poel* or *Agens*, meets the Arab objections by calling God both the *sibah* and the *poel* 'הטעם אשר בראשונה קבעו הראשונים לכנות שמו ית' עלה או סבה ולא פועל כמו שרצו קצותם היה מפני שמלת עלה כולל יותר ממלת פועל כי פועל לא יכלול רק שהוא הסבה הפועלת אמנם עלה כוללת היותו הסבה הפועלת והצוריית והתכליתית' The reason why the early philosophers designated God as the first cause and not as the *Agens*, as some of them preferred, was because the word cause includes more than the word *Agens* since the latter implies that God is only the efficient cause while the former describes him as the efficient, formal and final causes.'[25]

Arama concludes the first part of his first sermon by adding to his logical arguments a moral argument in favour of the belief in creation, since a belief in the eternity of the world necessarily implies that all that happens to man also follows from necessary causes. The whole foundation of the fear of God and the doctrine of reward and punishment obviously falls away once we posit that a particular result must follow and that God cannot direct certain other results by his will. Hence the belief in creation is fundamental also to a proper fear of God. This argument is similar to that advanced by some of his predecessors who maintain that belief in creation was a basic doctrine in Judaism, for if the world were eternal then miracles would have been impossible, and great and extraordinary personalities such as Moses and the Messiah would be impossible. In fact, the only basis on which we can accept the occasional intrusion of the super-natural into the normal order of Nature is the belief in creation which has as its central feature a God who can create by an act of his will all phenomena and who alone can therefore control by his will the course of events.[26]

These two aspects of God's creative power by which the Universe is governed in accordance with natural law and providence are further treated by Arama in his fourth sermon. He argues that to hold to one without the other would lead to an incorrect view of creation. For if we believe only in the first, that the Universe exists and continues only in accordance with natural law we would be logically led to the theory of the eternity of the Universe. On the other hand without the stable and permanent natural law the Universe could not exist at all. But with the permanent laws of nature, God also acts, on occasion, through his knowledge of individuals and providentially intercedes to direct the affairs of man.

Arama puts it this way. There are two aspects of God's creative power. First, there is the aspect which makes God the necessary first cause of all existence. He is the immovable mover and from him all things proceed as of necessity. Again, since God is continuously in action it follows that motion is continuous and the process of creation evolves through the established law of cause and effect. From the first cause, through to the separate intelligences, the heavenly spheres and the planets down to the smallest existence in the sublunary world of matter—all things are produced in accordance with necessary natural law. There is no way in which natural law can be broken or changed—this immutability of natural life is in itself a law of creation. There is only one way really by which the law of the Universe can be suspended and that is by the intervention of God himself who is responsible for that law. This introduces the second aspect of God's creativity which shows God not so much as the first cause but as the Creator who produced the Universe by an act of his will and who has knowledge of all his creatures for whose sake the laws of Nature can be diverted at his will.

Arama insists that both natural law and the suspension of natural law by God's will are to be joined together to form the complete view of the world order. At the end of Sermon Three he remarks that the designation of the Creator as *Elohim* in chapter one of Genesis refers to him as the God of natural law whose Universe is governed by the immutable law which alone makes ordered life possible.[27] The designation of God as *Yahweh* in the second chapter refers to another aspect of God, viz., his knowledge, mercy and kindness which is extended to all.[28]

Arama illustrates his point from the story of Abraham. He remarks that at the start of his career Abraham thought of God after the first idea. That is why he calls God *Koneh* 'the possessor, i.e., one who can exercise the power of a remote owner,[29] whose law is universally static and who does not have knowledge of the small details in his possessions. Then when God showed his power to upset natural law by granting Abraham and Sarah a child, then Abraham realised for the first time, the complete concept of God as Creator. The argument of Arama is one that was used by Maimonides to support the belief in creation. If the Universe is eternal, then ' everything in the Universe is the result of fixed laws ; Nature does not change, and there is nothing supernatural ; we should necessarily be in opposition to the foundation of our religion, we should disbelieve all miracles and signs.'[30] Maimonides thus regards a belief in the eternity of the Universe as clearly opposed to a fundamental principles of Judaism. This applies only to the Aristotelian theory of eternity. But what of the Platonic theory of the eternity of matter ? Here Maimonides believes that such a theory is not against Jewish belief and that the occurrence of miracles can be reconciled to the Platonic theory. He will not hold such a belief himself however, only because the theory of the eternity of matter has not been proved.[31] This passage in the *Guide* is referred to by Arama as having been a stumbling block for Jewish scholars who misinterpreted or misunderstood Maimonides' real meaning and thought that the theory of eternity was acceptable to Judaism.[32]

It must not be thought, however, that Maimonides held the Platonic theory to be correct for despite his admiration of Greek philosophy, Maimonides held his view in strict opposition against all theories of eternity. We have already noted his clear statement that belief in creation *ex nihilo* is a fundamental principle of Judaism.[33] But he is at pains to narrow the gap between Aristotle and himself. He states that Aristotle was aware that he had not proved the eternity of the Universe[34] while on the other hand he admits that his own theory of creation cannot be proved by logic.[35] The furthest he will go in his claim is that although both theories are admissible, his own theory is more acceptable, especially as it has the authority of prophecy.[36] Of course, he does not rest only on biblical support[37] for his arguments against Aristotle are also based on reasoning from cosmological and ontological hypotheses, from the nature of the Universe and from the nature of God.

His opposition to any theory of eternity is directed also against the Platonic theory with its prime matter which he understood to have been taken as eternal in such a manner ' that neither God existed without that matter nor the matter without God.'[38] But only foolish people, he says, can assume that Plato's doctrine can be harmonised with the belief in creation *ex nihilo*. Maimonides defends his theory which was the doctrine of most Jewish scholars who followed or preceded him, but he has the unique advantage over others in that he clearly states the Aristotelian and Platonic theories that were being discussed by medieval scholars. He explains their theories giving them fair treatment, and shows up their weaknesses while attempting to prove the superiority of the Jewish view of creation *ex nihilo*. Nevertheless, it would seem that Maimonides' apparent hesitancy and reluctance to repudiate outright the Aristotelian and Platonic theories as being both against the Scriptures led to some confusion and brought a few at least to a sympathetic attitude to the Platonic theory. Arama pours the fury of his invective against such people[39] who turn aside from a simple belief in the creation of the Universe as an act of God's will in a definite point of time. That Arama regards the Platonic theory equally as erroneous as the Aristotelian is clear when he says that the institution of the Sabbath serves: להוציא מלב כל בעל דת אפיקורוסות הלזה הן בכללו הן בהמצא חומר או שום התחלה קודמת אבל שיאמינו אמונה שלימה ואמיתית שחדוש העולם היה בריאה חדשה לגמרי יש מהאין המוחלט... הנה למדנו שהיה חדוש מוחלט מאפס ותהו גמור 'To remove from the heart of every man of religion the heresy of the theory of eternity, whether it be the idea of complete eternity or the belief in the existence of some matter of eternal principle. But they should believe with a true and perfect faith that the creation of the world was brought about by an entirely new act of creation out of the absolute nothing. ... We have now learned that it was an absolute creation out of nothing and out of the perfect void.'[40] The *klalo* is obviously the Aristotelian theory of eternity while the *homer* or *hathalah kodemet* the Platonic theory of existing matter.

Having shown his stern opposition to those who hold to any theory of eternity, Arama pronounces his own belief and explains his view of the process of creation in three stages.

1. Creation out of the absolute nothing. This was the bringing forth of first continuous[41] matter from the absolute non-existence into existence.

2. The creation of a positive substance from this hyle.[42] This was the bringing forth of a completed essence out of relative nothingness.

3. The development of one substance out of another substance by means of the transformation of the egg from the drop, and the bird from the egg.[43]

Stage 1 took place on the evening of the first day of Creation. The second stage was carried through from the beginning of the first day till the end of the sixth and the final stage commenced in the evening of the seventh day and continues thereafter. This latter stage, while in itself it embraces an activity, is a quiescent activity and is 'rest' or *m'nuha* in relation to the activity of the other days.

This theory puts us in mind of Nahmanides who states his view in the beginning of his Commentary on the Bible. God created heaven and earth, though not in the completed state, but merely the hyle from which there ultimately grew the entire Universe. According to Nahmanides there were two kinds of hyle—that from which the heavens were made and that from which the earth was made. Our own author refers to the hyle as the prime matter from which were created both the upper and the lower worlds. 'He brought forth the first substance (the hyle) for the translunary and the sublunary worlds.'[44]

### III

In accordance with Arama's system, his exposition follows the strict order of the text so where an ordered philosophical work might treat each subject separately and in a clear order, his book suffers from the complications and repetitions which arise from a close following of the text. Nevertheless, in our examination of the present subject it is worth while following Arama at every point which he raises in the complicated pattern of his treatment of the creation.

The first thing created, according to the Bible, was the *shamayim* or heavens. What does this include? Further, what differentiates the heavens from the earth? The proper meaning of the Hebrew terms *shamayim, eretz, rakia,* as well as others which are found in the first verses of Genesis, engaged the attention of medieval Jewish writers, and Maimonides devotes an entire chapter to the definition of the terms.[45] Arama does not follow a line of subservience to Maimonides in this particular matter and defines *shamayim* and *rakia* in an independent manner. *Shamayim* or heavens refers, properly speaking, to the entire body of heavenly spheres which revolve as the ever-moving agencies of God. The *rakia* or firmament is simply a thin division which separates the heavenly bodies from the sublunary world. The heavenly bodies are changeless and their movements caused the mixing of the elements in the sublunary world of change.

From the first verse in Genesis we know that the heavens were created first. We have seen that the term 'heavens' is understood by Arama to include all translunary existences by which he meant in the first place the heavenly spheres. According to medieval thought there are altogether ten spheres and each sphere moves in a constant circular motion. Most thinkers of the age, after Ibn Sina, counted nine celestial bodies. The diurnal sphere (free from stars), the sphere of the fixed stars, the seven spheres carrying planets—Saturn, Jupiter, Mars, Sun, Venus, Mercury and Moon. Finally, the sublunary sphere carrying all existences on the earth. Each sphere is moved by or is motivated by a separate intelligence—*sekel* or *sekel nifrad* or *sekel nivdal*. There are thus as many intelligences as there are spheres. These intelligences were often identified in medieval philosophy with the angels.[46]

It was observed by the ancient philosophers that the natural movement of sublunary objects is in a rectilinear direction, up or down, and the four elements, fire, air, water and earth which are basic in all sublunary existences have this characteristic: fire and air travel upwards while water and earth travel downwards. Now the circular and constant movement of the spheres presented a unique kind of movement which was not to be easily explained. It was held that the spheres have a movement of their own and that they are not dead masses but living beings.[47] This Aristotelian doctrine was pronounced with great conviction by Maimonides. 'Scripture supports the theory that the spheres are animate and intellectual, i.e., capable of comprehending things; that they are not, as ignorant persons believe, inanimate masses like fire and earth, but are as the Philosopher asserts, endowed with life, and serve their Lord, whom they mightily praise; "The heavens declare the glory of God." '[48] Arama is himself against this view and argues that just as some things move up or down, others from east to west or from west to east in accordance with the laws inherent in their nature placed in them by God, so the heavenly spheres have been created with the power of circular motion. It is not necessary to argue that they are living entities or to hold, as the philosophers do that they are inspired like intelligent beings in order to allow them to move in a circular manner by separate intelligences or angels. Besides, Arama considers it lowering to the greatness of angels to ascribe to them the regular burden of movers of the spheres מציאות המלאכים המזכירה אותה התורה הוא ענין מעולה מאוד מהיותם נפשות או מניעים לגלגלים 'The existence of angels described by the Torah is too exalted a thing to allow them to be made "souls" or movers of the spheres.'⁴⁹

Nevertheless, Arama does not choose to remain alone in his view and in any case the authority of Maimonides is too great for him so that at the end he also submits the view of Maimonides and of the majority of thinkers that the heavenly spheres are animate beings and that the final cause of their movement is the separate intelligence or angels.⁵⁰ Further, when necessary he even uses the very theory of the intelligent spheres as a proof for his own arguments. Thus, for example, in another context he submits that the intelligence of the spheres moves them to revolve faster or slower in their desire to reach unity with God. It was known that with the exception of the uppermost diurnal sphere which moves from east to west at a greater velocity than any of the other spheres, the higher a sphere was in the heavenly order the slower it moves. The reason for this, says Arama, is that the nearer the sphere to its Creator, the more sublime is its intelligent soul and it will recognise that it can never hope to unite with God, hence its movement will not be so great in its desire for its source because it knows that it cannot reach it. The lower spheres, however, have a greater velocity since they feel, with their lesser intelligence, that the faster they move the nearer might they come to God.⁵¹

Arama now proceeds to answer the question whether the angels were created before the heavens and earth or after. Though there is support in the Midrash⁵² that they were created after the heavens and earth so that none could say that God had a co-partner in creation, nevertheless, the majority view is that they were created first, and this view, besides finding support in other midrashic statements also conforms to the belief just stated that the angels are the final cause for the movements of the spheres.

The position arrived at thus far is that the first existences in the order of creation were the separate intelligences or angels, together with the heavenly spheres and the hyle of the material world. Two questions are now referred to by Arama, both of which exercised the minds of the ancient philosophers. The first is relevant to the method by which the angels themselves were created. Were they the necessary eternal result of God's existence and consequently eternal with him, or were they created deliberately by a special act of God's will and in a point of time? The first alternative we recognise again as the standpoint of Aristotle and of those who held the view that the world is eternal and necessary. The second, is the view of creation consistent with Scripture. The other question refers to the problem of the plurality of angels. If we assume that these angels are pure spirits then how is it possible that there is more than one? Only material or corporeal things differ one from another, but pure spirit cannot differ from pure spirit. What is it then, that differentiates the individual intelligences, notwithstanding they they do not possess the ordinary differences of corporeal beings.[53] Now Arama has his mind made up on both these points. With regard to the first, he categorically states that God created the intelligences and that they are not the necessary result of God's own existence. This, of course, is only consistent with his view of creation *ex nihilo*. ומעתה אין העולם קדמון ולא מחויב 'Consequently the Universe is not eternal and not necessarily existing'[54] but is the result of God calling it into existence out of nothing by a definite act of his will. On the second question, Arama is not so clear. In one place he holds that God created a variety of intelligences, but in another place he appears to hold the view that one emanated from another. This seems to be a combination of two different theories in support of which he refers his reader to Maimonides' *Yesodei Hatorah*.[55]

The real intention of Arama, however, is to make clear that even if we assume that one intelligence proceeded from another intelligence, no part of the result was necessary, but the whole sequence came into existence through God's will which he made manifest by planting in the intelligences the power to influence the emanation of other intelligences and set the spheres in motion אף על פי כן לא הושפעו אלו השמים מאלו הנבדלים על דרך החיוב כי אם ברצונו יתברך 'Nevertheless, the spheres did not emanate from the intelligences through necessity, but by God's will.'[56]

Our author is now able to state his interpretation of the first verse of Genesis, 'In the beginning God created the heavens and the earth,' in the following way בתחילת הכל הוציא מהאין המוחלט שמים וארץ. במלה שמים כוון אל שני ראשי הבריאה... העולם הרוחני שהוא ראוי שברא ראשונה... וכולל גם היולי גרמי הכדורים שהוא הראש הקרוב אליו בסדר 'In the very beginning God brought the heavens and the earth out of absolute non-existence. The word "heavens" points to the two elements, the spiritual world (intelligences) which had to be created first and also the hyle of the spheres that was closest to God in the order of creation.'[57] From the word 'earth' Arama supposes that the four elements[58] of the earth were part of the first act of creation. But these four elements were not yet in their proper existence but rather in a mere state of potentiality, or earth hyle, which was later worked upon by the movements of the spheres.[59] The hyle of the spheres is not the same as the hyle of the sublunary world for there is this essential difference between the sublunary and translunary world. That while the sublunary world is composed of the four elements—air, fire, water and earth, the heavenly bodies are made of entirely different matter. Arama comes back to this point later on when says that the heavens are a 'fifth element' *yesod hamishi*.[60]

## IV

Among the various questions which Arama seeks to answer is the question: 'How could there have been a "day," that is a unit of time measurement before the fourth "day" when the luminaries were not yet in the heavens to measure the night and the day?' Could there have been time before the heavenly spheres commenced their movement? In answer to this question Arama refers to the two main views of time. First, there is the famous definition of Aristotle[61] that time is the measure or the number of motion in respect to what is earlier or later. There can be no time without motion. First the spheres move and time measures or numbers that motion. Just as there can be no empty space, so there can be no such thing as empty time or a concept of time that does not measure an already existing movement. This view that time is a measure of motion was accepted by Maimonides. 'Time is an accident ... connected with motion. This must be clear to all who understand what Aristotle has said.'[62] It is clear to us by now, however, that in accepting Aristotle's view of time, Maimonides rejects his view of the eternity of motion. To the Greek, time is eternal as the eternal measurement of movement which is also eternal. To Maimonides, of course, the motion of the spheres commenced with creation, and at that moment time was created. 'I told you that the foundation of our Faith is our belief that God created the Universe from nothing, that time did not exist previously, but was created: for it depends on the motion of the sphere, and the sphere has been created.'[63]

This is the first view of time as the measure of motion and following Maimonides, Arama postulates that this is the true kind of time, and in so far as we believe that the movement of the spheres was created, so we must believe that time was created with it. התחלת הבריאה והתחלת הזמן נמצאים יחד. 'The beginning of creation and the commencement of time came together.'[64] But there is a second definition of time which describes it not as a measure but as a duration. This is the view of Crescas. Time is not the measure of motion, but rather motion is the measure of time. Time is independent and its existence is not related to any other object but only to the thinking mind. Given this thinking mind that grasps the concept of time as duration then time exists.[65] Time as duration is also found in Saadia[66] and in Abraham Bar Hiyya.[67] This view presupposes, of course, that time could exist even before the spheres, and even Maimonides, firm Aristotelian though he is, admits that we must grasp hold of a kind of time that existed before God created the Universe. 'We say that God existed before the creation of the Universe, although the term "existed" appears to imply the motion of time; we also believe that he existed an infinite space of time before the Universe was created; but in these cases we do not mean time in its true sense. We only use the term to signify something analogous or similar to time.'[68] Maimonides himself does not explain what he means by 'something analogous or similar to time.'

The point is made clear by Isaac Albo in his discussion.[69] Albo follows the view of his teacher Crescas, both of whom were influenced by Plotinus.[70] According to Albo's treatment of the subject, there are two kinds of time. One kind is 'measured duration, which is conceived only in thought, and has perpetual existence, having existed prior to the creation of the world and continuing to exist after its passing away.' This kind of time is what he calls absolute time and would probably fit into what Maimonides called 'analogous to time,' i.e., the 'time' we think of as in existence before creation.[71] The other kind of time is that which is 'numbered and measured by the motion of the spheres and in which there is the distinction of prior and posterior, of equal and unequal.' According to this treatment, we now find the view held that there is a time which is described as a 'duration' or 'analogous to time' which is not dependent on creation at all but which still existed or rather which can be thought of as being in 'existence' before creation. That Arama is aware of this better description of time as a duration is clear from his reference [72] to Crescas' proposition where that view is stated. Arama furthermore makes the very valid point that if time is thought of as in being before creation then how much more so after the creation itself! For all we are concerned with really is the possibility of time after creation but before the movement of the spheres. In this respect, of course, Arama is open to no criticism at all, even from the Maimonidean standpoint or that of Crescas, since none would argue against the existence of time once the process of creation had started, although the luminaries were not yet functioning as instruments for the normal measurements of time. Arama, however, at this point offers a second solution to the existence of time before the fourth day which is rather bold, but perhaps unnecessary in view of his first solution. In this matter of Time before the motion of the spheres the Bible, he says, records it all retrospectively, after it has all happened. אעפ״י שנודע שלא יצויר הזמן כלל בלא תנועה גלגלית כלל הנה לא מפני זה ימנע הכתוב מלשערו עם שם העתיד. כי האלהים ידבר ומשה כותב... כי למה שהזמן השלם הוא מצוי בחכימתו ית׳ הזכירו הכתוב ושערו טרם המצאו כמו שיהא שיעורו אחרי מציאותו השלם. 'Although it be known that Time cannot be created at all without the motion of the spheres nevertheless Scripture will not, because of this, refrain from describing it in terms of the future. For God speaks and Moses writes. . . . For in so far as proper time exists in God's wisdom . . . Scripture mentions it and defines it even before it comes into existence in its final description.'[73]

Arama then goes on to find some support for these two solutions to the problems of time before the fourth day from an interpretation of a passage in the Midrash *Bereshith Rabah*, III. The passage reads as follows: 'And there was evening. R. Judah b. R. Simon said it is not written "let there be evening" but "and there was evening" hence we know that a time order already existed.' There are several ways in which this Midrash might be understood. The first is to take it as a deliberate statement of R. Judah's actual opinion, that is, that his words are to be understood in their literal sense. This would imply that R. Judah held that time is independent of the creation existing before creation as a duration and in this way Crescas takes the Midrash as a support for his theory. The second view is to dismiss the Midrash as a mere homiletic exercise and of no scientific value whatsoever. This is the view of Maimonides who says in his *Guide*: 'We find some of our sages are reported to have held the opinion that time existed before the creation. But this report is very doubtful . . . and is objectionable. Those who have made this assertion have been led to it by a saying of one of our sages in reference to the terms "one day" a "second day." Taking these terms literally, the author of that saying asked, what determined the "first day" since there was no rotating sphere and no sun? He continues as follows: Scripture uses the term "one day" and R. Judah b. R. Simon said: "Hence we learn that the divisions of time had existed previously."[74] Maimonides then goes on to infer that this view necessarily carries with it the view of the eternity of the Universe. 'But every religious man rejects this.'[75]

According to Maimonides, time is generated by motion and therefore there could be no proper time before the creation of the spheres. Whatever R. Judah meant by his statement, it cannot be taken literally as postulating the doctrine of the existence of proper time before the spheres. Joseph Albo also discusses the statement of R. Judah. As we have already seen he recognises two kinds of time, an unmeasured duration which exists in the thinking mind and an 'order of time' measured by the physical motion of the spheres. He takes R. Judah's statement to mean simply that there was an order of time even prior to the fourth day since the spheres began to move immediately they were created.[76] Arama's view is stated thus: R. Judah teaches from the text the truth of the first view (i.e., that time existed after the creation though before the fourth day) that time can be estimated without the motion of the spheres. Since in so far as creation was begun and brought with it the concept of prior and posterior, the order of time is already possible,[77] The concepts "day" and "night" need not be taken in their exact literal sense but as expressions which cover the supposition of a period of darkness which came first and a similar period of light which followed. This is not exactly measured time but it is a valid concept of a definite duration of time, which, although the movements of the spheres had not yet begun and consequently independent of the movement of the spheres, is nevertheless properly called time.

It will be seen that Arama is independent in his interpretation of the Midrash. While repudiating Crescas' view of time as a duration before creation, he still holds to a concept of time before the fourth day. Neither does he follow Albo's interpretation that the spheres were in motion from the first day, a view which is perhaps not entirely ruled out by Maimonides.[78] For Arama, there was no time before creation, not even a concept of duration. Nor was there a proper order of measured time before the fourth day. What there was between creation and the fourth day was a kind of sequence of prior and posterior which could be supposed to fit into the concepts of periods of time equivalent to night and day.

Arama then connects the second half of the Midrash to his second suggested solution to the existence of night and day before the fourth day, viz., that Scripture records the events of the future as though they had already happened. Rabbi Abahu said: 'This proves that the Holy One, blessed be he, went on creating worlds and destroying them until he created this one.' Arama expounds this rabbinic homily by saying that since God knows all things the idea of building one world and destroying another can be taken only figuratively. What we might understand from it is that God's preferential action over another alternative action represents the 'building' and 'destroying' respectively. But since he knows all possibilities from the beginning, one world is made and another is destroyed in his mind from the very commencement of things. In the same way the proper order of time is made from the beginning since it is all part of God's knowledge from the origin of creation. The exegesis seems to be rather forced and there is a strong suspicion that Arama is constrained to fit this part of the Midrash into his second solution for the sake of completeness of treatment alone.

Having offered his explanation of the division of time before the movement of the spheres, Arama now reverts his attention to a statement of Maimonides which he finds utterly unacceptable. In his *Guide*, II, 30, Maimonides repudiates the view of R. Judah, mentioned above. In answer to the question how there could be night and day before the fourth day, he appears to suggest that everything in creation was in existence from the first act of creation on the first day. Consequently, since the spheres existed, there could be a division of time. In support of this theory, he says that the particle *et* in the first verse of Genesis signifies 'together with' and means that 'God created with the heavens everything which the heavens contain, and with the earth everything which the earth includes.' Further, in support of this idea, he submits the illustration of the sower who lays down his seeds all at the same time, some springing forth one day and others the next. Later on in the same chapter, Maimonides quotes the talmudic expression 'When the Universe was created, all things were created with size, intellect and beautifully developed.'[79]

Now all this is interpreted by Arama to signify that Maimonides believed that all things were created in their final form on the first day and against this supposition Arama argues most vehemently complaining also that Maimonides is inconsistent since the illustration of the sower tends to upset his thesis. It is, however, doubtful whether Arama correctly understood Maimonides. For Maimonides nowhere says that everything in existence was created at once on the first day. To say nothing of the biblical story, he is too devout and earnest an Aristotelian in his theory of the natural development by cause and effect to suggest anything of this kind. On the contrary, his very statement that even when the sages say that 'all things were created together' is concluded by the phrase 'but were separated from each other successively.' This last phrase is of greatest importance since it lays down the theory that there was a time order in creation. Whatever we may suppose to have been the original source of an existing thing, it appeared in the Universe in accordance with a proper order in the chain from cause to effect. Indeed, in the same chapter Maimonides makes it clear that the Universe in its totality came into existence as a result of a series of successive causes and effects. 'Our sages have already explained that the herbs and trees which God caused to spring forth from the ground were caused by God to grow after he had sent down rain upon them.' Arama is justified in assuming that this should be taken as an indication of Maimonides' recognition of the incidence of cause, effect and priority in the order of creation.

He would, however, appear to be mistaken in assuming that the quotation from the Talmud about all things being created with size is an indication that Maimonides held that the Universe was created perfect and all at once in its completeness. There is positively no foundation for this, and the reference in Maimonides neither leads off from such a subject nor leads towards such an inference. In fact, it is written, more or less, as an isolated quotation and if it has any direct reference at all to what goes before it, it can possibly mean that when each part of creation came into existence on the *appropriate day* of creation and in accordance with its proper order in the sequence of creation then it came into existence in its final form. On the fourth day, for example, the luminaries existed in their final form just as on the fifth day the creatures of the waters and the fowl of the air were created in their final form.[80] If it is true that Arama misunderstood Maimonides in this chapter, we are still left to explain the answer Maimonides gave to the question of the existence of time before the fourth day. Arama took

Maimonides to mean that the spheres were already complete by that first act of creation. This seems to be Maimonides' meaning especially when we consider his approval of the teaching that 'God created with the heavens everything that the heavens contain' and the support he finds for the simultaneous creation of the heavens and earth from the text 'I call unto them; they stand up together.'[81] Against this, however, we must set his statement that 'they were separated successively' and the further midrashic statement which he quotes approvingly, 'these lights (of the luminaries mentioned in the creation of the fourth day) are the same that were created on the first day—but they came into existence in their *final form* on the day recorded in the Scriptures. This is consistent with Maimonides' general theory of evolution, with his talmudic quotation referred to above, and also with the text of the first verses of Genesis.

The answer to the problem of time before the fourth day, for Maimonides, would be in postulating the theory that he held the spheres as *completed* and in their proper stations only on the fourth day, but as being in *existence* by the first act of creation. Without being in their stations in the heavens they were nevertheless in existence and moved, thus creating light and darkness. If this view is correct, then it would seem that there is little difference between it and the first view of Arama stated above.

## V

### 1

It is of importance as well as of some interest to follow Arama's further exposition of the text in order to see how he views the various details of creation in their biblical order. Taking the rabbinic text, 'The world was created in ten sayings'[82] which the rabbis originally intended as a homily on the theme of reward and punishment, Arama takes the 'ten sayings' to refer to the expression *vayomer Elohim* 'And God said' which occurs ten times in Genesis I.[83] These he equates to the ten categories with which Aristotle defines the essence of a substance.[84] Arama is not really concerned with the philosophical concepts of the categories. It is, as we shall see later on, only in a very arbitrary way that he justifies the introduction of the ten categories into his discussion. His chief object, rather his only object, is to expound the first chapter of Genesis in a way that presents an ordered and reasonable sequence of events in the story of creation. To achieve this he merely uses the technical aid of the ten sayings and proceeds from one *vayomer Elohim* to the next.

At the beginning God created the intelligences and the hyle, or original matter. This latter is not a substance but a mere potentiality without substance or form. This corresponds so far with the first verse of Genesis; 'In the beginning God created the heavens and the earth.' In this opening verse the heavens and the earth represent *shne ktzot ha-briah* 'the two extremes of the creation.' But for this original act of creation out of nothing there is no *ma'amar* or saying since there is yet nothing of material substance in being. The intelligences are pure spirit and the matter of the four elements is not yet in substantial existence. Then God created the light which is signified by the first saying *vayomer Elohim yehi or.* ' And God said let there be light' when the intelligences then began to cause the motion of the spheres and to bring into existence the luminaries of the heavens although these were not yet in their stations in the heavens until the fourth day of creation. But before the appearance of light on the earth, God allowed a darkness to cover the prime matter of the elements. The period of darkness lasted the length of a night [85] and then light was created. When the light had shone for a similar interval, the period of the darkness and the light constituted the measure of a day.

Since this first creation represents the beginning of the substantial world its appropriate category is *Etzem* or Substance.

2

The terms *shamayim* 'heavens' and *rakia* 'firmament' have been variously interpreted and we have already noted how the former term has been taken to include the entire host of separate intelligences or angels as well as the hyle of the heavenly spheres. The latter term is explained by Arama to mean that part of the upper world which separated the heavens with their intelligences and heavenly matter from the sublunary world of the four elements.

This definition of the 'firmament' as the division between the translunary world and the sublunary world is found in the writings of Isaac Israeli which Arama quotes with approval. The interpretation given by Arama to Genesis I, 6 is now as follows:

After the creation of light the next step was to make the moving spheres so that they could impress form upon the matter of the sublunary world. The heavenly spheres are then created through the emanation of the intelligences and are set inside the firmament. These heavenly spheres are now in their setting forming the completed firmament which divide the *mayim elyonim* ' upper waters ' (intelligences) from the *tahtonim* ' lower waters' (four elements). Thus, there was first of all, the *rakia* without the heavenly spheres. This is represented by the phrase *yehi rakia* ' Let there be a firmament' and then the completed *rakia* with the heavenly spheres is represented by the phrase *vaya'as Elohim et harakia* ' And God made the firmament.' מים העליונים אשר מעל לרקיע למעלה והם עולם השכלים והמים התחתונים אשר מתחת לרקיע והם עולם ההויה וההפסד והמים האמצעים הוא הרקיע הכולל כל גרמי השמים ושהוא תקרתו של עולם. ' The upper waters which are above the firmament represent the world of the intelligences. The lower waters beneath the firmament represent the material changing world, and the middle waters and the firmament which includes all the heavenly spheres and which is the ceiling of the habitable world.'[86] What was the substance of the firmament itself? Arama suggests that it was formed of a hylic matter והוא כנוי נאות להיולי השמים שאמרנו שנברא ראשונה אמצעי בין קצוות הבריאה ושממנו נעשה הרקיע ' And this is a proper description for the heavenly hyle which, as we said before, was created first as an intermediary between the two extremities of the creation and from which the firmament was made.'[87]

Referring to a midrashic comment that the firmament was formed of water and that ' the middle drop congealed to form the heavens '[88] Arama believes that this is an appropriate reference to the heavenly hyle of the firmament.[89] The seperation of translunary and sublunary existences places the second act of creation in the proper category *Anah* or Place.

3

After the heavens and the earth had been formed in general the Creator proceeded to fashion the particulars of the Universe and continued with the earth. The waters are gathered together and dry land appears. This dry land is given the name *erets* ' Earth.' But this is a homonym since the same term was also used in the first sentence to connote all the sublunary world. The gathering of waters is given the definite term *yamim* ' Seas.' The category Arama gives to this part of the creation is *Matsav* or Position.

## 4

Three different kinds of natural vegetation are mentioned in Genesis I, *desheh* grass, *esev mazria zera* herb-yielding seed, *etz oseh p'ri l'mino* fruit trees bearing fruit after its kind. Arama sees the essential characteristics of these three kinds of growth in the following way.

1. Grass represents that which grows spontaneously without any seed.
2. Herb-yielding seed represents the annual plants which grow only as a result of sowing their seed and which die annually requiring a fresh sowing before a new crop can grow.
3. Fruit trees bearing fruit are the perennial kind, lasting through the years.

The significant remark is made that in the case of natural vegetation the pronouncement 'And the Lord said let the earth put forth grass' is followed by the words 'And the earth brought forth grass.'[90] This means that God implanted in the earth itself the power to produce vegetation of itself without any external agent. Not so, however, in connection with the creation of the creatures of the waters or the living beasts of the earth. There the pronouncement 'Let the waters swarm'[91] and 'Let the earth bring forth living creatures'[92] is followed by 'And God created'[93] or 'And God made.'[94] Although he does not say so in this section, the implication of the remark is that there could be no inherent power in the waters or in the earth to bring forth any living or sentient creature. The evolutionary powers inherent in the earth stopped short of such a possibility and living things could come into existence only by the deliberate and separate act of God's creativity.[95]

The special activity of the earth which produced the vegetation of God's command gives this section of creation the fitting designation of *Yifal* or Action.

## 5

Arama makes it clear that he holds the order of created things as recorded in the Scriptures to be accurate *v'hare hu nakon baseder. En mukdam um'uhar bo.* 'The order is correct and there is nothing in it that should come either before or after.'[96] This question arises from the order in which Scripture places the luminaries in the heavens. Gersonides, for example, holds that in fact the luminaries were completed before the dry land but are placed here in the scriptural account of the fourth day in order to help us to avoid the mistake of believing that the activity of the stars assisted in creating the dry land. The objection of Gersonides to the literal order will be obvious since the luminaries with their consequent light and dark are really necessary, also for their heat and cold, in order to help the vegetation to grow. Arama, however, is adamant and argues that the effects of the luminaries are not essential for the growth of vegetation but only for the living creatures. Therefore, it was necessary for the sun and moon to be in their stations in the heavens only before the creation of living things.

It will be remembered that Arama held that the luminaries were actually created on the first day giving light and darkness to distinguish night from day. It was, he said, only on the fourth day that they were set to move in the heavens to perform their full function over the entire world. Because of this the biblical pronouncement is 'Let there be lights *in the firmament of the heaven*' and not just 'let there be lights.'

The whole calculation of proper ordered time and seasons comes under the category of *Matai* or time.

6

After the spheres moved in the heavens the next step in the sequence of creation was the appearance of animal life and the material or bodily part of their existence was caused by the motion of the spheres. The life element in the animal creatures, however, could be the work only of God himself. ממלאכת התנועות הגלגליות היה הנעת היתודות וערובם בהיות גופי הב״ח לבד. אמנם תת בהם הרוח החיוני וזרוק נשמות לפגרים היה דבר מיוחד לאלוהי הרוחות לבדו ולו נתכנו ולא זולתו 'From the activity of the movement of the spheres procceded the mixing of the elements and the formation of the various substances necessary for the bodily existence of the living creatures. However, the endowing of these creatures with a living spirit and the granting of souls to bodies was the work of the God of Spirits, and no other factor was involved in that.'[97] Since the full life of the creatures could not evolve from the waters, the Bible records a second clause *vayivra Elohim* 'And God created.'[98]

Since the creatures of the sea and the air were brought forth in abundance and were blessed with the pronouncement 'Be fruitful and multiply,' the category associated with this act of creation is *Kamah* or Quantity.[99]

7

The next stage was the creation of the living creatures that are upon the earth. The differences between the animals of the land and those of the sea is the difference between the higher and lower species, the former being more perfect in their structure and ability. Since the Creator acts on the earth and the living creatures are perfected by him, they are the complete subjects of his activity and therefore fit into the category of *Yitpa'al* or Passivity.

8

The heavenly spheres and the sublunary world are now complete. With the creation of man, the higher and the lower parts of the Universe are joined together since man contains in himself elements of the Divine spirit—*vayipah b'apav nishmat hayim* 'And He breathed into his nostrils the breath of life'[100] as well as the ingredients of the material world—*afar min ha-adamah* 'dust of the ground.'[101]

Arama then expounds the Midrash *Bereshith Rabah* in which four statements are made to explain the phrase 'let us make.' One view is that God consulted heaven and earth, another that he consulted his own heart, a third that he consulted the angels and fourth that he consulted the souls of the righteous. In Arama's exposition, these correspond to the four causes of existence, material, efficient, formal and final.

The creation of man further differs from the creation of any other living creature in at least five respects.

1. God created man himself without seconding a part in his creation to any other element in the Universe, as was the case in the creation and evolution of living things of the sea and beasts of the earth.
2. God 'consulted' prior to the creation of man.
3. Man was created as a single person.
4. He was created in the Divine image.
5. He was given dominion over all other creatures on earth.

These points of superiority, which added to the fact that he has the power to exercise a free will to raise himself to the fullest heights of human potentiality, clearly gives the creation of man the category of *Ech* or Quality.

## 9

Propagation is a precept for man rather than an inherent instinct. In this, too, man's place in the scheme of things distinguishes him from other living creatures. His excellence and dominion over all other living creatures illustrates the category of *Mitztaref* or Relationship.

## 10

There remains one category not accounted for yet and that is *Lo* or *Kinyan*, Possession. To the very end Arama's skill never fails him and he finds that the tenth 'saying' in which God grants his living creatures permission to eat of the vegetation of the earth is the most appropriate section to fit into the category of Possession. With this, Arama completes his interpretation of the creation story in accordance with his plan to relate each of the ten pronouncements of God and what follows it to one of the ten categories.

## VI

Before concluding his subject, Arama attempts to solve one or two outstanding problems. First, why did Scripture not include the phrase *ki tov* 'that it was good' after the creation of man? Arama is not satisfied with the rabbinic view that such a phrase would have been inappropriate since man's final perfection is in his own hands. Arama prefers the suggestion, the source for which he does not quote, that the ultimate phrase *tov m'od* 'very good'[102] which on the surface applies to the totality of God's work, really refers more specifically to the creation of man since man represents the logical development and completion of the animal world for which in all earlier stages the applied word is just *tov* 'good.' However, when the whole work was brought to a climax in man the Bible states that it was 'very good.'

Finally, God instituted the Sabbath which, in itself, is also proof of the creation since it shows that God rested from a period of creation which was completed at the end of six days. The Sabbath is the end of the whole process of creation, the seal to the ring, which establishes before all mankind that the Universe bears the stamp of God and that the work of creation is the act of God who made the Universe out of nothing.

Perhaps, as we reach the end of the subject, it might be appropriate to refer to the discussion of Arama's fifth sermon. Here he is concerned to show that of all created things in the Universe, man is the highest. Aristotle's teaching that the intelligences were living spirits which endowed the spheres with the power of motion was taken over by Arab and Jewish thinkers. But even the spheres themselves were considered to be alive, consisting of body and soul. Their motion is not natural, but voluntary, the spheres being rational with intelligent souls. Not only so, but these spheres are of a higher order than man in the chain of existences in the Universe. Arama refers to four reasons why Arab and some Jewish thinkers—among whom are Maimonides, Gersonides and Ibn Ezra—held that the spheres were on a more important level than man. First, the spheres were created before man in the order of creation and consequently may be considered on that account to be of greater worth and importance being nearer to the first cause of all existence. Secondly, they are made of purer substance than man who is fashioned out of common earth. Thirdly, they exist in a higher plain than man whose abode is only in the sublunary earth. Forthly, they are indestructable while man is individually mortal. Arama, however, counters these four arguments by pointing out that if everything created later was less important than a creature which preceded it in order of creation, then it would follow that man is less important than animal and animal less important than vegetation—which is, of course, absurd.

The rabbinic dictum *kol hanivra ahar havero shalit ba-havero* 'Whatever was made after another, prevails over that thing,'[103] is a further support for the supremacy of man.[104] Also the text *na'aseh adam b'tzalmenu* 'Let us make man in our image'[105] signifies the God-like character of man. For Arama, the purpose of the earlier creatures, including the intelligences and the spheres, was all for man since he was the final object of all that God created. In themselves the spheres and the intelligences might be of superior matter and form, but as for the final purpose, they are without a doubt subservient to man.[106] Although Arama is a resolute opponent of Maimonides and Gersonides in this particular matter, he is by no means alone in holding that man is the final and supreme purpose of creation. Talmudic teaching already places man higher than angels,[107] and among the medieval philosophers Saadia clearly enunciates the view that man is the ultimate purpose of God's plan in creation.[108]

Arama devotes the rest of his fifth sermon to several lengthy but ingenious expositions of the texts, all of which, whether from the Scriptures or from rabbinic writings, tend to support his view that when man rises to his full spiritual stature he is the highest and the noblest of all God's creatures.[109] The heavenly spheres, he has already stated, are not really animate beings at all, although he is prepared to cede to the majority view on this. Nevertheless, even if they are animate then they are on no account to be regarded as more precious than spiritual man who is the highest part of God's created Universe and the end for which God brought the Universe into existence.

# 4 THE SOUL

## I

Greek philosophy which enriched Arab and Jewish thought in so many directions is nowhere so evident as in the medieval discussion on the human soul. What is the soul? Whence does it come? What happens to it on the death of the body? Is the human soul different from the vital soul of an animal and if so, what constitutes this difference?

The most comprehensive definition of the soul was that given by Aristotle who defined it as the first perfection of a natural body possessing organs.[1] This definition implies that the soul is not an independent entity outside the body. For when Aristotle says that the soul is the first perfection or 'entelechy' of a natural body, he does not mean that at first there is an organised body which is then entered by the soul, it is rather that the soul is an immanent principle which organises the body and is the form of the body making it what it is. In this sense the soul does not exist without the body any more than a body is complete without the soul. 'The soul cannot be without a body'[2] and the body cannot be without a soul since 'the soul is the cause or the source of the living body.'[3] Yet Aristotle taught that there are parts of the soul which are nevertheless separable from the body. There is in the soul a potential intellect to know all things while there is an influence which makes this potential into an actual intellect. The former, the potential intellect in the soul, is often referred to as the passive intellect; the latter element of the soul is called the active intellect which is 'separable, unmixed . . . superior to the passive factor. . . . This alone (the active intellect or mind) is immortal and eternal.'[4]

Thus it would seem that we might see in Aristotle two kinds of soul, one coexistent with the body and the other separable from it. The first is simply the organisation or form of the body and as such it is inseparable and cannot exist without it. It is to the body what sight is to the eye. This soul perishes with the body since the connection between them is organic. But then there is a higher soul, a thinking soul which is, so to speak, independent of the body and exists after its death. This is the active intellect or reason, imperishable and eternal. On the relationship between the active intellect and the passive intellect and between the latter and other aspects of the soul Aristotle is notoriously obscure. Further, despite his theory that the soul is the form of the body he is not quite free from the Platonic doctrine that the soul is a distinct entity coming into the body from a spiritual world and using the body as its instrument on the analogy of a pilot using his ship.[5]

This confusion and obscurity led Aristotle's commentators to interpret him in several different ways. Among these interpreters there are two who are mentioned by Isaac Arama and who adopted opposite interpretations of their master's teaching. These are Alexander of Aphrodisias (third century) and Themistius (fourth century). The former found Aristotle's definition of the soul as both the form of the body and an independent substance clearly contradictory. The soul is the form of the body only and exists with it and perishes with it. While living, it is a mere potential intellect or disposition. Themistius held the Platonic implications in Aristotle's theories to be the more valid and he regarded the soul as an independent and eternal substance that pre-exists the body and survives after its death. Finally, there were those who tried to reconcile both theories fusing them into an harmonious whole. Among this last group we must place Isaac Arama.

## II

Arama devotes the whole of Sermon VI to his exposition of the subject.[6] At the outset he is concerned to show that if man is to understand his true purpose on earth and, what is more important, if he is to try to fulfil that purpose in life, then it is essential for him to grasp the secret of the soul; he must understand what it is and what is its ultimate purpose and real power. Only then will he begin to understand his great potentialities and will be able to pursue his objects in life with greater success. All this he illustrates from the scheme of the heavenly spheres. With the exception of the uppermost starless sphere which is governed by laws special to itself the other spheres move faster the further they are placed from their Divine source. Thus, the topmost sphere moves slowest and the last sphere of the moon revolves fastest. This is because the nearer they are to their heavenly source the clearer they will understand their real possibilities with their limitations. The higher the sphere the clearer will it understand that it cannot approximate to God, hence it will not revolve at such a furious rate as the lower spheres which, in their lesser knowledge, assume that they can become one with their source rushing along in their pursuit after such an objective. We shall not be detained here with a criticism of this piece of medieval astronomy nor with the inconsistency involved in his earlier preference for the view that the heavenly spheres are not living substances with souls of their own. We may simply note in passing that Arama shared the pre-occupation of his age with astrological matters and sought in the heavenly spheres and their systems an illustration of what might be true in philosophy.

In approaching his own examination of the human soul, Arama first of all places before us the two views of what we found among Aristotle's interpreters, viz., the theory of the organic unity of body and soul which joins soul to body as the form of the matter and describes this soul form as merely a potential intellect, as well as the second theory of anthropological dualism which held that the soul comes from a source outside the body. The first view, he says, is held 'by the majority of thinkers' while the second view he credits to Themistius and his followers. וזה שלא תמלט משתהיה זאת הנפש כח והכנה בלבד הווה בהויית הגוף ומתחדש בחדושו כמו שחשבוה רוב המעיינים או שתהיה עצם נבדל עומד בעצמו בלתי הווה עמו אלא שמתחבר אליו הקשר מציאות בהוויתו כמו שחשב זה טמסטיוס וסיעתו 'The problem is whether this soul is merely a potentiality and capacity which exists only with the existence of the body, created with its creation, as is held by most thinkers, or whether it is a separate substance, existing independently of the body but which is joined to it on its generation by a union of inexistence as was considered by Themistius and his followers.'[7]

Arama then notices the difficulties inherent in each theory. If we hold to the view of the organic unity of body and soul then it would follow that with the death of the body the soul also dies. In this case there is no difference between the human soul and the animal vital soul, implying that man and beast are on the same level. On the other hand, the theory of anthropological dualism is difficult to maintain since it means that the separate substance of the soul coming from an outside source moves towards the material body. But since a thing that moves can only be composed of matter, this is impossible since the soul is not matter, but spirit. Further, if the soul pre-existed the body we have no answer to the question whether it is an individual soul or part of a universal soul.[8] If it is an individual soul, what constitutes its individuality? If it is part of a universal soul then how comes it that there can ever be such a thing as a complete individual soul? Again, if there are individual souls existing in their pre-existent state then it would follow that man is not a free agent since he gets a particular soul with already defined characteristics. On the other hand, if all pre-existent souls are the same then by what method of justice does God decide that one shall go to a righteous and another to a wicked person? Finally, says Arama, let us assume that something does pre-exist the body in the form of a separate spiritual soul and that this something—the soul—is then joined to the body, we might reasonably ask, what purpose at all did God see in planting the soul in a body which might be the cause of its downfall and destruction? On the surface it would seem that it were better had the soul remained in its pure state undefiled by any contact with the perishable body.

In proceeding to expound his own views, Arama is gracious enough to admit that he is about to say nothing essentially original. 'At the outset let it be known that what I shall say I have not thought out from my own heart, but I have chosen it from various opinions and theories expressed by several of our sages and which I have examined by the standards of the traditions of our Faith in order to purify them like purifying fire. . . . The results, therefore, will not be anything strange or new but a compilation and ordered statement of what is found scattered about in books.'[9]

Having made this honest acknowledgment he does not give the sources upon which he drew to formulate his composite theory. In the event, it is difficult to state with any degree of certainty to whom he is indebted for his own theories, particularly, since he admits that he combines several different teachings into his system. As we proceed in our present examination, however, we shall attempt here and there, to draw certain parallels between the views of Arama and those of his predecessors in order to indicate, if only tentatively, some of the chief sources that may have been drawn upon by our author.

### III

All philosophers recognised different classes of soul. Plato spoke of the difference between the vegetative, the animal and the human souls, with different seats in the human body.

Medieval psychology sometimes followed this plan, or taking the soul as a unitary substance divided the single soul into separate faculties. At all events, it is possible to talk of a vegetative soul which is responsible for the body's growth, nutrition and reproduction; of an animal soul which is responsible for locomotion and sensation; and of a human soul which, in addition to the functions of the preceding two souls, is distinguished by the rational faculty. The human soul is clearly superior to the two lower souls since it takes in their functions as well as containing the higher faculty of itself which is unique. When Arama speaks of the human soul he treats it as a single substance composed of several faculties. He defines it as the 'first form'[10] of the human body. It is the best of all 'hylic forms'[11] just as the human body is composed of the finest of all material substances put together in the most 'harmonious mixture.'[12] In stating that the soul is the 'first form' of the body Arama comes close to the famous Aristotelian conclusion which was already generally accepted by many of his predecessors, including Saadia, Halevi, Ibn Zaddik, Ibn Daud, Maimonides and others.

In calling it a 'hylic form' Arama adopts the terminology of Avicenna who taught that the basic soul which is found in every human being is only an intellect in potential and which he calls the intellectus materialis 'in view of the resemblance to primary matter which in itself does not possess any of the forms but is the substratum of all forms.'[13] His comparison between the excellence of the human soul over all other souls and the excellence of the human body over all other bodies includes the thought that the human body is made of a harmonious mixture of the elements and suggests that the substance of the soul is, of course, much more than merely the harmonious mixture of elements. Here, too, he may be following the lead of Avicenna, whose psychology was so well known to Jewish medieval scholars.[14] The soul is brought into existence by heavenly powers acting upon a harmonious mixture of the elements, but the soul is nevertheless above this mixture.[15]

To show how the human soul is recognised as the highest of all forms in created things, Arama writes that all existences are classified in their different groups in an ascending order of excellence. The lowest form is that of the four elements, then the form of minerals, then of plant life and then of animal life. On top of this ascending scale is human life in a state of supreme excellence. There are certain intermediary stages which are easily discerned, giving added proof to the truth of this system. Thus, we see that the monkey stands midway between the human species and the animal, the marine sponge stands midway between animal and plant life, and the coral stands midway between the plant and mineral life.[16] The general theory of the development from the inanimate through the animate and the transition from the lower to the higher form of life is in good Aristotelian tradition and was acceptable to medieval Jewish philosophy. The outcome of this theory is that man is both in his body and in his soul the most perfect of all living creatures. As a result of the excellence of his soul he surpasses all other creatures in his ability to discern what is good and evil, and even more so, he can exercise his reason in his choice of good and evil so that he might even reject an immediate good in order to escape from a remote evil or deliberately embrace what seems an evil for the sake of enjoying a resultant good in the future. This ability to choose by an act of will and intellect is peculiar to man alone.

On examining the human soul a little closer, Arama follows the well-known plan of dividing the soul into different faculties. Sometimes, he divides the soul into two main divisions, the sensory and the intellectual showing that each is again divided into two parts, a higher and a lower.[17] Perhaps his clearest treatment of the division of the human soul is found in Sermon 17.[18] Here Arama remarks that man's complete soul is the result of the combination of three souls, *nefesh tzomahat* the vegetative soul, *nefesh hiyonit* the animal soul and *sekel* the human intellect. The first two comprise three main faculties each and the last is divided into two. Thus, the vegetative soul comprises the three faculties *zan* nutritive, *m'gadel* growth and *molid* reproductive. The vital or animal soul contains the powers of *hergesh* perception, *t'nuah* locomotion and *ratzon* volition. Finally, the human intellect is described as of two kinds *iyuni* theoretical and *maasi* practical. The entire treatment is identical with Avicenna's description.[19]

This intellectual part of the soul differs from the lower faculties since while the latter depend on the body for their realisation the thinking soul can be said in a way to have a certain independence from the necessity of bodily strength, and a body in a state of weakness or great age can still be the vehicle of a strong thinking or intellectual soul.

Sometimes this theoretical thinking soul of man is thought of as being of two different kinds, the passive and the active

intellects. Arama makes the following distinction. The passive intellect is given to every man and is the basic form of the human soul or the hylic soul already referred to and which he describes as the 'first form' of the body. In this form it is found in all men and is designated the universal *intellectus materialis*.
והנה הצורה הזאת ההיולנית אשר כן תארנוה היא הצורה המינית המשותפת למין האדם בכללו ואשר יקבלו אותה כל אחד ואחד מאישי המין
'And this hylic form which the philosophers have described is the generic form for the whole human species and which every member of the human species receives.'[20] This universal passive intellect is a mere potential—*koah hakanah* capacity, or disposition—which can change into an actual intellect through the exercise of personal endeavour and Divine influence. The passive intellect can apprehend only individual things and external objects while the active intellect can comprehend pure form and the essential nature of an object. The passive intellect, or that part of it which does not become identified with the active intellect dies with the body while that which is active intellect is the only immortal part of the soul.

But two notes of caution must be sounded here. First, for Arama, the passive intellect is not altogether in an undeveloped state of primitive ignorance. Indeed, always the lover of rabbinic homily, he finds some value in the quaint talmudic saying which suggests that an infant learns the whole wisdom of Torah before birth but is made to forget it at the moment of birth.[21] It would seem then, that what is actually involved in the struggle for soul perfection is for man to recollect the wisdom and the goodness which were part of him before birth. Education then takes on the interestingly modern character of 'drawing out' the full potentialities which are dormant in the human spirit.
ואולי שהחוקרים שאמרו שכל מה שישכילהו האדם הם על דרך ההזדכרות כוונו אל הכחניות הזה אשר רמזהו חז״ל ויצדק מאמרם
'It is possible that the statements of the philosophers that whatever man understands intellectually is in the nature of recollection points to the (soul) potentiality to which the rabbis have referred. And what they say is right.'[22] The passive intellect is 'potential' then because it already has inherent all the qualities and characteristics which can be turned into perfection. Those qualities only need to be 'drawn out' to become actual.

In this connection also, one should note the doctrine that the soul which comes to man at birth is morally pure and untainted with sin. כל בעל תורה ראוי להאמין שהנשמה מתחילה ומעת היותה באדם היא מראה מלוטשת ומזה בה ידעו ויזכרו כל הענינים האלהיים כמו שאמרנו

## THE MEDIEVAL JEWISH MIND

'ולא נתן לנו אצלה משא הזכוך רק אזהרת השמור Every man of Torah should believe that at the beginning and from the time it came to man the soul is like a polished and clear mirror in which all Divine matters could be seen, as we have said. Nor have we been given the task to purify it but only to preserve its purity.'[23]

This does not really contradict what Arama has already said on the subject of the actualisation of the potential soul since this development of the potential towards the actual soul relates not to moral but rather to intellectual perfection. With regard to its moral purity a man should endeavour to return his soul to his Maker in its original state of purity from sin, but with regard to its intellectual perfection the ideal is for the early soul to be completely transformed. אמנם זה יובן בענין הזכוך אמנם בענין המירוך רצוני ההתעצמות שכתבנו שהוא הכרחי לשלמותה בענין הנפש (שער ו') ראוי ומחויב להשיבה ביתר שאת ומעלה ממה שנתנה לנו בלי ספק 'However, this the return of the soul in its original state will clearly apply to the question of its purity but in connection with its development or actualisation, of which we wrote that it is essential for its perfection (Ser. 6) it is clearly proper and necessary to restore it in a state of greater excellence and higher worth than it was when it was given to us.'[24]

The second point that ought to be made here is that when the Jewish philosopher ascribes immortality only to the highest developed form of the soul it must be recognised that this is not the same as the philosophic concept of Aristotle which holds forward the idea of immortality only by virtue of the excellence of the intellect. Arama knows of this philosophic point of view and in a subsequent sermon[25] he places this theory together with those of the non-believers. When Arama maintains immortality only for the highest form of soul, it is not that the highest soul has reached its excellent grade through the exercise of its intellectual capacity, important as this may be, but through the discipline of the Torah which is of even greater importance. This distinction between the Jewish and the Greek attitudes has always to be recognised.

Now leaving aside these last notes of caution, there are in Arama's whole approach to the subject of the soul several ideas which are worth emphasising. First of all, it is clear that the identification of the passive intellect as a potential intellect, a mere capacity or disposition which is co-existent with the body belongs to the teaching of Alexander of Aphrodisias who attempted to rid the Aristotelian doctrine of all Platonic encroachments. On the other hand, we noticed that Arama believed that the potential intellect can become actualised through an influence acting outside the soul. In this way, he seems to hold forth the view that the highest development of the human soul comes, so to speak, from without, so that in this composite view we see the teaching of Themistius joined with that of Alexander into something of a whole. In another place Arama interprets the Garden of Eden as the external active intellect which influences the four rivers, symbolic of the four faculties of the soul—two sensory and two rational.[26] We can now take note of the view that this external active intellect which acts from without on the passive intellect is not part of the human soul but the last of the angelic substances. This was the unanimous view of medieval Jewish philosophers.[27] In his treatment of the influence of this external active intellect upon the human passive intellect it may be assumed that Arama followed closely on the heels of Maimonides who submitted in his *Guide* that the existence of the active intellect 'is proved by the transition of our intellect from the state of potentiality to that of actuality . . . for whatever passes from potentiality into actuality, requires for that transition an external agent of the same kind as itself.'[28]

We have now reached the following conclusion in Arama's concept of the rational soul. First there is the potential intellect, of the kind which is universal to man. Then through self-discipline and hard training the individual may bring down upon this potential intellect an influence from the external active intellect. When this happens his potential intellect becomes actualised and in so far as it rises to this higher grade then it becomes immortal. עד אשר יתעצם הכח ההיא הראשון עם זה השפע האלהי... והוא הולך ומתחזק עד היותו עצם רוחני נבדל בלתי נפסד בהפסד הגוף כלל 'This first potential joins with the spiritual influence of the Divine and the soul proceeds in strength until it becomes a separate spiritual essence which is not affected by the subsequent destruction of the body.'[29]

The transition from the potential to the active intellect shows, according to Arama, a development in three stages. The first grade in the theoretical intellect is the material or absolutely potential intellect which can rise to the second stage through self-discipline and the influence brought to bear on it by the Divine spirit. It can then rise above this second gradation to the more sublime grade of the active intellect through perseverence in its religious and spiritual discipline and the further influence of the Divine. In this third gradation the soul comes closest to God and as a fully inspired soul is a pure prophetic spirit. Most Jewish philosophers recognised the simple two-fold division of the rational soul, viz., the potential and the acquired active intellect. Schmiedl is perhaps justified in asking who were the Jewish philosophers vaguely referred to by Arama as having recognised three gradations of the rational soul.[30] אמנם התחכמנו עם המתפלספים מחכמי אומותינו כשהניחו במהות הנפש ג' מדרגות 'Moreover, we agree with our Jewish philosophers who supposed three gradations in the essence of the soul.[31]

It is more than probable that he found such a division only in Ibn Daud's *Emunah Ramah*,[32] though he must have been aware that among non-Jewish writers Alfarabi and Avicenna recognise a similar multiple division of the human intellect. The following brief quotation will show the similarity of views between Arama and the later Arab philosopher. 'In the transition of the potential intellect into actual intellect we may likewise distinguish three stages. The first stage is that of the material intellect which actually thinks nothing but is a mere potentiality of thinking. The second stage is that of possible potentiality and marks only the possession of the principles or axioms of knowledge. The third stage is that of the perfection of this potentiality. Here the process of acquisition ceases; all the forms of it exist in the intellect which is in a state of habitus where it can by itself perform the act of thinking. . . . The actualisation of the potential intellect presupposes another external intelligence which is always in actuality and which makes the potential human intellect actual. This is the active intelligence.'[33]

Arama speaks of the religious philosophers who adopt this three-fold division of the soul but before stating the theory in his own words he puts the doctrine into a more specifically Jewish context and so remained faithful to the aim which he set himself at the outset of his task, to collect the various views of other thinkers and 'to pass them through the test of traditional religion purifying them like purifying fire and nitre.'[34] In doing this, he relates the three gradations of the rational soul to the three biblical concepts *nefesh, ruah, neshamah,* and by scriptural quotations he attempts to show that each of these terms can be understood as the equivalent of each soul gradation in ascending order.

'The *nefesh* is that which is with man at the beginning of his life and is the soul's first designation. Then after he becomes a little older and wiser in the ways of the Torah and the Divine commandments his intellect becomes stronger and the *ruah* rests upon him so that the first substance becomes actualised into a separate spiritual substance as has been said. Then should man increase in spiritual strength and habitually occupy this gradation with complete earnestness and with the desire to mount higher and to perceive the presence of his God, the *neshamah* will come upon him as the most perfect of all gradations.'[35]

Among Jewish writers, the terms *nefesh, ruah* and *neshamah* are used in a similar but not in precisely the same way as is done by Arama. Thus Albo interprets *nefesh* as denoting the animal soul of man.[36] In another place he seems to interpret the word *ruah* as pointing to the vital soul of the animal, to be distinguished from *neshamah* which means the human soul.[37] Again Maimonides seems to suggest that *neshamah* is the lower mortal soul of man while his *nefesh* is the higher immortal faculty.[38] Perhaps in this respect at least, Arama shows his independence of all his predecessors since in matters exegetical he is strong enough to show an independent and often penetrating mind. At all events, this division of the soul into three gradations must not be confused with the Platonic trichotomy which found zealous Jewish followers from the time of Philo. According to this theory there are several souls in the human organism, each with its separate power and usually each with its separate seat in a different part of the body. Philo, for example, held that the appetative soul was seated in the abdomen, the spiritual soul in the chest and the rational soul in the heart. Pseudo Bahya in the *Torat Hanefesh* taught that of the three souls, the vegetative soul has its seat in the liver, the animal soul springs from the heart and the rational soul resides in the middle brain. So, too, Joseph Ibn Zaddik. For Arama, however, the soul is a unitary substance, simple and indivisible. While its first state is one of mere potentiality and its latter state may be one of actual intellect— it is still the same soul. The important thing to note is that it has been transformed and has taken on a new chapter through the process of actualisation *m'kabel hitatzmut*.[39]

## IV

Since reference has been made to the doctrine of immortality it is perhaps necessary to add a note on Arama's general view of the doctrine of the existence of the soul after death *hasharat ha-nefesh*. There is nothing new or original about it and he is quite unphilosophical in his approach. The clearest idea of his attitude can be gained from Sermon 70, where, while ostensibly dealing with the problem of reward and punishment, Arama introduces a lengthy discourse on the subject of the highest spiritual reward—immortality.

Four views, he says, can be discerned among people who discussed immortality. The first is the view of the philosophers for whom everything follows a law of Nature. To them, immortality as a reward to the deserving soul is impossible. For if Nature allows soul existence after death then all souls, both of the good and the impious, will necessarily survive as a law of Nature. If, on the other hand, there is no universal law for soul existence after death, then all souls, both of the righteous and of the wicked, must necessarily die with the body.

Second, there is the view that immortality is the fate of that soul which by its intellectual power is identified with the universal active intellect. According to this theory, if there is immortality then it has no reference to God's reward to the pious but is the direct result of the identification of the soul intellect with the external angelic source which is eternal. Arama brackets both these views as non-religious.

Thirdly, there is the belief of the followers of others faiths, such as Christianity and Mohammedanism, which clearly holds forth the belief in immortality for the pious among their own particular religions. Arama indirectly answers the criticism of Christian theologians who pointed out that while immortality is the reward explicitly stated in the New Testament, no reference is made to immortality in the Torah. This objection to the Hebrew Bible and its teaching is unreasonable. First, because the Torah is realistic enough to hold out only such rewards as could be understood by ordinary people. Few would grasp the significance of the promise of soul existence after death while all people would readily understand and act upon the promise of material reward. In this way the Torah is in fact a greater educative force in the life of the ordinary people. But, in any case, says Arama, the heavenly reward of soul immortality is in the Torah although it is only faintly or implicitly understood from the text. There are, he points out, numerous passages which hint at the reward of immortality.[40] This biblical teaching is carried in the writings and in the lives of the sages, many of whom deliberately rejected the pleasures and the material rewards of this world in order to be more secure in the promise of eternal reward after death.

All this leads to the fourth view which is the proper Jewish view on immortality which is that a man of faith knows that the righteous soul will go back to its maker; what is required is that people should be warned that God's grace will not extend over the wicked and that the soul of the sinner will be cut off. That is why the Torah contains stern warnings about the destruction of the sinner's soul[41] and it would be true to say that the Torah is more explicit in stating the destruction of the soul of the sinner than in declaring the immortality of the righteous soul. As if for good measure, Arama now adds an additional support for this view of the doctrine of immortality. This is that over and above the element of encouragement we find from the lives of the martyrs and saints; even irrespective of the veiled references contained in the Scriptures, the Jewish belief in soul immortality can be supported by an appeal to reason. Every existence has a final purpose and the more superior the existence then the more superior will be its final end or purpose. Now the soul is the most sublime form and therefore its final end or purpose must be of the most excellent. This can only be immortality.

From the above discussion we have noticed in passing that Arama seems to hold the view that the soul of the wicked receives some form of punishment after death. Wherein lies the punishment? It may be that the death of the soul in itself constitutes the punishment, or it may be that the sinner's soul survives in some way to receive a more direct punishment. The first view may easily be inferred from Arama's writings on the soul's development. Thus, the first grade of soul which is with man at his birth and develops no further dies with the death of the body and there is absolutely no future for it, of any kind כי הצורה ההיולאנית היא הווה בהוייתו ונפסדת בהפסדו ככל שאר הצורות ההיולניות 'For the hylic form is generated with the generation of man and is destroyed with his destruction, like all other material forms.'[42] The inference from this is that the lower soul dies with the body, and there is no doubt that such also is the theory held by Maimonides[43] which was certainly known by Arama. The problem arises, however, what happens with the theory of retribution and wherein lies the future punishment of the wicked? Maimonides is consistent in his view that the absolute destruction of the sinner's soul in itself constitutes its punishment.[44]

It would appear however, that Arama is not nearly so consistent in maintaining the theory of the destruction of the lower soul, for in addition to what has been said above he seems to leave the door open for some kind of existence for the lower soul in which it would receive the punishment due to it. אם שתאבד ולא תשאר כלל או שתשאר מצטערת לעד 'Either it perishes and has no further existence, or it remains in a state of eternal existence in suffering?'[45] Arama's equivocation may be an indication of his own deep uncertainty on this point or it might be that we have here an illustration of the conflict between the philosopher and the religionist, the philosopher maintaining that the lower soul perishes with the body and the religionist in Arama requiring that the soul still be kept in existence to endure its punishment.

Within the same area of discussion we can show an example of the same kind of conflict within Arama. According to the Aristotelian doctrine that everything that is generated is subject to destruction it would follow that the soul, being generated at birth, is also by the very physical law of its beginning subject to destruction. Now Arama is aware of this view and without criticising its validity he attempts to reconcile it with the view of the immortality of the higher soul of man. How can this be done? The answer Arama gives is that when the higher soul is in a state which merits immortality it is not really the originally generated soul at all which becomes immortal, for that original soul has now become completely transformed through the Divine influence and has become something else. In this sense then, it cannot be said that the higher soul was generated or produced *ab initio*, it is that the old one has been transformed and in the process, the lower soul has coalesced or changed into something higher and different.

In this way the philosopher makes room for the theory of immortality without having to give up teaching that everything produced is subject to destruction. But even at this stage Arama has second thoughts. If what he has said is true, it must follow that if a man's lower soul remains in a state of undevelopment then that soul will necessarily perish with the death of the body. What happens then with the theory of retribution which may require the sinner's soul to remain in some state of existence in order to receive its due punishment? As if to forestall such a question, Arama goes on to say, that in any case it is not necessary to believe that everything which is generated is subject to destruction and he refers with approval to Maimonides who shows that such a belief is contrary to proper Jewish teaching.[46]

# 5 FREE WILL

## I

Jewish religious teaching has always recognised free will as a fundamental doctrine. Man is of flesh and spirit and through the spirit he is able to discern between the good and the bad, between the higher and lower values of life and nearly always man has freedom of will to choose for himself the path which he will take. Indeed, so insistent is the Bible on this teaching that it is dogmatically expressed in clear unequivocal terms. 'Behold, I set before you this day a blessing and a curse: the blessing if ye shall hearken . . . and the curse, if ye shall not hearken. . . .'[1] It is, of course, true that the Bible contains a few references which seem to indicate that man is not free, but close examination reveals a particular point which the Bible there wishes to stress and which does not in fact negate the fundamental teaching that man has the freedom to choose between right and wrong and to act in one way rather than in another.[2] So, too, in his solemn farewell warning to his people, Moses declares, 'See I have set before thee this day, life and good, death and evil; and ye shall choose life.'[3] Again, in the story of Cain and Abel, the Bible speaks of 'sin crouching at the door' like a beast of prey ready to spring on a weak victim, 'but you shall rule over it.'[4] Perhaps one of the clearest expressions of the same idea in extra-biblical literature is found in Ecclus. 15, 'Say not then, it is through God that I fell away. . . . He himself made man from the beginning, and left him in the hands of his own counsel. If thou wilt, thou shalt keep the commandments; and to perform faithfulness is of thine own good pleasure. He hath put fire and water before thee; thou shalt stretch forth thine hand into whichever thou wilt. Before man is life and death; and whichever he liketh it shall be given to him.'

In early philosophical literature Philo was the first to set the pattern for subsequent Jewish teaching on the subject. In opposition to Plato who held that the Universe is governed in accordance with immutable laws of nature which cannot allow any alteration of the destined course of events, Philo wrote, 'God gave to the human mind a portion of that free will which is his most peculiar possession and most worthy of his majesty.'[5] The rabbis of Midrash and Talmud expounded the identical doctrine with a steady insistence. Typical of their exposition is the following homily. . . . 'God deliberated how to create man. He said to himself, "If I create him like angels he will be immortal; if I create him like the beasts he will be mortal." And so God decided to leave man's conduct to his own free choice.'[6]

Of course the question inevitably arises how such free will can be reconciled with God's foreknowledge of events. God is omniscient and knows all things that are to happen in the future. He is, too, the ultimate arbiter of man's destiny. But if this is so, then how can it be said that man is free? On the other hand, if man is completely free, how can it be said that God has pre-knowledge of all man's actions before he does them since man's conduct to be free must not be bound to a particular pattern known first by God. This is the difficulty against which all thinkers fought hard, in an attempt to reconcile two equally precious doctrines since they are loath to let go of either. Philo is the first to be keenly aware of the problem, although he does not discuss the apparent conflict between the two theories and the difficulty of holding both at one and the same time.[7]

He simply states both doctrines and in different places asserts that God has foreknowledge of all things that are to happen and that man has free choice to do as he wills. The same attitude is adopted in the Talmud. Thus Rabbi Akiba taught 'everything is predestined, nevertheless free will is given.'[8] This, on the face of it seems as amazing a paradox as one is likely to find. Clearly, Akiba, like most of his rabbinic colleagues, was faced with two directly opposing teachings, each of which, on its own, was held to be true. In general, the rabbis were prepared to hold on to both theories, with the implication that freedom and providence are the joint authors of man's destiny. In the result this might mean that in some things the conduct and affairs of man are in God's hands but in most things man is the sole author of his conduct.[9]

The problem of God's foreknowledge and man's freedom was one which was keenly debated by medieval philosophers and it is here that we shall see how an attempt was made at a solution for nearly all medieval Jewish philosophers from Saadia and onwards were deeply concerned with this question and gave it a position of centrality in their writings. Abraham Ibn Daud wrote in his Introduction to his *Emunah Ramah* that the exposition of the problem and its solution was really the sole purpose of his book.

## II

The general discussion among medieval writers hinges upon three chief points. God's knowledge, God's providence and man's freedom. God is perfect and therefore no deficiency can be allowed in this knowledge, for lack of knowledge, even of contingencies or of individuals, would amount to a deficiency in God. Again, faith in God who is good and all powerful demands the belief that he directs and controls all the affairs and the destiny of man. But if this is so then two problems immediately arise. Since God knows also the contingent it is impossible that man should do anything other than that which is in God's knowledge. For if he was to act in any other way it immediately follows that God's knowledge is incorrect—which is an impossibility. Since, therefore, man can perform only those acts which are in God's knowledge, it follows that his actions are not really free. Again, what happens to the justice of God when the righteous suffer and the wicked prosper, for God must know the true merits of each class?

In their attempts at reconciling God's omniscience with a belief in man's freedom we can distinguish three main shades of thought. There are those who fervently hold on to both horns of the dilemma and proclaim that God has foreknowledge and also that man is free. The chief exponent of this school is Maimonides who follows most of his predecessors, including Saadia and Judah Halevi. This is the view generally shared by most Jewish writers after Maimonides, including Joseph Albo as well as our own author, Isaac Arama. Differences are to be found in details, not in principle. The second view is the celebrated view of Gersonides, and to a much lesser extent, even of Ibn Daud who, in his attempt to safeguard the important principle of man's freedom sacrifices some of God's knowledge in order to leave man absolutely non-determined. The third point of view is that which finds it necessary to hold fast to the doctrine of God's knowledge even if it means giving up some of man's freedom. Hasdai Crescas approaches such a viewpoint; and even with him we cannot be absolutely certain on all points that this was his intention. It is significant therefore, to note that with the single possible exception of Crescas, all other Jewish writers insisted on man's freedom of action.[10]

Let us now first of all examine the views of Maimonides which form the basis of Arama's own exposition.

Maimonides gives us a clear outline of five different theories concerning God's providence in relation to man's freedom.[11] The first is the extreme view of Epicurus and his followers who deny altogether God's providence and hold that there is no order of determination in anything in the Universe, since everything owes its origin to chance. The second theory is that of Aristotle who believes that providence exercises its management directly only in the translunar world of the spheres, but these higher existences transmit their influences into the lower world and establish life in accordance with the laws of Nature. These laws ensure the existence and the future of all things as a species but not as individuals. The human kind is subject to providence but not the individual man. Vegetation is protected by the laws of providence in Nature but not the separate tree which may be uprooted by a storm or by accident.

Thus, says Maimonides, Aristotle makes no difference 'between the case of a cat killing a mouse that happens to come in her way, or that of a spider catching a fly, or that of a hungry man meeting a prophet and tearing him.'[12] All these occurrences to individuals of the species are accidental and in no way the result of providence. The third theory is that reported of the Mohammedan Ashariyah. According to them every single thing that happens in the world is predestined by God. It is God who not only causes the wind to blow but also makes the leaf to fall in one place and not in another. With God there can be no such thing as possibility since a thing is either necessary or impossible. Contingencies exist only in relation to man but not to God. When man acts he does only what is necessary in God's knowledge and providence. When the innocent suffer it is likewise a necessary occurrence in God's providence. Against the fatalism of the Ashariyah, the Mutazillah believed in a limited free will for man. This is the fourth theory in Maimonides' exposition. They hold that God knows everything and that he is just; when the righteous are slain it is so that they might receive greater reward in after life. But even while these things are believed, man still has free will—although it is not absolute. The fifth and last view is that of the Torah. Man has perfect freedom; indeed, it is part of Gods' wisdom that all creatures were given power to move and act of their own will. Further, all things that happen to man, whether to the individual man or to the community as a whole, are a manifestation of God's justice. 'Even when a person suffers pain in consequence of a thorn having entered into his hand, although it is at once drawn out, it is a punishment that has been inflicted upon him (for sin), and the least pleasure he enjoys is a reward (for some good action). All this is meted out by strict justice; as is said in Scripture "All His ways are judgment" (Deut. 32, 4); we are only ignorant of the working of that judgment.'[13]

Having emphasised that Divine providence is exercised over each individual human being, Maimonides then proceeds to explain his view of God's knowledge of the individual.[14] God is perfect in everything and since a deficiency in his knowledge is impossible it must follow that he knows everything. God knows, of course, each individual since we have already seen that his providence extends over each human being. But because God's knowledge cannot change or increase, i.e., he cannot at one stage know something that he did not know before, it follows that 'he constantly knows them, and therefore no fresh knowledge is acquired by him.'[15] He knows, that is, all events before they take place. God's knowledge extends over the past, present and future and is part of his essence.[16] But if God knows all things, even the contingencies, what happens to the free will of man? Is he not destined to act in a particular manner that agrees with God's knowledge of contingencies? Maimonides, of course, is clear on the doctrine of man's free will and accepts no limitation of this freedom or compromise with it. 'Free will is granted to every man. If he wish to direct himself to the good way and become righteous, the will to do so is in his hand; and if he wishes to direct himself to the bad way and become wicked, the will to do so is in his hand. . . . Let there not enter your mind the assertion of the fools of other peoples and also of the ways of the uninformed men among the Israelites, that the Holy One blessed be he decrees concerning the human being from his birth, whether he is to be righteous or wicked. The matter is not so.'[17] Maimonides asserts, furthermore, that it is all part of God's wisdom that man is endowed with free will. 'Just as God willed that man should be upright in stature, broad-chested and have fingers, likewise did he will that man should move or rest of his own accord and that his actions should be such as his own free will dictates to him, without any outside influence or restraint.'[18]

From all this is can be clearly seen that Maimonides (like others before and after him) clung to both theories though he was fully aware that logically it is hardly admissable to do so. When attempting to solve the problem he seems to hide himself behind a cover of agnosticism. God's knowledge, he says, is of a special kind. It cannot be understood by us, no more than God's essence can be properly defined.[19] The important fact, however, which is borne out by the Scriptures, and by philosophical enquiry is that God's omniscience in no way acts as a determining cause of man's conduct. It may be pointed out that Maimonides was severely criticised for his weakness and vagueness in raising questions which he did not satisfactorily answer.[20]

Yet it is difficult to see how any solution to the problem could be found on the basis of holding as inviolable doctrines both the teaching of God's omniscience and man's freedom. Indeed, all subsequent philosophers, including Arama, who maintained both theories together, were compelled to follow Maimonides in his agnostic attitude towards the problem of God's knowledge.[21] We just cannot know how God can have full knowledge of all contingencies and yet leave man perfectly free to act by his own unhampered choice. Saadia and Judah Halevi came to a similar conclusion, though neither of them attempted to examine the problem as deeply as Maimonides.[22]

Leaving aside Gersonides who gave up the idea of God's knowledge of particulars and Crescas who compromised with the pure doctrine of man's freedom, those who followed Maimonides hardly deflected from his general treatment of the subject or from his views in any material aspect. Joseph Albo devotes about twenty chapters of the *Ikkarim* to a lengthy discussion of God's knowledge, his providence and man's free will and with the addition of some non-important references to the place of the stars as determining factors in man's destiny he contributes no suggestion that is not already found in Maimonides. What are these theories which were formulated by Maimonides and are found also in Albo? They may be listed as follows:

1. God must be free from defect, therefore he must know everything.
2. God's knowledge is infinite and embraces the non-existent.
3. Freedom is a true doctrine and is essential to Divine law.
4. The first two principles can be reconciled with the third point, only on the admission that we can never know the nature of God's knowledge.[23]

We have here all the theories of Maimonides repeated by Albo. The same is true of Isaac Arama who also incorporates into his system several minor ideas not referred to above since they do not seem to affect the main problem. We shall notice them, however, more carefully in our closer study of Arama's treatment of the subject. It is to this that we must now apply ourselves.

## III

Arama's treatment of the subject of free will is contained chiefly in Sermons, 19, 21, 22, 26, 28 and 103. Like Maimonides he is concerned at great length to explain the character of God's knowledge and like his great predecessor his starting point is that there can be no deficiency in God so that we cannot conceive of any absence of knowledge in God. If knowledge is essential to the wise man—and without knowledge he is no longer wise—how much more so must we postulate complete knowledge as inseparable from God והנה מפני היות הראשון הוא יתברך החי בהחלט והחכם על כל והמשלים כל אשר בו רוח חכמה הנה היא מהמבואר תכלית הביאור שהוא יודע 'And since God is the first and absolute living Being and is wisest above all, and he perfects man in whom there is a spirit of wisdom, it must clearly follow that he has knowledge.'[24] But among those who agree that God has knowledge there are different views about the character of this knowledge. There are those who believe that since God's knowledge cannot change he can have knowledge only of that which is constant, i.e., himself. Consequently, knowledge in God can only mean that he has knowledge of himself כי זה מה שיפיל שום שנוי ושום רבוי שידיעתו בעצמותו אינה נוספת על עצמותו והיודע והידוע דבר אחד 'For then there can arise no change or plurality since his knowledge of his essence cannot increase and the known and the knower are one.'[25] Then there are those thinkers who are not satisfied with the view that God can know only the constant essence of himself and wished to ascribe to God knowledge of particulars and contingencies. They do that, says Arama, by putting forward the view that God has knowledge of universals only and, that his knowledge of particulars is implied and follows from his knowledge of universals. Further, that which is contingent is possible only in our own limited knowledge, but in God's knowledge there is really no such thing as the contingent or possible since everything is necessary as the effect of a cause and that cause from a preceding cause and so on until we come to the ultimate constant universal cause which is in God.

Thus, from God's point of view what we call possible is really necessary and since his knowledge and his essence are one and necessary it follows that it embraces all the particulars and future events which we call contingents. God knows the particulars then, but not in their separate individualities but as part of one constant and unchanging knowledge of the universal.[26] Then there is a third view which Arama attacks with great force. This is the well-known view of Gersonides that God knows only universals and not particulars or individuals. Indeed, God has knowledge of particulars only when they happen. For a thing is either necessary, impossible or possible. If it is necessary then God knows it as part of the constant universal law which he established. If it is impossible then the concept of knowledge cannot in any case apply to anything which does not exist. If it is possible, then God cannot know it before it happens because if he does know it then it is no longer merely possible but it must happen.

On the basis of his exegesis of Job 10, 3-6, Arama attempts to explain five reasons that have generally led philosophers of the above view to deny God's knowledge of contingencies.

1. Knowledge makes the possessor of that knowledge more perfect. But God has no need of such additional perfection since he is altogether perfect.

2. When anyone has knowledge of a particular thing, that knowledge becomes part of his essence so that the subject and the object of knowledge become one. But knowledge of unimportant details, of individuals and contingencies, cannot be thought of as part of God's essence.

3. Knowledge of particulars can be gained only through normal sense perception which cannot apply to God.

4. Contingencies occur with changing circumstances and at a point of time which is different from the past and future. But God's knowledge cannot be subject to such occurrences within the limitation of time change.

5. The strongest objection to a belief in God's knowledge of particulars lies in the hard reality of the existence of evil. If God knows individuals and contingencies then how can he allow righteous individuals to suffer or the wicked to prosper?

The exegesis is faulty and forced since Arama tries to fit five philosophical objections into four phrases of the scriptural text. He also claims that Maimonides mentions these five arguments of the philosophers against God's knowledge of particulars in his *Guide*, III, 16. In fact, Maimonides refers only to three. Arama, it would seem, merely puts up the skittles so that he can knock them over before stating his own opinions. This he proceeds to do and he bases all his arguments on two main theories, viz., that lack of knowledge, even of contingencies, would amount to a deficiency in the all powerful Creator. Secondly, that the omniscience of God is ultimately something we can only ascribe to him but cannot understand because man's knowledge can never fathom the character of Divine knowledge.

We can now state Arama's own view on God's knowledge a little more clearly. They may be conveniently listed as follows.

1. Since God is perfect we must ascribe all knowledge to him.
2. This knowledge embraces the past, present and future. שהוא יתעלה יודע הכל הדברים העוברים וההווים והעתידים ידיעה אמיתית שלמה מכל צד 'The Most High knows all things past, present and future in one complete and true knowledge in every respect.'[27] שלא יתואר בשום חסרון עד שזה מה שיתחייב ידיעתו כל העניינים הנמצאים בין עוברים בין הווים ועתידים מאיזה מין שיהיו 'He may not be described with any deficiency at all so that it must follow that he knows of all existence of whatever kind whether past, present or future.'[28]
3. God's knowledge extends directly over individuals and particulars. הוא יתברך יודע אלו הנמצאים כלם הנצחיים עם רוב חלופיהם לסוגיהם ומיניהם וכל הדברים האפשרים המתחדשים לא ע"ד הכללות והחיוב מסיבותיהם לבד כי אם ג"כ ע"ד האישיות המעוין 'He knows all existences which are consistent with their numerous changes in a generic way but also all contingencies that occur he knows not as a result of the universal and necessary cause but also as separate individualities.'[29]

## IV

We must now proceed to see Arama's standpoint with regard to man's freedom. As has already been noted he is most emphatically on the side of human freedom. He adopts the well-known argument that God's own perfection really implies that he gave man freedom since otherwise man would be an imperfect creation—an idea which we may not hold. Furthermore, we believe that God gave the Torah with all the commandments and prohibitions together with promises of reward and punishment. Surely, asks Arama, it would amount to a serious failing

in God were he to have given such instructions and yet not have createad man free to choose his way in order merit either the appropriate reward or punishment. אמנם הנחת שלמות הידיעה הנה
לא תכחיש החפשיות בבחירה אבל יקיימהו לפי שהנחת הידיעה השלימה אנו
רק כח החיוב שתחייב השכל לסלק ממנו יתעלה כל העדר וכל חסרון וזה עצמו
מה שיחייב חיוב הבחירה האנושית ואמיתת החפשיות שאם תאמר שידיעתו זאת
מכרכת אותנו בפעולתינו היה בכח חסרון בה שלימותו להטפל אלינו על ידי נביאיו
ולהורות לפנינו תורה מצוות ליעד שכר וענש עליהם אחר שאין רשאין לעשות
גדולה וקטנה כי אם אשר נתחייב מפי הגזירה מהאל ית׳ 'Now this supposition of God's perfect knowledge need not negate our belief in free will. On the contrary, it should confirm it, since our supposition of God's perfect knowledge means that we must remove from the Supreme Being any deficiency or failing ... and this in itself must lead us to a belief in human freedom and its truth. Because if you were to say that God's knowledge determines our actions it would amount to a deficiency in his perfection. Since he has concerned himself with us through his prophets and given us Torah and commandments appointing reward and punishment in respect of them though he knows that we are not permitted to do aught, big or small, except what is determined by Divine decree.'[30] הנה הידיעה השלמה היא בו ית׳ מחויבת ועליה אנו
סומכים על אמתת חפשיות הבחירה כי לא דבר רק ובטל יוצא מתחת ידו ית׳
'Indeed God's own necessary perfection in knowledge is a basis on which we rely for our belief in the truth of free will.'[31] God therefore knows all things, even contingencies and individuals. At the same time man is free in all things. How are the two theories reconciled and acceptable as one whole?

Arama admits the difficulty of the problem and seems to suggest at times that it is really insoluble. It is fundamental to our Faith that we should believe in God's perfect knowledge of details and in man's freedom—although we cannot explain the matter and reconcile both parts of the proposition rationally. *af al pi hadavar kasheh al ha-sekel ha-anushi.* 'Although it is difficult to understand by reason.'[32] Basically then, Arama follows the approach of Maimonides in his attempt to answer the difficulty by declaring simply 'We cannot know.' God's knowledge cannot be understood because we have no measuring line for it: it is a different kind of knowledge that bears no relation at all to human knowledge and so we cannot ever hope to understand how God's knowledge of individuals and future events can still leave man free to choose and act.[33] This is an illustration of Arama's attitude which is at the forefront of his entire treatment of the problem.

## THE MEDIEVAL JEWISH MIND

As an argument, that is really final and nothing that Arama says in addition is of much assistance. When he writes, for example, that God knows contingencies because they will happen; they don't happen just because he knows them, then he does not add anything to the solution. ידיעתו ית׳... נמשכת ממה שיצא אל המציאות לא מציאותם ממה שידעם 'God knows because those things will happen; they do not occur because he knows them.'[34] It is succinctly put, but we are still left wondering what kind of knowledge is this which is God's, which embraces future contingencies and yet has no causative power in the sense that man is still free to choose from a variety of possible plans of action. Can he, we ask, choose to do that which is not in God's foreknowledge? If free will is to be maintained it is arguable that he can choose to do something contrary to God's knowledge, but that would immediately upset our belief in God's knowledge. We are compelled then to fall back on the answer, 'We cannot know.' We believe that God knows all but that his knowledge still allows man to be free in the details of his conduct.

Before concluding this section it might be worth pointing out that medieval scholars knew of the discussion on our limited free will, i.e., the freedom to act badly but that good conduct was the necessary result of the gift of God's grace. Thus a man does good because God has bestowed his grace on him. Arama explains this view in his smaller work *Hazut Kashah*.[35] According to this view expounded by a 'certain wise man' who is obviously a Christian scholar, God first blesses a man with his grace and then the man does good. In the sphere of good conduct there is really no freedom. Free will exists, however, in the power of man to choose and to do evil. The whole chapter is interesting as an example of Arama's firm but polite method of debating with non-Jewish theologians and also as an illustration of the atmosphere of scholarly disputation which characterised some medieval Jewish Christian discussions into which Arama was drawn. Our author resolutely opposes anything short of complete freedom for man to do good or bad and against this Christian doctrine of grace he offers four clear arguments.

1. Although the Christian theologians recognise the truth of Aristotle's ethical teaching, they fail to realise that such teachings which limit man's freedom is against the views of Aristotle and the philosophers.

2. If God does not extend his grace to a particular man,

then the very witholding of it may be the condition for a man to act badly. So there is no true free will even in bad conduct.

3. According to this theory of Divine grace there would be no possibility for a good man to become evil, just as there is no real freedom for a bad man to become good.

4. The whole of this doctrine of grace is against the main teachings of Scripture. Thus, says Arama, God delighted in Noah, Abraham and the Patriarchs because they did good: they did not act righteously because God chose them first for the blessing of his grace. At every point Arama is firm. Man is free at all times to choose his own conduct, good or bad.

V

The character of man's fate or destiny, says Arama is not altogether the result of free will nor entirely the result of providence: there is something of both involved. But of the two, freedom is the factor of greatest importance since the detailed actions of man in which he has complete freedom will necessarily influence Divine providence in his favour or against him in accordance with whether he deserves a good or bad fate.

In his twenty-sixth sermon Arama explains from this point of view the biblical account of Jacob's preparation before meeting Esau. It is an old, but always interesting question which Arama tries to answer. Since Jacob was worthy of Divine protection why did he go to great lengths in arranging for the physical safety of himself and his company? Surely providence would exert its saving influence to rescue him from Esau. On the other hand, if God willed that Jacob be slain at the hand of Esau then what profit all his small preparations?[36] Arama begins his exposition by stating that when looked at closely, we realise that reason, Torah and man's experience all testify to the apparent fact that man's fate is the result of Divine providence, the heavenly constellations, his own diligence and sometimes even pure chance. והשכל והדת והנסיון כלם יחייבו שלא יהיו בדרך אחד מהם לבד הנה אז יחייב שתיעשינה ע״י כלן ' Reason, religion and experience force the conclusion that (man's destiny) is not controlled by one of these factors alone (Divine providence, stars, diligence or chance) but they are the necessary result of all factors.'[37]

It might seem strange that he includes chance at all in his list of causative factors, particularly after his agreement with the Aristotelian refutation against the incidence of chance.[38]

Still, he soon states that the element of chance is really rare and consequently insignificant. His purpose in including it in his list is not at all clear, particularly when he proceeds to ignore entirely the incidence of chance and concentrate on the other three factors.

With regard to providence, little need be said here since it will in any case be perfectly obvious that Arama leaves ample room for the workings of Divine providence in the lives of individuals and groups. The stories of the Patriarchs and other good men and women prove that God has care of their destinies; the records of Israel's history is further support for the belief in God's providential care over whole peoples. The more worthy the people or the individual the greater the degree of providence. That is why he suggests that Divine providence is extended more particularly over Israel.[39] In yet another place[40] Arama develops the thought that although God's providence is extended over all, nevertheless it varies in accordance with merit. God's providence is smallest over the gentile nations, is greater over Israel and is greatest over the individual man who follows in love the teachings of Divine law and precept. There are, he says, three degrees of providence. The first is shown to the gentile nations and is illustrated in the stories of the Flood,[41] the Tower of Babel,[42] the destruction of Sodom,[43] and the story of Jonah. Here God intervened in history in order to right a wrong. The expression used in the Bible for this type of providence is *r'iyah* that is, God sees, and in these instances he delegates great responsibility to angels and other intermediaries, including stars. A second and higher form of providence is recognised under the biblical term *panim* that is, God's 'face' is turned towards or against the people[44] and it is Israel alone which is the object of this kind of providence. The third and highest kind is reserved for those select individuals who live in accordance with God's law. To them the expression applied is *en Adonai* or the 'eye of God' which is always compassionately turned to those who fear him.

A word must now be included in connection with Arama's reference to astrology. In the Middle Ages particularly, it was extensively practised by Jews and the most notable scholars were firm believers in the validity of astrology. Man's fate, they maintained, was decreed in the heavens and largely depended upon the particular constellations under which he was born. We shall shortly see how a belief in astrology could be reconciled with the greater and more important truths of

Divine providence and man's freedom. Nevertheless, it remains for the time being to notice this widespread popularity of astrology—ideas which were accepted as true by the greatest Jewish minds of the age, including Abraham Bar Hiyya, Abraham Ibn Ezra (the most enthusiastic astrologer of all), Abraham ben David of Posquieries, Abraham Ibn Daud, Joseph Albo and our author, Isaac Arama.[45] Indeed, Maimonides is said to be the only authority who was opposed to astrology and who was outspoken against the 'absurd ideas of the astrologers' which he connects with witchcraft.[46] But the power of astrological beliefs was too strong to be upset by even such criticism and it remained a constant element in Jewish philosophical writings long after Maimonides.

This raises some doubt against the principle of free will in an even stronger form. If man's character and destiny are decided by particular constellations then it immediately destroys the whole basis of man's freedom of action. The answer given is that the stars only create a tendency in man to act in a particular way: they do not provide him with his final character and destiny. So Arama can say that although man has נטיה בפעולות מפאת הגרם השמיימי או מפאת המזל לא יחויב שיהיה כן על כל פנים 'an inclination in his conduct because of the heavenly spheres or his star; it does not follow that in every event he is destined to follow a particular path.'[47] The extent of the power of the spheres lies in their ability to create in man a particular disposition or leaning towards one kind of action rather than to another. Man is therefore still free to rise above this tendency and although his fate is described by the stars, it is a fate which would only be realised if he followed his tendency caused by the stars. If, however, he broke the causative influence of the stars to act independently and of his own free will entirely, then the fate decreed previously by the stars and subsequently upset by his independent action can itself be repealed by the Divine power which grants the individual freedom to act, even if it means that thereby the decree of the stars may be upset. אבל כי יד האדם תהיה תמיד על העליונה להתנהג כפי שכלו ועל פי חפשיות בחירתו הן לשבר הוראת המזל ההוא בלי ספק לגמרי או שיהפך הוראתה אל צד וצדדים שלא תזיק או שתועיל מעט או הרבה 'Nevertheless, man will always be more powerful to conduct himself according to his reason and free will whether entirely to break up the indication of the star or to deflect its indication so that it be rendered entirely ineffective.'[48] Again he says,

ואם יש די זכות תורה ומצוה ביד האדם ודאי הוא שליט על מזלו
'And if a man has sufficient merit in Torah and good deeds he can certainly prevail over his star.'[49] So, too, his emphatic statement שכל האדם על הכל אין המזל כדאי להכריחן אדרבה המזל נמסר ביד השכל לתכן או לעוות 'Man's intellect is supreme over all (conditions). The star is not powerful enough to compel him (to actions); on the contrary the stars are subservient to human intellect which may confirm or reject (the stellar indications).'[50]

Taking all three points together—free will, the stars and providence—Arama lays greater stress on free will. For in all ordinary cases man's own voluntary efforts can earn him the merit that the fate of the stars is even upset in his favour by Divine providence. This power to act and to bring about a definite result in most things is the whole justification for man's *haritzut* or diligence and effort. For what other purposes, asks Arama, would the Torah give man explicit instructions with details of conduct to be observed and of other things to be avoided if not so that man can influence his own fate by voluntary good or evil conduct. True it is, that the stars exercise an influence, but Arama holds that free will means that an individual can break out from the state of subservience to the stars. Arama continues this part of his astrological theme by examining the following cases.

A man may be born under (a) a good star; (b) a bad star; or (c) a neutral star. His conduct may be (d) good; (e) bad; or (f) medium. Now he notices the following combinations.

1. If there is a combination of (a) and (d) then God's providence lends man all support to confirm the indications of the star and to make that man eminently successful. Such a person need not be over careful to guard or protect himself with *haritzut* for his good fate is secure.

2. If there is a combination of (a) and (e) then the good indication of the stars is set at nought through the intervention of providence.

3. In a combination of (b) or (c) with (e) then his position is certainly without hope. Nothing he can do will be of avail to him.

4. If there is a combination of (a) and (f) then the indication of the stars is not likely to be confirmed by providence since there are not enough voluntary good deeds. In such cases the individual should exercise great personal diligence and care in

order to protect himself from possible harm. Personal diligence in this group is a saving factor.

5. If there is a combination of (b) or (c) with (f) then providence will certainly not intervene on his behalf and he needs to exercise in his personal affairs all the care of which he is capable.

6. If there is a combination of (b) or (c) with (d) then providence will watch and assist, but he is warned at the same time to avoid obvious dangers and to employ a measure of *haritzut*.

From the above series of combinations it is clear that Arama credits greater power to good deeds than to good stars. The last possibility, for example, implies that an evil star may be overcome by good deeds and careful conduct. Arama concludes this section by advising every man to consider himself born under a neutral star and with only indifferent conduct to his credit. In this event, he cannot directly draw upon himself a special manifestation of God's protection and he must be conscious of the fact that his own diligence and efforts are required to keep him safe.[51]

None will suggest that such a system is without inherent contradictions and that it does not conflict with Arama's own insistence on the teaching that God has direct knowledge of each individual. It is unfortunate that medieval Jewish philosophy had to be tied down even to such an extent to astrological beliefs. That Jewish philosophers in general were able to maintain a working belief in man's freedom as well as in God's foreknowledge, was due to the fact that each doctrine in itself was too precious to give up. Also because those thinkers who held to both views together could always take refuge behind the agnostic attitude adopted by Maimonides, or by postulating the reservation that God's knowledge is in any case not causative of the events of which he knows. In their astrological beliefs, however, they were faced with no religious authority or sanction for persisting in the belief that the stars have a causative effect on man's life. At the same time, once holding such a belief, they are not easily presented with a reasonable way out of the impasse of constellary determination. For the stars are either causative or not. Astrologers believed that they are. Furthermore, it is difficult to see how their indications could be changed since they are part of the laws of Nature. To the modern reader it all seems rather strange. Yet, perhaps the attitude of Arama[52] can be understood by a modern reader who substitutes for the influence of the stars the factors of heredity and environment. We are then faced with the modern discussion of freedom versus determination. In this discussion it is clear that even those who uphold the view of man's freedom are still aware of the fact that man is subject to certain conditions not of his own making. These are the conditions of heredity, social factors and environment which, while not of his making, nevertheless combine to create very powerful influences in his life, often shaping his conduct and consequently his fate. Yet it is felt that these conditions create only a tendency and a disposition in his character, sometimes a powerful one, it is true, but one never so strong as to determine without doubt man's character and conduct. For above everything else man still has freedom to break away from the bands of circumstance and to assert himself as a free individual. Cases are on record of twins who were subjected to the same set of circumstances, but who, nevertheless, act in different ways and lead different lives. One has allowed his circumstances to govern him; the other has risen over them and rendered them purely external.

This view of self-determination which is current in modern idealistic thought seems also to be recognisable in the medieval Jewish writers. The only difference in treatment is that while the modern writer talks about heredity, social circumstances and environment as the semi-determining factors, the medieval theologians write about the stars. But the problem is the same and the approach to a solution seems to be the same.[53]

## VI

When we say that man's actions influence providence either to confirm or to annul the fate destined in the stars it should be made clear that this applies only as a general rule. For there are exceptions, when God wills a particular end which has little or no relationship to the sequence of antecedent events. In other words, the final end takes place not necessarily as an end event in the chain of cause and effect of man's free behaviour but as a result of God's special will.

A man may perform an act of good intent but the result may not seem good to him. Conversely, the intention may be bad, but the result may seem good. Arama interprets the story of Joseph as an example of such an instance where the agent had one intention while the result bore no relation to what was intended. This is because the result is in the hands of God and the final outcome is in accordance with God's plan. This is not to say, that because the result is God's work that in such cases at least man is devoid of freedom. No; the point is that God's result in no way determines man's free choice of particular actions, since in any case God's will can be carried out in so many different ways. כי תשאר הבחירה האנושית חפשית לגמרי בכל חלקי המעשים האנושיים אם היות קצת ענינים כוללים ונמשכים מהם מיועדים מפאת החפץ האלהי 'Human freedom remains for all the details of man's conduct, although some general results which follow from them are determined from the point of view of God's wisdom.'[54]

It is of importance to note that the range of even such limited determined results is clearly restricted to 'some' general results. But the supremely important conclusion for Arama is that even in that determined class of event which occurs because it is God's will the freedom of man in his particular actions is inviolate. Thus, Arama insists הרצון האלהי בכמו אלו הענינים אינו מכריח הרצון האנושי החלקי 'Divine will in such matters does not in any way determine man's free choice in particulars.'[55] Again, he says כוונתו יתברך בענין הכולל אינה מכרחת חלקי המעשה הפרטים לאנשים אבל כל אחד הולך לתומו ועושה כפי חפצו ורצונו 'The general intention of God does not determine the particular or individual action of man but everyone is able to conduct himself according to his perfection and act according to his desire and will.'[56]

Along similar lines Arama explains the statement of Rabbi Akiba, 'Everything is foreordained (i.e., the final general result) but free will is given' (i.e., in the details of conduct). When the final result does not fit in with man's actions, then we must still believe that man will ultimately receive his proper reward in full accordance with his own actions, good or bad, irrespective of the result which may have been brought about through the separate will of God. For God is just; therefore, reward and punishment will be meted out in strict justice.[57] But here we seem to be about to encroach on the subject of Divine retribution and justice which is a subject to be examined in the next chapter.

# 6 REWARD AND PUNISHMENT

## I

Jewish religious philosophy is generally agreed on the principle of God's knowledge, man's free will and Divine providence. The next logical step is to believe that man receives from an all-knowing God just retribution for his voluntary conduct.

The doctrine of Divine retribution is consequently a fixed belief in Jewish theology and is an essential pillar in the religious philosophy of all representative Jewish thinkers.[1] The source of every Jewish exposition is found explicit in the Scriptures and in the Talmud which hold out the unambiguous doctrine that there is reward for obedience and punishment for disobedience. Man's fate, then, is directly connected with his conduct and he receives the reward or punishment he deserves.

The eleventh principle of Maimonides lays down the general statement with which no Jewish teacher would disagree: 'The Creator, blessed be his name, rewards those who keep his commandments and punishes who transgress against them.' Maimonides further states, 'Wrong cannot be ascribed to God in any way whatever; all evils and affliction as well as all kinds of happiness of man, whether they concern one individual person or a community, are distributed according to justice; they are the result of strict judgment that admits no wrong whatever.'[2] Thus far, everyone is agreed. The difficulty arises when the details of such a just working are examined. If God metes out justice why do some wicked people prosper and some righteous people suffer? Does God dispense justice in this world or in the next? Is retribution in the form of material reward and punishment, or by an external spiritual reward and parallel punishment? Maimonides is prepared at the outset to adopt an agnostic attitude and having set down the fundamentals of the belief he remarks 'We are only ignorant of the working of that judgment.'[3] This frank attitude towards the impossibility of a full solution has a parallel in rabbinic teaching of the second century 'It is not in our power to explain either the prosperity of the wicked or the afflictions of the righteous.'[4] It is an attitude adopted also by modern scholars. Thus, M. Friedlaender writes, 'We understand the doctrine of retribution only in its general outlines . . . but how the law is applied in every single case is known to God alone. It is presumptuous on the part of short-sighted man to criticise God's judgment and to find injustice in the seeming misery of the righteous.'[5] So, too, Isidore Epstein writes, 'The character of this retribution is not known. Judaism being chiefly interested in doctrine for the sake of their significance—moral and religious— is satisfied with the mere definitive establishment of the belief in retribution, without being much concerned as to the manner and circumstance in which it would be effected.'[6]

Nevertheless, in spite of the great difficulties involved, Jewish teachers often attempted an explanation of the working of Divine retribution in accordance with God's justice. Generally speaking their attempted solutions fall under two chief headings. First, that God rewards the righteous and punishes the sinful in this world and consequently physical happiness or affliction have a clear relationship to man's conduct, i.e., there is physical reward for righteousness and physical affliction for sin. When it became evident that such a theodicy cannot always be maintained in view of the suffering of the righteous or the prosperity of the wicked a second approach to the problem was propounded which suggested that true reward and punishment are in the next world after death. Various secondary views can be observed under the two headings just given. Thus, the view that children may suffer for the sins of their fathers or enjoy a reward because of the merit of their fathers[7] will easily come under the first heading, while under the second theory will be noticed the view that the righteous often suffer affliction not on account of sin but because God loves them and chastises them as a loving father trains his children.[8] In the course of our exposition we shall need to notice both main theories and their subsidiary ideas a little more closely, particularly as Arama, here as elsewhere, is eclectic rather than consistent in one theory.

The first view is that of 'measure for measure' and is maintained on explicit scriptural authority that the promise of retribution is physical[9] and is meted out in strict return for sin or righteousness. The historical record of Israel in the Bible amply illustrates this theological doctrine since it is seen that national affliction always followed sin against God's law.[10] In the book of Job, which is entirely devoted to the problem, Job's comforters hold firmly to this doctrine and seek to explain Job's calamity by alluding to some early sin. The speeches of Moses in Leviticus 26 and the whole theme of the proclamations in Deuteronomy are modelled on this philosophy. Many teachers in rabbinic literature expound the same doctrine. 'There is no death without preceding sin, nor affliction without preceding transgression'[11] is a comment on Ez. 18, 20 and Ps. 89, 33. In a similar way the afflictions which occur in the life of entire peoples are seen by them as a direct result of infraction of the laws of God as set down in the Bible. 'Pestilence comes into the world for capital crimes mentioned in the Scriptures. . . . Noisome beasts come into the world for vain swearing and for profanation of the name of God. Captivity comes into the world for strange worship and incest, and for shedding of blood and for not giving release to the land.'[12]

This philosophy of 'measure for measure' both in the apportioning of reward and punishment is often translated into what seems the most unlikely events. Thus 'Because the Egyptians wanted to destroy Israel by water (Ex. 1, 22) they were themselves destroyed by the waters of the Red Sea (Ex. 14, 28).' At times this rough and ready philosophy is carried to extremes, as when we read 'Samson rebelled against God with his eyes (by lusting after a Philistine woman Jud. 16, 4) therefore his eyes were put out by the Philistines (Jud. 16, 21).' Again, 'Absolom, whose sinful pride began by his hair (II Sam. 14, 25) met his fate by his hair (II Sam. 18, 9).'[13]

## II

It is at this point that we might conveniently turn to our own author because his views fall very largely into this first theory of 'measure for measure.' In this particular respect he shows some independence of his medieval contemporaries and is not afraid to adhere quite dogmatically to the biblical teaching of material retribution on a strict basis of 'measure for measure.' We shall see later on how he tries to answer the difficult problems involved in this point of view but in the meantime we need to say that, as far as possible Arama tries to follow the strict implications of the biblical and rabbinic views just mentioned and only introduces other solutions as secondary ones when he is forced to do so because of the obviously difficult task to hold consistently to the theory of 'measure for measure.'

Every instance of suffering, Arama maintains, is first to be explained as the just punishment of God for sin. Arama quotes the statement in the Talmud[14] in the name of R. Hunna that if a man become a subject to suffering he should examine his conduct. The probability is that he has sinned in some way and his suffering is then a clear case of just retribution sent by God. If, having examined his conduct he finds nothing wherein he has sinned then he should assume that his punishment is the result of his neglect of Torah study. What, however, if the sufferer has in no way neglected the study of Torah? In that case, there can only be one explanation and that is that his suffering is a chastisement of love sent by God to those whom he loves in order to train and refine them for a higher reward. Arama's view is based on the clear faith that everything that happens to an individual happens with God's knowledge. Further, since God is just and it is unthinkable that anything should occur with his authority which is not just, then it must follow that there is really a just reason for all individual suffering. The problem very often is to find out this reason, but if a man searches hard enough he could find it. Most suffering must be assumed to follow on from some sin or other since it would be extraordinary for a man to be perfectly free from all guilt. Viewed from this aspect, suffering is to be regarded as an essential instrument for spiritual improvement because it is like a barometer indicating how a man stands with God.

הייסורין הזמניים הם נר דלוק ביד האדם לדעת מה טיבו עם בוראו ושאין דרכם לבוא כי אם בביטול המצוות המרחיק נפש אדם מאלהיו ושעל ידם ישוב אליו ויתוקן עניינו... אם לא מצא במעשה יבדוק בדעות ובהתרשלות השתדלות התורה והשכלתה וכאשר יקרה שלא יחטא באחת מהנה מה שיהיה על צד הפלא הנה באמת הוא ענין אהבה יתירה כעניינו של איוב וכדומה וכמו שאמר את אשר יאהב ה׳ יוכיח. 'Temporal suffering is like a flaming torch in man's hand to show him his relationship with his Creator since suffering does not usually come except as punishment for man's neglect of the commandments, a neglect which estranges man from God. But through suffering he can return to God and his position can be remedied. . . . If he can find no wrong deeds which he has committed, he should examine his mind (his beliefs and the quality of his faith) and his reluctance to aspire to Torah and the understanding of it. But should it transpire that he is not at fault in either of these two matters—which would be something of a miracle—then his suffering is indeed a manifestation of God's special love as was the case with Job and others like him, as it is said "Whom the Lord loveth He chastiseth."[15]

Arama's interesting parenthetical note 'which would be something of miracle' reveals his true mind since from this we may assume that he is convinced that few people, if any, are blameless. Hence nearly all suffering has sin as an antecedent.

This is Arama's chief theme and it is a corollary of his oft-repeated teaching that God constantly concerns himself in the affairs of man. He is not merely the Creator of the Universe, who, once having set the world in motion leaves everything to follow its original law with cause and effect, but he is God who can interrupt at will the natural law in order to bring just retribution on the world and on the individual.[16] It is unthinkable then that a man should suffer or enjoy temporal punishment or reward as a matter of chance, or as a result of antecedent fortuitous circumstances not of his making. For then man would be subject to an unfair or arbitrary fate which is impossible in a world governed by a just God. It must be affirmed, maintains Arama, that everything that happens to a man happens as a result of God's justice; hence his fate is brought about primarily as a result of his conduct. The sinner will suffer punishment for his sins and the righteous man will enjoy his proper reward.

Commenting on Lamentations 3, 37-40, he relates the passage to those who foolishly believe that suffering can come to man without Divine providence, i.e., 'When the Lord commandeth it not' since 'out of the mouth of the Most High proceedeth not evil and good." וזה הענין לא יאמר מצד שנמשך מהסדר השמיימי העליון אשר ברא השם לעשות עד שנאמר שמה שנמשך ממנו הוא מה שצוה להיות תמיד על יד הרצון הקדוש הן בשיסכים עם המעשים הבחריים או לא רק שהוא חפץ בדבר עתה בעת שיסכים המקבלים הן שיסכים עם הטבע הקדום או לאו וא״כ חויב שלא ימשך זה הרצון רק מפאת המעשים האנושיים כי לא ישדד האל ית׳ הטבע חנם ואם כן מה יתאונן אדם חי על מה שיבוא עליו מהרע כי אם על חטאיו. 'This matter (suffering) cannot be explained as a natural sequence of the order of the heavens which God created so that whatever develops from that original act is in a sense what God commandeth to happen as an effect of his first act of will, whether it fits in with man's free conduct or not. Surely, he wills the particular thing to happen now in accordance with the new act of man at each time whether what happens is consistent with the original laws of Nature or not. Hence God's will is connected with human behaviour. For God will not upset the law of Nature for no purpose. So wherefore doth a living man complain on account of the evil that befalls him except it be for his sins?'[17] Hence the text continues 'Let us search and try our ways,' for the evil that befalls a man is connected with his 'ways,' i.e., his sins, which are the cause of his suffering.

With regard to the *philosophical* problem of the existence of evil, Arama shows little or no further interest since he is chiefly concerned with the problems of theodicy or of God's justice. From the above, however, as well as from the general direction of his remarks on sin and suffering, it must be assumed that he would regard sin and evil as an absolute and not just the negation of the good as was believed by Ibn Daud and more particularly by Maimonides.[18]

The purely philosophical problem of the existence of evil appeared as a stumbling block to the concept of a God who is all good and from whom nothing evil, physical or moral could proceed. The answer that Maimonides gives is that evil is not positive, it is simply the non-existence of the good, as darkness is the absence of light. Since God makes that only which is positive, i.e., that which is good, he cannot be said to produce evil which is merely the absence of the good. Arama, it would seem, would hold quite a different view and he makes moral evil the positive choice of man while physical evil is the positive punishment sent by God in retribution of sin.

### III

This, briefly stated, is Arama's theory of temporal suffering and quite clearly there is nothing original or new about it since it is the classical theory of representative rabbis of the Talmud[19] and it is a view of punishment which maintains a strong body of support in Jewish religious literature of the Middle Ages. But hovering above this approach to Divine retribution there is the gnawing problem raised by the suffering of the righteous and the prosperity of the wicked. How can such hard realities be accommodated by the side of the belief in God's justice? In answer to this problem some thinkers brought to the front the teaching that true reward and punishment exists only in life after death; material welfare is of no importance, or at best it is only of infinitisemal value. The idea that the righteous suffer in this world for their few failings so that they reach their fullest reward in the world to come while the wicked enjoy worldly prosperity for their few good deeds so that in the life after death they suffer unmitigated punishment for their evil conduct is a theory which is well known[20] and one would naturally expect to find it in Arama who follows the classical rabbinic theology in this discussion.

In general, however, Arama is anxious to make physical retribution something really important and meaningful. He agrees, of course, with the greater value by far of spiritual reward in the world to come, but he will not use this as an answer to the problems just stated, simply because he also believes that a substantial element of Divine justice is recognised in this world.

In his discussion on life's true values, Arama makes both points of man's life of real importance—the material and the spiritual. The spiritual is without doubt the greater and more significant, but it could not be achieved without the former which acts as an instrument by which man can achieve a state of spiritual worth all the more effectively. To take the acquisition of wealth as an example, Arama refers with agreement to Aristotle's discussion[21] on the definition of a 'good and the Good.' The Good is that which is ultimate, the final happiness or *summum bonum* for man; a good is that which can serve as an aid towards reaching the Good. Now wealth, while not the Good is nevertheless a useful aid—it is a good and consequently it can be legitimately desired, not, of course, for itself, but as a help towards final happiness.[22] This final happiness is spiritual and hence the force of the rabbinic maxim 'Where there is no bread there is no Torah. Where there is no Torah there is no bread.'[23] In this sense material prosperity is something which should be legitimately desired, though, of course, in moderation, and it is both foolish and unrealistic to turn one's back against this pursuit which must be recognised as a perfectly proper activity for man.[24] In this view Arama finds support from rabbinic and biblical texts, the most explicit of which is perhaps his reference to Ecclesiastes, 'It is good that thou shouldst take hold of the one: yea, also from the other withdraw not thy hand.'[25]

Throughout Arama's writing there is this healthy insistence on the importance of physical well-being and happiness as a worthy aim and a good for man הוא מהמבואר שהצלחת האדם וטובתו נשלמת בב׳ דברים ראשיים האחד טיב הנפש והצלחתה הנקרא בלשון הכתוב דבוק בה׳ באומרו ואתם הדבקים בה׳ אלהיכם ובו תדבק (דברים י׳) והיא תכלית הכל והב׳ טיב מצבו וספקו מהטובות הזמניות העזרות ומשרתות אליה כמו שזכרנו ראשונה ובהרבה מקומות 'It is clear that man's happiness and good is fulfilled by two chief ends. The first is the welfare of his soul and its happiness which is described in the Scriptures as cleaving to God, as it is written "And ye cleave

unto the Lord your God," and, " And ye shall cleave to him."
This is the final goal. And secondly, by his personal welfare and
his satisfaction of temporal goods which assist him towards such
an end, as we stated before and in many other places.'[26]

Divine reward and punishment similarly is of both kinds,
spiritual and material המצות התוריות האלה נתנם לנו האל הנאמן
להנחיל אוהביו יש ולמלא אוצרותיהם מהצלחות שני העולמים ' The faithful
God gave us these commandments of the Torah to give his
beloved ones inheritance and fill their treasurers with the happiness of both worlds.'[27]

In all this we find nothing really new in Arama since most
Jewish philosophers maintain that reward and punishment is
given both in this world and in the next. Even Maimonides,
Gersonides and other Jewish Aristotelians would scarcely deny
that there is reward in this world. All that they would maintain
is that the chief reward is spiritual and in the future world,[28]
which is really what Arama himself says and is in general accord
with classic rabbinic doctrine on the subject.[29]

The problem now posed by Arama is this. Since reward and
punishment extend to material retribution in this world and
spiritual retribution in the world to come, why is it that the
Bible seems to stress in so many places the promise of only
material reward and punishment, particularly as it is spiritual
reward which is really the chief aim of religious endeavour?
אחר שהיותר שלמה שבהצלחות הוא הצלחת הנפש והשארותה בעונג מתמיד
בעולם הנשמות היה ראוי ומחויב שיהיה הוא הכוונה התכליתית לכל מצות
התורה והשכר המיועד אליהם ' Since the most perfect happiness is
the happiness of the soul and its immortality in eternal bliss in
the world of the spirits, this should have been the proper and
necesesary purpose of all the commandments of the Torah and
the reward promised for them.'[30]

Our author makes much of this particular question since to
him it had rather important implications in his defence against
Christianity and Islam which claimed superiority over Judaism.
לא הוזכרו הייעודים הנפשיים בתורת משה כמו שהוזכרו בדתותיהם
' Spiritual promises are not mentioned in the Law of Moses as
they are in their own religions.'[31]

His answer to this problem is twofold. First it is a denial that
the higher kind of spiritual retribution is not found in the Bible:
it is only that it is not as explicit as reward and punishment of
a material kind. Arama then gives a number of illustrations from
the Scriptures which point to the heavenly reward after death.

Among such verses he quotes the following 'If I had not believed to look upon the goodness of the Lord in the land of the living,'[32] and similar verses where the phrase 'the land of the living' is understood as the eternal life with God after death. 'For Thou wilt not abandon my soul to the nether-world, neither wilt Thou suffer Thy godly one to see the pit,'[33] where the reference is to the destruction of the wicked in that he can enjoy no after life. There are numerous places in the Bible where the reward held out is purely spiritual, but the Bible does not deal with such matters in detail since they are not subject to physical proof. גלתה אותם גלוי מספיק ונאות כפי טבעם כי מהטבע הדברים אשר כאלה שלא נראו מציאותם לחוש שלא להתפאר בהרחבת הדבור בהם רק באופן אשר ישכילם מעצמו ימצא אותם בכתובים וירגישם הרגש שכלי חזק 'The Bible has revealed these things sufficiently well in accordance with the nature of such matters which are not subject to sensorial apprehension. So it has not expounded the matter extensively but only to the extent that whoever discovers it by himself can find evidence in the Scriptures and comprehend it with a strong intellectual perception.'[34]

The second answer Arama gives for the apparent preponderance of material reward over spiritual reward in the books of the Bible is a realistic admission that the Bible speaks for the average man for whom the profound mysteries of spiritual reward would be unintelligible and therefore a promise of such reward would be without much purpose. The true reward, Arama agrees, is the reward of immortality but most people will not understand promises of spiritual bliss in an after life: they can grasp only the everyday material things of the tangible world. And when God does, in fact, reward and punish people in this world it serves as a salutary reminder of the reward and punishment after death and provides man also with a guide by which he can aspire to the higher spiritual reward. Arama uses the analogy of an archer's target which contains many wide circles around the central point or 'bull's eye.' Very often, he says, the marksman finds that he cannot aim directly at the centre point because it is too faint or small. He will, therefore, use the outer circles as a guide and regulate his aim for the centre by reference to them. So too is the connection between temporal and and eternal retribution. Both are real and both are the just workings of a just God, but the Bible is realistic enough to hold out in the first place that kind of reward which is more easily understood and which will consequently be a clearer target for the average man.[35]

Other philosophers have emphasised that the true reward is the spiritual reward and have pointed out that the promise of material gain is a sort of educative technique to train the immature person to do well. Maimonides uses the example of the lad who is urged on with his studies by the promise of a sweet: the youngster studies hard but is all the time consciously aiming at the prize. This in itself represents only a stage in the boy's training, but it is nevertheless an important stage.[36] For man, in all his weakness will find it easier to aim at the true spiritual reward by aspiring to redeem his conduct from all culpable actions deserving of a physical punishment.

Arama, it is now clear, recognises the validity of this argument, but goes perhaps further in an acceptance of physical reward and punishment as a distinct reality which exists, so to speak, for itself. Put in another way, we may say that God orders physical reward and punishment not only as a tempting good or warning for the immature but as a real element in Divine retribution.

It is this part of Arama's theory, the reality of material retribution which opens up so many problems which Arama, like others, is unable satisfactorily to answer. But before we notice these problems in the context of Arama's writing it would perhaps be as well in a sentence or two briefly to review his position thus far. First, he holds that ultimate retribution is given after death. Second, there is a lower form of retribution—which is still a real part of God's justice—which decrees material reward and punishment on earth. Third, the cause of reward and punishment in both cases is the righteousness of the good and the sins of the wicked for which they receive their just payment from a just God.

## IV

Arama really fails to see that his position thus far contains irreconcilable contradictions. As we saw, he holds that physical reward and punishment is a measure of Divine retribution sent by God to the righteous and the wicked respectively, but quite obviously he is unable to leave it as simple as that. In the first place, how does one explain the suffering of the righteous? We have seen that Arama insists that in most cases this can be understood with reference to some sin committed by the righteous man. But what if he is altogether without sin? Then, says our author, it is a 'chastisement of love' sent to the truly pious as an indication of God's careful refining of the righteous man's soul. But this would mean that every perfectly righteous man should suffer chastisements of love. This is a position that could hardly be maintained since it would rule out the possibility of an altogether good man enjoying physical happiness and prosperity in this world. Such a view, it is suggested, would be absurd in theory and cannot be reconciled with the known experience recorded of many pious men who lived without suffering. If it is true that a material reward may be the lot of the righteous then it cannot also be true that the righteous will undergo 'chastisements of love.' It is one or the other, but it cannot be both. For if he enjoy material prosperity as a reward for his righteousness then he is without suffering. But if he be without suffering, is not this a proof of the absence of God's love since 'He who God loveth he chastiseth'? If, on the other hand, the righteous man suffer the 'chastisement of love' then he is without material happiness and in that case what happens to the theory of the reality of physical reward and punishment for the righteous and the wicked? This is strong enough an objection to such a composite theory suggested by Arama.

Of course, Arama could attempt to defend himself by holding that the suffering of the righteous is not such a great problem after all because 'There is not a righteous man on earth who doeth only good and sinneth not.' We saw before that he maintains that a completely righteous man is something of a phenomenon *al tzad ha-pele* and consequently every man will deserve some punishment. But part of the problem, however, undoubtedly remains, particularly when the sufferings of the righteous man are long and severe. Further, the real problem is seen when the sufferings of the righteous are compared with the material happiness of the wicked.[37] For Arama, material well-being can be the corollary only of righteous conduct. Why then do the wicked prosper? Of course, we ought not expect to receive a more satisfactory answer to the intractable problem posed here any more than we receive a satisfactory answer from any of the other thinkers who have applied themselves to the search for a solution. The most we can expect, however, is some large measure of consistency in Arama's treatment of the subject. Unfortunately, there is room for criticism here, since, forgetting his earlier emphasis on the reality and the worth of material happiness he joins forces with so many others who have faced the problem of the prosperity of the wicked by belittling the importance of material prosperity in any case.

Thus, we can adopt the well-known view that material welfare and prosperity is only transitory and the apparent success of the wicked is fleeting. Interpreting Psalm 37, 1, Arama says, 'Fret not thyself to join those men, workers of iniquity, who choose this imaginary (material) happiness. For even if a man like that exists for a short while he cannot continue for long.'[38] The real reward and punishment is spiritual, not material and man should not concern himself for more than his minimum physical requirements. This is the lesson of the Succah which indicates by its flimsiness the insubstantial values of material goods and which brings to the front the lesson of spiritual bliss and happiness as the all-important factor in man's life.[39]

In this way also, Arama argues that the purpose behind the laws of the Sabbatical and Jubilee years as well as a purpose which motivates even such social laws as the prohibition of usury is to warn man and to prevent him from the folly of spending all his time and energy in the acquisition of material wealth.[40] Here Arama does no more than fall in line with the well-known theory that since true reward and punishment are spiritual and meted out in the life after death, the wicked receive their reward in this world for the little good they perform, while the righteous receive their punishment here in this life for the few sins which they commit. This leaves the full reckoning for the other world unhampered by the small unpaid accounts.[41] But Arama is no more satisfied with this answer to the question than we would really expect him to be. He knows clearly enough that the prosperity of the wicked is a great problem and one which was a stumbling block to real faith.

He refers to those in his own day who murmur against God's justice 'when they see the prosperity of the wicked and say "Why is not the earth destroyed on account of that evil man's crimes? Why is not his house destroyed over him, or why does not the earth swallow him up?" Such mockeries are proclaimed by those people who cry out "Let God hasten and speed up his work that we might see something." And so this unbelief is the great barrier against faith in Divine providence and they choose the path of atheism.'[42] Arama offers in the context of this passage, which is part of his exposition of the Flood story, two further suggestions which are worth noting. First, that the destruction of the wicked is kept back till the very last moment in order to give them a chance to repent. God after all, is the Father of all creatures, so shall he not deal even with sinful children as a merciful father? God's patience in dealing with the wicked is part of the Divine compassion. *l'haarik la-r'shaim ulai yashuvu* 'To deal patiently with the wicked in case they repent.'[43] Hence the fact that so many generations elapsed between Adam and Noah in which wickedness filled the earth, yet God withheld his punishment.[44] Even at the last moment, a further chance was given to them because the instruction to build an ark was carried out in public in the hope that others would see Noah's preparation for the Deluge and would repent even at the last moment. It was only when the wickedness of the people was complete and unredeemable that God brought the Flood to destroy them. Therefore, says Arama, in examining the problem of the prosperity of the wicked we do well to distinguish between those who are so evil that they have gone beyond the point where there is hope for return and those others who are also wicked but for whom there is yet hope of redemption from sin ...רשעים שאינם גמורים אלא שהם רשים ממעשים טובים ועדין לא נחתמו לאבדון אבל הם תלויין ועמדין לראות אם ייטיבו מעשיהם אם לא אמנם לרשעים הגמורים אין דבר עומד בפניהם. כמו שהיה הענין בזה ובזה בדור הרע הזה שנשטפו במי המבול.' These people are not out-and-out sinners, but are merely without good actions and are not yet finally decreed for destruction. Their case is indetermined in the chance that their behaviour might improve. However, for those who are thorough sinners there is no obstacle to their punishment as we have explained in connection with this evil generation that was overwhelmed by the waters of the Flood.'[45]

The second suggestion that Arama makes in the discussion is that God may refrain from punishing the wicked since often the innocent is involved in the suffering. This, of course, was the force of Abraham's plea for the cities of the Plain[46] and was the argument used by God himself when he spared Nineveh which contained much innocent cattle.[47] Only when it is clear that God's punishment of the wicked will not result in unjust suffering to innocent bystanders or others who are innocently involved, only then is the punishment of the wicked decreed. למנוע הרע מהזכאין הנלוים אליהם כאשר א״א שלא ימשך להם רע מרעתם יחוייב לבא אצל אלו הפורענות בקושי גדול 'God withholds punishment from the wicked in order to withhold evil from the innocent ones who are associated with them. Since it is impossible that some evil does not attach itself to them from the evil of the wicked it follows that such punishment would be an unfair hardship for them.'[48] This answers the complaint against an apparent injustice of God by an appeal to his justice and its validity is perfectly clear.[49] The same argument which explains God's apparent leniency towards the wicked can of course be extended to explain God's affliction of the righteous. For sometimes an individual may appear to suffer although he be righteous so that through his personal suffering a great good for a large number of people is realised. This is the obvious interpretation of Joseph's reply to his brethren 'Ye meant evil against me; but God meant it for good, to bring to pass as it is this day, to save much people alive.'[50] Arama makes a special point of this and states that God's plan was not so much for the individual *ki im l'maan ha-tov ha-klali* 'but for the common good.'[51] Thus, Arama uses with good effect the doctrine of the good of the large number as a greater good than that of the individual.

It is, of course, possible to connect these two secondary ideas to Arama's main thesis which relates sin and suffering as a matter of cause and effect. In the present two subsidiary theories, he still retains this main thesis, that sin is the antecedent of material punishment, but it is modified. Sometimes, a wicked man will continue to prosper because he is not altogether sinful and God gives him a chance to repent. Sometimes the wicked man will not suffer so as to avoid innocent dependants suffering in his destruction; they are innocent therefore God's justice demands that they be left unharmed even if it involves the escape of the individual sinner, since the benefit of the larger group is more important than the punishment of the individual. On the same basis, an individual righteous man may sometimes be called upon to suffer for the good of the wider community when the larger group is worthy enough to receive such a benefit.

Old Testament theologians are fond of using the term 'corporate personality' to describe the totality of the Jews as a single social unit.[52] It is the idea of the 'corporate personality' of Israel which they suggest lies at the basis of the early dispensation of a rough justice on the family of an offender against the law since the members of the sinner's family were to be held in almost equal responsibility with the sinner within whose crime they had been caught up.[53] In the present discussion, however, we see the principle working in reverse, that is, not that the individual's conduct must bring suffering on the community but the community's welfare can guarantee that the individual sinner shall, on occasion, remain unpunished. So, too, the righteous man's conduct may at times, far from bringing him material reward, actually result in great personal suffering if thereby the community as a whole stands to benefit.

The theory is attractive on the surface, but it is soon seen to suffer from two faults. First, it seems to come rather close to the Greek theory of God's providence which extends over the species and not over the individual. This is a very serious criticism, particularly in view of Arama's oft-stated opinion that Divine providence extends over every individual. God is the great Creator and all creatures stand in relationship to their Maker who knows them as separately known and individual creatures whose personal acts of righteousness or sin will not be ignored. Secondly, even on the basis of the theory that the welfare of the community is of greater importance than the retribution of the individual, an omnipotent God of justice could still reward and punish an individual without upsetting the Divine will in respect of the entire community. We ought to be able to conceive of the wisdom of God which can punish an individual sinner without affecting the larger group just as we can conceive of God's wisdom bringing about the safety of the community without inflicting suffering on an individual righteous man. The theory that partial evil can be universal good is really no answer to the problem of evil because the individual selected to suffer may well ask 'Why select *me* rather than anyone else?' It may be that partial evil can lead to a greater good, but the problem still remains in its distribution.

The easiest way out of all these inconsistencies and difficulties would, of course, have been to maintain that this-worldly prosperity and suffering are of no account at all and that true reward and punishment exist only in the next world. But our author rejects such a view. The nearest he comes to such a position is in an interesting passage where he argues that if God immediately rewarded the righteous and punished the wicked then there would be no room at all for the exercise of true free will since the wicked man would immediately alter his ways as soon as he saw that his sins brought him no profit but punishment. God, therefore, having set the laws of Nature, allows affairs in the world to proceed on the basis of cause and effect so that everybody, wicked and righteous, enjoy or suffer under the same cosmic laws and man is therefore left with no selfish motive in his choice of good or evil. But the universal laws of Nature which benefit the righteous and the wicked impartially can go uninterrupted only for a limited duration of time since at a certain stage God will certainly interrupt those laws to punish and to reward. והנה לפי זה הרשעים כי תצליח דרכם ולא פנו ולא שתו לבם לאמר מה זאת עשינו להוסיף רשע יום יום עד אשר יחרה אף

'השם וקנאתו עליו ויטה ידו על הטבע הזה העומד עלינו And so, when the wicked prosper and do not consider what they do but continue more wickedly each day, God's anger and zeal is finally kindled against them and he stretches his hand to interrupt the laws of Nature which protect us.'[54]

But the relevant point is that in spite of Nature's laws which protect the righteous and the wicked alike, at some stage in human affairs God does interrupt the law of cause and effect to give to each his due merit on this earth. Physical reward and punishment in this world are therefore realities for Arama and so long as he insists on recognising a relationship between them and man's deeds then he is constrained to parry the blows of criticism with a number of answers which are not really strong enough to explain the great problems which still remain unsolved.

# 7 THE PURPOSE OF DIVINE LAW

All writers on Ethics assume that there is a highest good—a *summum bonum*—to which man should aspire, and that his happiness is achieved in relation to his approximation to this ultimate good. What this highest good is has been a subject of philosophical controversy from earliest times, but suffice to say that as far as Jewish thinkers are concerned this good had always been identified with a spiritual good, that is, with an ultimate development of the human soul to its highest point of perfection. This does not necessarily exclude the temporal and physical happiness of man, but the latter is always of secondary importance before the final and highest good which is spiritual in character and which redeems man from the animal world of the flesh to raise him to the level approaching the angelic creatures. In common with all Jewish philosophers, Arama is found to emphasise this spiritual perfection as identifiable with man's greatest good and happiness.

From this first and basic consideration we can move to the second step where the Torah or Divine law and teaching is recognised as the means through which man can arrive at spiritual perfection. Man is quite unable to arrive at a state of such spirituality without a more powerful aid than his own human spiritual powers and it is for such a purpose that God intervened in history in order to provide him with the appropriate means for his salvation. So, Arama in his forty-fourth Sermon[1] commences part I with the key statement: אחר שהאושר האלוהי והטוב העליון הוא זר ורחוק אל המין האנושי לפי טבעו ומזגו באמת צריך הי׳ לתחבולה גדולה אלהית לתקנן ולהכשירו עד שיבוא כדאי להשיגו 'Since ideal happiness and the supreme good is foreign and distant from human kind because of man's nature and temperament, it was indeed necessary for a great and Divine plan to correct and improve man so that he would be able to achieve it.' Again, commenting on the scriptural phrase 'God is unto us a God of deliverances'[2] he relates it to this idea by saying that God provided us with the means of salvation

' to cast off from us the death which is ordained through physical nature and to place our souls in life.'³ It is clear, says Arama, that without this means of spiritual or soul redemption, man would be no better than the beast of the field, for in all other matters man and beast are the same; they eat, drink, procreate and die. What then is the pre-eminence of man over beast except it be in the nature of his soul which can achieve salvation. Hence the power and purpose of Torah which is like the oil which lights the wick (the soul) in the lamp (man).⁴ Without it the soul would be useless, but with it the soul can illumine the life of man in this earth and live to eternity in the next.

So, in a general approach to the Divine law Arama understands that it was God's purpose to provide the means for man's perfection. In this light every law can be examined, both those which seem to have a bearing on the individual as well as the social laws. At the beginning of Sermon 81,⁵ the author explains that the law to help our enemy by releasing the burden from his ass is intended to eradicate from our hearts the sin of hate. This is only one example of many and from this point he develops his theme that the spiritual wholeness of man and the happiness of society is the immediate aim of the laws.

But if Torah has as its purpose the perfection of man then it has to be of a kind that is readily available, easy to possess, universal in its application and not quickly lost. As Arama states, its practicality as an agency for man's good depends on whether it is *noah liknot, karov, kolel, kasheh hasarato*.⁶ This explains the special method of Torah which is not simply a method of philosophical or ethical teaching but is a ready and practical guide made up of numerous positive and negative commandments. The ordinary man who is not a scholar would not always follow the teaching of Torah unless there were practical precepts to direct his conduct along the desired path and to help him to avoid evil. This provides us with a rationale for the precepts and prohibitions of Divine law since only by doing things can man be guided into right conduct and only by following the clear law and doing so constantly will man gain the advantage of the fundamental teaching of Torah.

By means of the commandments the Divine lawgiver made the Torah easily accessible to all since everyone is able to follow a clear command. Further, since the commandments enter into every aspect of man's daily life it becomes a very difficult thing to reject and there is thus the greater chance that man will grasp many commandments and observe them. ...הוא במה שהפליא

עצה ותושיה לשום עמודיו ואדניו יתידותיו ומיתריו כלם ענינים ומעשים
רצינים מצות ומניעות בכל דברי התורה הזאת כי על זה האופן לא לבד ימצא
זה השיתוף 'This (union with the Divine spirit) is remarkably effected with counsel and wisdom by God establishing as its pillars and sockets its pins and its cords, all of them occupations and voluntary tasks, that is, precepts and prohibitions, throughout all the words of this Law. For only by this means can the union be brought about.'[7] Or again,
הקירוב ההוא היה מצד שהכל תלוי במעשה... כללותם... שהמעשה הוא דבר
משותף לכל... וזה שהמצות באות וחלות בדברים אשר יפול עליהם החלק החמרי
ובכל מיני צורכיו ולא יכלו להמלט מהם 'This accessibility comes through the fact that everything is dependent on practical deed ... its universality ... since it is available to all men ... and in so far as it affects material things and enters into all man's needs it is not easily discarded.'[8] Without precepts and prohibitions Torah teaching would have been most ineffective. A teaching without commandments could never reach the masses or even if it were to touch them it would be for a limited time only since people could not live up to the high standard demanded on theoretical instruction alone.

It is not known whether Arama had Christianity in mind when he wrote this defence of the Torah commandments. His age was certainly one in which numerous disputations took place between Jews and Christians and it is highly probable that, as a well-known religious leader and preacher of the Jewish community, Arama himself may have been drawn into these disputations in a personal and active capacity. Certain it is that in his day and in his Community Jews were compelled to listen to Christian sermons. Indeed, it is believed that it was partly as a result of the effect which it was feared the Christian sermons would have on their Jewish listeners that Arama devoted himself to the task of presenting a clear and reasoned exposition of Judaism in the form of his weekly sermon. It must be assumed that at every turn he was mindful of his ultimate aim to redeem his people from erroneous ideas and beliefs which were spread about by false philosophy and non-Jewish teaching and also to give his hearers and readers the correct view of Judaism.[9]

In our present context no reference of any kind, even implicitly, is made to Christianity, but Arama's insistence on the necessity of commandments and his frequent repetition of the view that ethical teaching without commandments is valueless, leads one to the reasonable conclusion that in addition to explaining Judaism Arama is here by intention criticising Christianity. This view is appreciably strengthened by reference to the seventieth Sermon where Arama explicitly complains that Christian teachers spread the idea of the supremacy of the New Testament over the Torah because the former holds forth soul immortality as the heavenly reward while the Bible mentions only material rewards as a signal of God's blessing. Here Arama is quick to reply that the Torah is realistic and is in closer communion with the people by virtue of holding before them a sign of God's grace which they can more easily understand.[10] It is a question of educational method; and the Torah succeeds, while Christian doctrine because of its total separation from this world fails to help people to a recognition of God's loving care. So too, it would seem, the argument could hold in our present discussion for while Christianity lays no stress on the concrete law, Judaism sees in that very thing the convenient means of drawing its followers to God.

On the other hand, it must not be thought that Arama's view of the Torah and the importance of the practical laws leads him to a position in which he regards the practical laws alone as of importance and as an end in themselves. This is not so. For side by side with the practical laws Arama recognises the importance of correct beliefs and theoretical knowledge of the good. Commenting on the biblical phrase *na'aseh v'nishmah* 'We will do and hear'[11] he makes the well-known point that the term *nishmah* means rather to understand. In the reply which the Israelites gave to God they were thus right in proclaiming their willingness first 'to obey,' i.e., to perform the practices of Torah, through which they would then arrive at an understanding and intellectual appreciation of the moral teaching which underlies the Law. Here, he seems to suggest that the final aim is in the nature of intellectual perfection and the means to be employed is the practical commandment. This is clearly reminiscent of the intellectual approach of Maimonides which we will examine briefly below. If we have correctly understood the author's thesis so far stated (and the view has been expressed by him several times in the text in addition to the references quoted above) it is clear that of the two parts of Torah, the practical means and the theoretical end, the latter can be achieved only by the former. On the other hand Arama at times appears to indicate that correct views and intellectual perfection must come first and can lead to the observance of the Law. As an indication of this theme Arama expounds the

Midrash[12] which is a rabbinic homily on the phrase *na'aseh v'nishmah* 'We will do and we will hear.' The Midrash connects this phrase to the subsequent sin of Israel with the Golden Calf. Had the Torah been comprised of practical commands only, or theoretical teachings only, then a breaking of either would have involved a serious crime of an almost irredeemable kind. The matter could be compared to a servant who broke one of two goblets and stood trembling before the king. The king then consoled him and told him to be careful with the second goblet. Thus, when Israel broke the second commandment—the *na'aseh*—God told them to be careful with the *nishmah*, which represents the theoretical and intellectual instruction. Our author then carries on from that point to make the remark that if the theoretical teaching is maintained then practical observance may follow. Not so, however, if the idea and beliefs are absent, for then the practical observances can never be restored. As an example, the life of Elisha ben Abuya[13] is mentioned. The inference here is that while a man holds correct views about God and other fundamental teachings of his religion then there is always the possibility of him returning to proper behaviour and observances. Elsewhere Arama states שהדעת את האלהים והיראה ממנו הם קודמים לשמור המצות, ואין ספק שהמצות התוריות המעשיות נמשכות מהחלק העיוני שבאדם כמו שביארנו בשער ל"ג 'Knowledge of God and fear of him take precedence over observance of the commandments; and there is no doubt that the practical laws of the Torah follow on from the theoretical capabilities in man, as we have explained in the thirty-third Sermon.'[14] In the latter Sermon, just referred to, Arama argues that a belief in God and a proper fear of him is, in fact, the essential prerequisite for good conduct as defined in the Torah. This is so, because so many of the Torah laws have no apparent reason and will therefore only be observed by a man with proper faith.[15]

This attitude, however, is not typical of Arama's treatment of the subject and it would be fair to say that viewing his attitude as a whole, his central thought is that God gave the Torah for man's perfection and the method used in the Torah is the practical commandment and prohibition, i.e., its practical laws. It is this aspect of Torah which Arama generally stresses rather than the aspect of its theoretical implications.

## II

We must now consider the following question. Assuming that

the Torah was given by God to lead man to perfect well-being and that the detailed laws are the working tools of the Torah, how do they act on man? What is the exact effect which they have on the person who performs the commandments? We have already seen that the Divine purpose is the perfection of man, but how does this plan act from the point of view of man —the doer?

Of course this question cannot be applied to all the commandments of the Law for there are many for which a clear purpose is either explicitly stated in Scripture or is evident to the normal intelligence. The commandment relating to the observance of Passover, for example, is intended to serve as a reminder of a great historical crisis in the story of Israel. Again, the laws relating to the giving of charity have reasons which are self-evident. But what about so many others for which no reason is given or is apparent? Among these 'non-rational' laws one might list, say, the laws of sacrifices, diet, prohibition of shaving the corners of the beard, against mixing diverse seeds or mixing wool and linen. It was clear that the wise Lawgiver would not make arbitrary laws; they must have a reason and that reason must somehow be related to the doer of the commandments. That is to say that they must have some effect for good which is related to the ultimate good of man and these laws must be necessary for the useful effect they have on the doer.

Let us understand the question through a simple analogy. Suppose we find that the lock on the door is broken and the door cannot be opened. In order to open the door we obtain the services of a carpenter who understands such things. The carpenter brings with him a screwdriver and several other tools to carry out his work. Now we are still left with the question: what particular function do these tools serve? what does the carpenter do with them? does he employ them to unscrew the door hinges, or to remove the lock, or even to break the door down? All these possibilities are open to him and each one would lead to the result of opening the passageway. Now let us agree that the desired end to open the door corresponds to the desired end to rid man of all imperfections. The wise carpenter is the wisdom of Torah and the tools are the practical and useful commandments without which Torah could not function. We are left now with the question comparable to the one touching on the precise function of each tool and what it will do to the door. This is: what is the exact function of the commandments and what is their detailed work on man which leads to the final and highly desirable end?

We are now facing an old discussion which has been considered by religious thinkers since earliest times and continues even in our own day. 'What is the function or purpose of the commandments?' In Jewish philosophical thought the problem is recognised under the general heading *Ta'ame hamitzvot* (The purpose of the commandments) and there are several different attitudes which are represented in the debate, usually corresponding to the view taken as to what is the ideal perfection to be aimed at. At the outset, however, it is well to point out that Jewish teachers do not accept one clear point of view to the exclusion of all others. The noteworthy fact is that they are generally eclectic in their approach and embrace several theories in their philosophical systems, since one view need not necessarily conflict with all others. The most that can be said is that is is fair to ascribe to representative Jewish teachers a tendency to emphasise one theory more than all others without necessarily excluding all others.

A further observation must, of course, be added here and that is that we are concerned now only with such teachers who actually sought a purpose in the commandments of the Torah. It is well known that there were others who believed quite decidedly that it is not our responsibility to look for any purpose in the commandments. It is sufficient that God by his will has given us the Law and ours is the duty to love and obey the Law unquestionably because it comes to us with Divine authority.[16] This is not to say that the others doubted the Divine origin of Torah. Every Jewish religious teacher held firm to the cardinal principle of God's authorship of Torah. The important qualification, however, for those whose views we shall now discuss is that in larger or smaller measure they recognised that God gave the commandments for a purpose and that it is right to find out that purpose.

Now what are the main views that have been advanced as to the purpose and function of the commandments? Generally speaking they may be noted as follows:

1. That the commandments inculcate virtues and develop a virtuous character.

2. That God wishes to give man a free opportunity to merit the Divine reward of grace, therefore the commandments were given to him to enable him to obey and earn for himself such heavenly reward.

3. That the laws which are Divine are to be obeyed so that man can thereby serve God, his maker, with love.

4. That there is a great intellectual truth which underlines each law and the purpose of the commandment is to train man to correct beliefs and opinions.

It will serve our purpose best if we briefly examine each of these views through the eyes of four different Jewish teachers. After that we ought to be in a better position to note the standpoint of Isaac Arama on this question. The four views have been set down in the above sequence because of the chronological order of their representative exponents, not because the first are more important or more widely held than the latter.

1. Our first view is that represented by Philo. He classified all the commandments under the headings of virtues and taught that the purpose of each law was to inculcate a particular virtue, whether of the body (such as health, efficiency of the senses, dexterity of mind and strength of muscle), or virtue of the soul (such as prudence and temperance). This is the standard that can be applied to any of the laws of the Torah since each and every one of them has this purpose in man's training. They are all held together in one fast system so that as a result of it man can become perfect in body and in mind.[17] In addition, the laws of the Torah, in so far as they can all be shown to be in accord with natural law, are based on reason. For natural law is the law of man's conscience arrived at by reason for his own good and for the good of society. In all laws there is a reason grounded in the final good which is the inculcation of the virtues.

It is true that this approach to Torah is rather close to the attitude of the Greeks who saw virtue as a final good for its own sake. Plato recognised that the purpose of the laws was to train man in all the virtues.[18] If one were to ask what purpose has virtue the answer would be that virtue needs no other purpose since it is good in and for itself. So Plato says 'Justice in itself is the best thing for the soul itself.'[19]

Another significant passage, touched upon also by Arama, can be quoted from Aristotle's Ethics. 'By choice-worthy in themselves are meant those from which nothing is sought beyond the act of working: and of this kind are thought to be actions according to virtue, because doing what is noble and excellent is one of those things which are choice-worthy for their own sake alone.'[20] Or again, the stoic precept, 'Virtue is worthy of choice for its own sake.'[21] There is here no question of reward and punishment and certainly no question of serving a higher authority since for the Greeks there was no such authority that imposed reward and punishment with the keeping or breaking of the laws.[22] The difference between the rabbinic and the Greek view is essentially the question of the source or authority of the law. For the rabbis this was, of course, God, while for the Greeks, it was the natural law based on reason.

When Philo seems to emphasise the importance of virtue for its own sake it might be thought that he does so to the extent of continuing the tradition of Greek philosophy and ignoring traditional Jewish attitudes. For example, the following passage is particularly Greek in its attitude. 'The man of worthy aims sets himself to acquire day for the sake of day, light for the sake of light, the beautiful for the sake of the beautiful alone, not for the sake of something else. . . . This is the Divine law, to value virtue for its own sake.'[23] To counteract this apparent stoicism it is therefore necessary to remind ourselves that in Philo the Jewish element always walks side by side with the philosophical and while Philo speaks of doing virtue for its own sake he also believed that virtue brings its reward in happiness and also that the laws must be observed because they are actions which please God.[24]

In another place he points out that the laws have an intellectual reason behind them and this intellectual meaning is the most important part of the law. But even if intellectual and moral perfection could be achieved without the law, the law must still be obeyed since they are God-given and therefore have an intrinsic value.[25] All this is stated to offset the strong stoic trend in the rest of Philo's approach, a trend which justified us in selecting him as the representative of the first view, viz., that the law is intended to inculcate virtue. It only remains to add that a similar view seems to have found its way into rabbinic teaching. The famous maxim of Antigonos of Soko immediately comes to mind 'Be not like servants who minister to their master upon condition of receiving a reward; but like servants who minister to their master without condition of receiving a reward.'[26]

2. Our second representative thinker is Saadia whose discussion on the nature and purpose of Divine law ought to be placed within the background of the tenth century Arab debate on the subject. According to the orthodox Ashariya, the Koran was altogether revealed by God, while the Mutazila believed that its basis is in reason. Saadia himself recognised two kinds

of law in Torah, that which is purely revealed and that which is valid on account of reason. There is no real gap between them since man would in time be able to evolve a moral code based on reason, but God in his goodness helped the process by giving us a law. 'His messengers established these laws for us by wondrous signs and miracles, and we commenced to keep them and fulfil them forthwith. Later we found that speculation confirms the necessity of the law for us. It would, however, not have been appropriate to leave us to our own devices.'[27] Here we find an indication that Saadia recognises the educative purpose of the laws for each of which there is a basis in reason. In his exposition of the laws of reason Saadia says either *min ha-hokmah* or *ha-sekel m'hayev* to underline that the revealed law has as its basis a natural law or some social value. At the same time it is proper to point out that with respect to the observance of the laws, Saadia sees them also as a means for serving God with gratitude. Certainly with regard to the revelational laws for which we do not always understand the reason, since 'The wisdom of the Creator and his knowledge is above everything human beings can attain.'[28] The only attitude fit for man is to perform the commandments with humility and through love and thankfulness to God. This is not to imply that Saadia does not attempt to find some acceptable reason underlying the revelational laws. Indeed he goes to some lengths to explain what he considers to be the rational aspect of the revealed Torah and he finds reasons for such laws as the institution of the festivals, the sanctity of the priests, the prohibition of certain foods and the prohibition of marriage to related persons, the order of the sacrifices, building of the Tabernacle and the ashes of the red heifer.[29]

But where Saadia is a little different in his approach is when he points out that the laws are a means to bring down the reward of God on the obedient. The world was created to show God's wisdom and also to bestow happiness on created beings.[30] But in order to reward man with happiness, man first of all had to deserve it and the means enabling him to do so was the Torah with its many commandments and prohibitions. 'Moreover, it would seem that in this way his goodness would have been more beneficial to men, seeing that they would have been free from making any laborious effort. My answer to this objection is that, on the contrary, the order instituted by God, whereby everlasting happiness is achieved by man's labours in fulfilment of the law is preferable. For reason judges that one who obtains some good in return for work which he has accomplished enjoys a double portion of happiness in comparison with one who has not done any work and receives what he receives as a gift of grace. Reason does not deem it right to place both on the same level. This being so, our Creator has chosen for us the more abundant portion, namely, to bestow welfare on us in the shape of reward, thus making it double the benefit which we could expect without an effort on our part.'[31] In this manner Saadia explains his view of an important purpose of the laws and it is a view which finds a prominent place in Arama's own exposition as we shall see below.

3. For Judah Halevi the chief purpose of the law is the pure service of God. It is, of course, true that he does not really discredit the place of reason[32] as a basis for Divine law, but this is of secondary importance only. For Halevi the secret of man's happiness lies in the love of God, expressed through worship and obedience to the laws which Divine wisdom thought best to ordain.[33] The ritual laws are not those that can be explained rationally, yet the pious man will turn to these actions which by their nature are difficult to perform and yet are performed with the utmost zeal and love.'[34] Dealing with the ritual of sacrifice, Halevi concludes 'It is commanded by God; and he who accepts it with all his heart, without scrutiny or scruple, is superior to the man who scrutinises and investigates.'[35] So, in general, the religious duties are valid because 'men cannot approach God except by means of deeds commanded by him.' His characteristic position is thus perfectly clear. Faith in God implies belief in a Divine Creator who is a benevolent God and desires man's good. The Torah is a revealed Law, given by God; and because we are to serve God in love, we should obey his Torah which is an expression of him. This is the essence of the religious life—the service of God and the worship of him. The way to the service of God is through his commandments. Hence the observance of the laws of Torah is an end in itself.

4. We have chosen Maimonides to represent the fourth approach to the commandments, the approach which sees the commandments as largely educative in their purpose. But before we note this we have to remark on the fact that Maimonides could also qualify as an exponent of another view, i.e., the third view just stated, where the highest ideal is the service of God with love. In this sense, as was seen before with Judah Halevi, the Torah serves as the means for providing man with the

opportunity for that kind of service of God about which Maimonides can say 'He who serves God from love occupies himself with the Torah and commandments. . . . For when a man loves the Lord with that love which is due to him, he will as a matter of course fulfil all the commandments from love.'[36] However, the key to Maimonides' special approach can be seen in the last section of that same chapter. Having emphasised that the great ideal is to serve God with love Maimonides then asks, 'But how is this best inculcated in man's heart?' The answer he gives is—by knowledge. Know God and then you can begin to love him. 'It is a known and clear fact that this love for the Holy One blessed be he cannot be secure in a man's heart until he completely devotes[37] himself to it and foresakes all else in the world, as he commanded and said "With all thy heart and with all thy soul." One cannot love God except through knowledge of him and man's love of God will correspond to such knowledge, whether small or great. Therefore, man should devote himself to understand and discern . . . those sciences and counsels which inform him about his Maker.'[38] Of course, in this as in so many other matters, Maimonides follows Aristotelian ethics which are purely intellectualistic.

For Aristotle, the *summum bonum* is the perfection of the rational faculty and man's real happiness is realised in relation to his approximation to this ideal. For Maimonides, the greatest ideal of man is the perfection of the soul but this can be achieved only by the holding of correct opinions and possessing great knowledge. To help him to acquire this is the main purpose of the Torah and its commandments. 'The general object of the Torah is twofold: the well-being of the soul and the well-being of the body. The well-being of the soul is promoted by correct opinions communicated to the people according to their capacity. . . . (This perfection) consists in man becoming an actually intelligent being, i.e., he knows about the things in existence all that a perfectly devolped person is capable of knowing.

This perfection clearly does not include any action or good conduct, but only knowledge which is arrived at by speculation or established by research. . . . It seeks to train us in faith and to impart correct and true opinions when the intellect is sufficiently developed.'[39] Reference in the above section to the practical value of the commandments as leading to man's physical well-being or to his social happiness in removing all injustice and improving social relations between man and man have been omitted since they are of secondary importance in the face of the educative purpose which Maimonides saw in the Torah as its primary aim.[40] This is his chief point which he keeps to the fore in his treatment of the whole subject and although we must beware from assigning to Maimonides the view that the *final* purpose of the Torah is man's intellectual perfection[41] yet the centrality of his intellectual attitude sets his method somewhat apart from other Jewish philosophers and we are justified in bracketing his name with this fourth view as distinct from those indicated in the treatment of Philo, Saadia and Halevi.

### III

We have now seen, at some length, the four main views which scholars have held with regard to the purpose of the commandments [42] and our effort has been worth while because we are now in a better position to understand Arama's own exposition of the subject. Like his predecessors he does not hold one view against all others but brings to his system a combination of views. His position may be briefly put as follows. Arama rejects unequivocally the Philonean view that virtue for its own sake is the purpose of the Law. This view, he would say, bears little relation to human nature and ignores the explicit statements of the Torah. But even here, the reader should be warned against the danger of generalisation, for Arama clearly recognises the purpose of character training which underlines many of the ethical commandments of the Torah.[49] The central point of the present discussion, it must be repeated, is that large body of laws for which there is no clear reason to be recognised. For Arama, these laws have several purposes which are reflected in a combination of views, principally those we saw in Judah Halevi and in Saadia. These are the two chief elements, love of God and man's reward from God, which Arama finds as the real purpose of the commandments. They seem, at first glance, to contain opposite elements, but we shall see how Arama attempts to effect a reconciliation.

Arama agrees that it seems to be reasonable to suppose that the supreme purpose of the commandments is the pure service of God with love. There can be no higher purpose of man than this, and the Divinely ordained Torah must, in reason, serve this highest end. We must at all events avoid the suggestion that man is more important than God's service. שחוייב אל הפועל היותר נכבד להיות לו תכלית יותר מעולה... וכאשר יאמן

## THE MEDIEVAL JEWISH MIND

אצלינו שהמצוות התורייות המסודרות מסדור האל יתעלה תהיינה הפעולות היותר מעולות שאיפשר הנה שיחויב מזה שתהינה תכליתו היותר מעולה שבתכליות והיא האל ית׳ לא זולת 'It must necessarily follow that action of a most sublime kind will have a most excellent purpose ... and when we believe that the commandments of the Torah which are Divinely ordained are the most excellent possible, then it must follow from this that its purpose must be the most perfect of all ends and that is none other than in the Lord, may he be blessed.'[44] And further on he says, לא תהיה השקפת המצות התורייות רק לעבודת המצות שהוא סבת הסבות ועלת העלות ב״ה 'The object of the commandments of the Torah can only be the service of the Lawgiver, who is the original cause, the first cause, blessed be he.'[45] In support of this first thesis Arama quotes rabbinic maxims which have the same implication. Thus the well-known teaching of Antigonos [46] as well as the aphorism of Ben Azzai [47] could lead to the same conclusion that the observance of the commandments is for the single purpose of the service of God. So, too, support for this teaching is found in the Midrash, 'A man should not say, now will I learn Torah to become rich or to be called "rabbi" or to have a portion in the world to come since Scripture states—"to love the Lord thy God," i.e., thou shalt not do these things except for love of God.' [48] All this is, of course, in the style of Judah Halevi's approach to the subject.

Against this, however, Arama suggests that it is not in accord with human nature for a man to do good without some expectation of a personal benefit. Even plant and animal life have their natural wants and desires by which they obtain their material needs for their own benefit. Why then should man be different? Surely it is reasonable to suppose that God has planted in man's very nature the will to act in such a way as to satisfy his own longings and thus work for his own immediate benefit? Further, even if we are to reject such *a priori* assumptions we know this to be true from experience since we see that men do not naturally do things for which there is no hope of a reward.

What Arama is trying to submit is that God in his wisdom could not have given the Torah and asked man to obey the commandments unless there were some definite good for the observer that must result. But the greatest argument in favour of this, Arama reminds us, is the important fact that the Bible itself contains numerous references and statements to the effect that when the Law is obeyed then God rewards with a long life or with some other apparent temporal blessing. This is the promise of God himself, so how can we argue against it and say that man must not look for any reward from observance of the Torah? As against the argument from the Midrash in support of the first view Arama counters with an equally definite rabbinic teaching from the Talmud that one who says I give this coin for charity that my son may live, or so that I may have a portion in the world to come, is a perfectly righteous man. So he concludes: אבל נתחייב להאמין כי חלף המעשים התוריים האלו יגיע לנו מהזכות והטוב שיעור מה שראוי לעשותם בעבורו בלי ספק 'It necessarily leads to the belief that reward for observance of these Torah laws will accrue out of the merit and good, in a measure that makes observance worthwhile. There is no doubt of it.'[49] Here we see that Arama is expounding the views which we associated before with Saadia.

Now it is clear that they seem to be opposing attitudes. Of course, one might hold both points of view as valid so long as one is predominant over the other, in which case one becomes the main purpose and the other a small and comparatively unimportant result which indirectly arises out of obedience to the laws of Torah. Indeed, such an interpretation is submitted in one place by Arama himself.[50] Of the two attitudes towards the observance of Torah Arama submits that one who observes from love of God is superior to him who obeys the Law only from a sense of fear of punishment. The hope of material reward is the lesser reward for the second kind of observance, while for the first kind there is the promise of the supreme spiritual reward of immortality. In this way Arama expounds Psalm 128.

The *yare* is lower in the religious scale from the man of whom the Psalmist writes *y'gia kapeka ki tokel*. So, too, in the story of Job, the whole force of Satan's first argument with God is that Job is righteous only because he is afraid to lose, by disobedience, his worldly goods with which God had 'hedged him around.' But let God deprive Job of his worldly possessions and see whether he will still remain righteous from love of God alone. Nevertheless, Arama is apparently not too happy about this difference in the motives of observers and in the passage we have been discussing he holds that both attitudes are valid and that one might serve God equally well from motives of love for him or in expectation of reward. Both are equally valid motives. שני הדרכים האלה מהחקירה שניהם כאחד טובים ונכונים ומסכימים עם מאמרי חז״ל... ושניהם אל האמת 'Both these ways derived from our examination are good and correct coinciding with the expressions of the rabbis ... and both point to the truth.'[51] There remains then the attempt that must be made to reconcile both points of view. In doing so Arama suggests that it is first necessary to correct two errors, one on each side. There is first the error committed by the followers of Aristotle, who assume that there is positively no reward at all outside the performance of a good deed. Virtue is good for itself and in itself. 'By choiceworthy in themselves are meant those from which nothing is sought beyond the act of working. ... Doing what is noble and excellent is one of those things which are choiceworthy for their own sake alone.'[52] Arama denies this. The commandments of the Torah, he says, are not to be explained like the philosophical virtues. For him the difference is clearly marked because the Torah has been Divinely appointed and because it contains definite promises of reward. 'אמנם אנחנו המאמינים ייעודי המצות התורייות בשכר הנפשיי הרוחני והי׳ האושר המיועד לנפשותינו אינו האושר המושג בפועל המידות אבל אחר נפלא ממנו שהוא תכלית כל המעלות כלן לזה ראה שתהיה המצוה האלהית מכוונת לנו להשגת התכלית ההוא הטוב לנו כמו שאמרנו' But we believe that the assurance of the Torah commandment is in a spiritual reward which is the happiness promised for our souls. It is not the happiness which is achieved in the workings of the virtues but is of another and more wonderful kind which is the final end of all the excellences. Hence God saw fit to direct the Divine command to us so that we could aspire to that end, which as we have explained is our good.'[53] Here we see straight away two important things: (a) that Arama has rejected the 'virtue for its own sake' theory; (b) that there is a reward for obedience but that this reward is primarily spiritual or soul happiness which is man's greatest good and for the attainment of which the Torah has been given.

The second point Arama makes is that this reward is of a kind not to be confused with payment in return for service. God does not benefit from man's service or obedience. Rather is this reward in the nature of an act of grace—a gift from God. Explaining in this manner the meaning of *p'ras* in Aboth 1, 3, he says that Antigonos relates the word to wages which, of course, is a concept that cannot apply to man's reward from God. On the other hand man can serve God in order to merit his grace. הוו כעבדים המשמשים לא ע״מ לקבל פרס על זה האופן רצוני שכר מה שהגיע לו תועלת מעבודתכם אבל שתקוו ממנו שכר טוב בעמלכם על דרך החסד והחנינה 'Do not be like servants who minister to receive a reward of this kind, i.e., a wage in return for a benefit he receives from your service but you should hope to receive from him a good reward for your labour by his grace and compassion.'[54]

By these two observations Arama believes that he has cut away the excesses of both points of view, i.e. (a) that there is positively no external reward and (b) that there is a clear 'payment' in exchange for good conduct. It appears that he believes he reached a fine compromise which results in disinterested service of God with the hope of meriting the blessing of God's grace.

At first glance it might seem that Arama has effected a modification of Saadia's view stated above, but on closer consideration it should be clear that in so far as he insists that the reward is not in the commandments or virtues in themselves but in something which is merited from God, then his view is substantially like Saadia's. The only thing that Arama has really done is to call the 'reward' the 'grace' of God: but it still has to be merited. Indeed there are indications that the actualisation of such Divine grace is found in material prosperity *ba-hayim ha-z'maniyim* provided for the temporal life' which Arama relates homilectically to the 'gold, even the pure fine gold.'[55] This, in addition, of course, to the spiritual reward referred to in the same Psalm. But whether material or spiritual, neither is inherent as a necessary result in the performance of good alone but in something which comes from God himself. It may be agreed therefore, that for all Arama's lengthy exposition his conclusion does not really represent an original conclusion. We have seen it before in Saadia plus Judah Halevi. This is, in fact, the point arrived at and stated quite explicitly by Arama.

שאם יושאל מזולתו לאמר מה העבודות הזאת תהיה תשובתו כי כן יסד מלכו של עולם ואין אנו רשאין לבטל ממצותו. וכאשר יושאל שנית ומה בצע כי תעבדו עבודתו אף הוא ישיב אמריו למען דעת בידיעה שלמה והאמין אמונת אומן שהירא אל דבר ה' והחרד אל דברו הוא הטוב והנרצה לפניו להטיבו בעולם הזה ולהשארו ברכה לחיי העולם הבא 'For if anyone should ask saying "What is the meaning of this service for you?" the answer should be that thus ordained the King of the world, magnified be his name, and we are not permitted to reject his commandments. And if it should be asked again "What benefit is there in serving him?" then one should reply that it is because it is known that he who fears the word of God and trembles before him the end is that he will do good to him in this world and keep him immortal as a blessing in the world to come.'[56]

Here Arama clearly states his credo in the matter. In the first part of the above statement he proclaims that the Torah with its commandments are to be kept unquestioningly as a form of service of God.[57] In the latter part, these same commandments are the means of earning a spiritual and eternal reward. Arama supports this twofold purpose of the commandments by reference to many biblical texts and is clear in his emphasis that the final purpose is man's own happiness and success. We thus arrive at the following definite conclusion. God gave man the means of meriting his grace through the service of him by the Torah and the commandments. Or to put it in another way, the immediate purpose of the Torah and commandments is the service of God and the ultimate result is the gift of God's grace.[58]

## IV

Reference has already been made several times in this chapter to the subject of sacrifices. These laws are an example of those Torah commandments, the purpose of which is not stated in the Bible and are accordingly representative of a class of commandment which have provided us with the subject of discussion in this chapter. Further, in view of the clear opposition found in the Prophets to some forms of sacrifice, the laws naturally assumed a unique place in religious discussions of many thinkers who sought to understand the purpose of such laws which governed the sacrifices.

Arama's attitude to the question is dealt with chiefly in his fifty-seventh Sermon which he devotes entirely to the subject. As will be expected, he adopts no single view to the exclusion of all others, but he includes several ideas within his treatment. It might be useful first of all to indicate the several views prevalent in different writings as to the purpose of the sacrifices. Of these four different attitudes can be clearly discerned.

There is first, the symbolical interpretation, adopted more than a thousand years before our period of study by Philo, who was the chief and most thorough-going exponent of this approach,[59] an interpretation which was followed by several rabbinic commentators, though with much less consistency and which saw in the details of sacrifice a number of acts which symbolised a great religious idea. Thus, Nahmanides[60] for example, submits that since sin is manifested in thought, speech and deed, the burning of the kidneys and other inward parts symbolises the purification of thought, the confession represents the speech of man which is to be cleansed and the laying of hands symbolises the act of man which is to be sublimated to holy purpose. The offering in all its details is, in this way, intended symbolically to touch on different aspects of man's weakness and to train him to be wholly cleansed from the taint of sin.

The second approach is that which sees the main function of sacrifice as an act which establishes greater religious harmony in man's life and by carrying out these Divine laws the worshipper draws to himself the awareness of God's presence. This approach is one adopted by Judah Halevi[61] among others. Thirdly, sacrifice may be seen as an act of vicarious punishment. Sin is transferred to the animal, and the sacrificer, in beholding the fate of the victim, is brought to the realisation of his own guilt and deserved punishment, which he pays for by submitting a sacrifice. This is a view held by Ibn Ezra[62] and Sforno.[63] Finally, there is the approach of Maimonides[64] in which he is supported by Abarbanel[65] that the institution of sacrifices was a necessary means of weaning the people of Israel away from paganism and from the barbaric and immoral practices which were associated with ancient sacrifice as carried out among the heathen nations. According to this view the ideal was a sacrifice-less worship of God, but such a step could not have been taken at an early stage in Israel's career and the development towards a form of worship that contained no sacrifice had necessarily to be a slow and gradual one. The biblical system of sacrifice was thus an essential stage in the development of Israel's religious life and was important in that while it accepted sacrifices as an integral feature of worship the sacrifices were spiritualised and completely rid of heathen influence. These are the four chief lines of thought along which medieval Jewish thinkers attempted to understand and to explain the sacrificial code. While accepting the laws as Divine enactments and therefore binding upon the Jews for that reason alone, they sought to look behind the law to find out its purpose.

When we remarked above that Arama incorporates several views in his own exposition rather than a single one, it will be readily understood that there is nothing really unusual in this as the subject is wide enough in its many facets to embrace several and different viewpoints. In fact, two or three of the above reasons can be easily held together and even in the references already made to other medieval Jewish thinkers they do not necessarily maintain one reason throughout. Thus, in addition to the view of Maimonides, referred to above, he seems to hold elsewhere that sacrifices have symbolic significance and that the ritual impresses upon man his own sinfulness.[66] In yet another place[67] he points out that sacrifices have no reason.[68] Again, Nahmanides joins with the symbolic reason the view that the fate of the animal is intended as a vicarious punishment for the sinner.[69] It is probable that the variety of sacrifices caused some concern to one who attempted a consistent theory. It was clear that some sacrifices were expiatory, others were thank offerings, others were a type of communion act[70] and no single theory could embrace all kinds of sacrifice.[71]

Arama commences his exposition of the subject by telling us first what the sacrifices are not and in so doing he sweeps away some ignorantly held notions that grew from heathen sacrificial worship. Sacrifices were not intended as a bribe to avert God's punishment of the sinner. This may have been the thought of the heathens in their sacrificial worship. Believing that they could appease their gods with gifts and that their gods stood in need of such gifts, their sacrifices were thought to be able to pacify the anger of the gods and to appease them as one would appease the anger of a man. But God, clearly, is completely detached from such material need. It is inconceivable that a gift of any kind could in itself bring pleasure to God as a gift. Whatever sacrifices are meant to achieve, they can have their purpose only for the worshipper and not for the gratification of God. Secondly, sacrifices must not be considered as a fine or a punishment imposed upon the sinner for his offence against God. This, Arama maintains, is explained by the fact that God himself cannot be harmed by man's sin and consequently the extent of man's offence against God is difficult to assess because no harm to God can be assessed, therefore the idea of a fine cannot be considered in such a context.[72] Thirdly, no one should imagine that sacrifice was instituted for the benefit of the priesthood. This will be clear to all and particularly when consideration is taken of the fact that in several kinds of sacrifice the priests have no share whatever. Fourthly, sacrifices were not intended as a means to limit the animal population. Arama dismisses this with a sentence as a proposition too absurd to need defending. God would on no account destroy his creatures.

Having cleared his path from some popular false ideas, Arama does not immediately tell us what the real purpose of sacrifice is but goes on to explain why the sin offering is brought only for unwitting sin. This is obviously a major difficulty, as we would have expected the Torah to have ordained a sin offering for the wilful sinner rather than for the one who sinned in error or in ignorance. First, because wilful sinners are in the majority and it is reasonable to suppose that the Law-giver would make a law for the majority. Secondly, because the wilful sinner clearly stands in need of atonement while the one who sins inadvertently has less for which to repent. In reply to this, Arama says that the wilful sinner is not given the means of atonement by sacrifice for two reasons. First, so as not to provide an evil example to the people who may be led to sin wilfully from the knowledge that it is possible for a man with full awareness of all the prohibitions to sin deliberately against God. Secondly, because such wilful sin is too serious to be atoned for by a sacrifice. The only effective repentance can be done by the sacrifice of the sinner's own soul in perfect spiritual return.[73] It is then only the unwitting sin that can be atoned for by a sacrifice. The purpose of the sin offering is really clear, it is to impress upon the sinner the seriousness of his error, for כאשר יראה שהקרבן הנקרב על חטאו ישחט ויופשט וינותח וישרף על האש אשר על המזבח כי ישים או על לבו שכן משפטו על חטאו וכן ראוי שיעשה בו לולי השם שרחם עליו ' when he sees the sacrifice that is brought for his sin slaughtered, skinned, cut in pieces and burned on the altar fire he will consider in his heart that such is really his punishment for the sin he committed and that all this would be done to him except that God had mercy upon him,'[74] and by means of the sacrifice he is made aware of the heavy punishment that he deserves and will accordingly appreciate his great guilt.

Through this realistic ritual then, he is brought first to a sense of guilt by recognition of his proper punishment and then to a fear of Heaven of a most perfect kind. Here we see already in this first class of sacrifice, a particularisation of one part of the general approach we saw before. The commandment is given by God as a means to help man to gain his heavenly grace and to avoid punishment. But this class of sacrifice is easier to understand and the purpose of its institution is comparatively clear. Not so, however, with another class of sacrifices which were brought as free will offerings.

We come then to the greatest difficulty inherent in the entire sacrificial system. Granted that there is a good reason for the institution of the sin offering, what purpose can there be for the second class of offering, viz., the peace offering, the free will and burnt offerings and those brought on festivals and other occasions, all of which have no connection with the idea of sin? At this point Arama quotes Maimonides' famous view that the sacrifices were ordained not for themselves alone but for the purpose of training Israel to a higher form of religious life and law.[75] Since Israel was so powerfully influenced by the sacrificial practices of the heathen of their day, and since animal sacrifice was so widespread and accepted a feature of religious life, it would not have been possible to wean Israel from sacrifices in a short time. God, therefore, allowed Israel to continue to sacrifice but the entire ritual was spiritualised and cleansed of any trace of heathen belief or custom. Against this, Arama purports to find support for his criticism from the commentators, among whom Nahmanides is particularly referred to,[76] on the grounds that if the sacrifices were ordained not for themselves but for some other purpose, i.e., to train the Israelites to accept a pure non-sacrificial religion, then why all the numerous and detailed ritual laws which govern the act of sacrifice? According to Arama this is a powerful argument against Maimonides, whose attempt at forestalling the difficulty fails when he suggests a parallel situation with the long roundabout way God took the Israelites that they might avoid the Philistines on the shorter route.[77] For Maimonides does not answer the question 'Why was it necessary if sacrifices were only a means to an end to have so many detailed laws as part of the system?' To this Arama asks a further question arising out of Maimonides' example. The two things are quite different from each other for whereas the long route taken by Israel in the wilderness was a temporary expedient to gain a desired end, the sacrifices were intended to last for all time and were consequently no mere temporary means towards a larger object.

Before proceeding to set down Arama's view it is perhaps not out of place to remark that he seems to have misunderstood Maimonides if he assumes that the latter's argument necessarily implies that the many detailed laws of the sacrifices would be superfluous. On the contrary, it could be argued that the very number and the detail of the sacrificial laws were regarded by Maimonides as serving the true purpose for which he thought the entire system was ordained, viz., to train Israel away from the idolatrous and superstitious beliefs of the nations of their day. The laws were the means by which Israelite sacrifice was made so very different from the sacrificial practices of other nations. While sacrifice may have been only a means to a greater end—a stage in the religious development of the people of Israel—they nevertheless must signify something in themselves and fit into the religious ideas of the people. It is quite clear that if Israelite sacrifice was intended to be, while it lasted, a meaningful religious form of worship it needed precisely these laws and details of ritual to make them such. Now Maimonides clearly recognised the need of the numerous and detailed laws of the sacrifices even though the sacrificial system in itself was but a step to a different form of worship and he states elsewhere[78] the separate purpose for each aspect of the many laws governing sacrifice.

The laws are all symbolic in their purpose and convey a religious teaching. He speaks here not of the sacrificial system itself, but of its detailed *laws,* and his treatment of the former does not necessarily do away with the need for the latter. The second of Arama's points however remains and is derived from the example of the wilderness route which was a temporary expedient only while the sacrifices were apparently intended to be preserved as a regular feature of Israel's religious life. But even here it would seem that Arama has not been wholly just to Maimonides' treatment of the subject. For it is clear that he anticipates this objection and meets it by proving that the sacrifices have been clearly limited by many restrictions on place and person precisely because it is a secondary form of worship. There is thus a great difference between sacrifice and prayer. The sacrifices 'have not been made obligatory for us to the same extent as it had before.'[79] In fact, it is prohibited for sacrifice to be offered except in the Temple and by a priest. 'All these restrictions served to limit this kind of worship, and keep it within those bounds within which God did not think it necessary to abolish sacrificial service altogether. But prayer and supplication can be offered everywhere and by every person. The same is the case with the commandment of *tzitzith, mezuzah, tephilin* and similar kinds of Divine service.'[80] Arama's subsequent argument, added to the former, that Maimonides' view is untenable since the Patriarchs sacrificed at a time before they were commanded to do so, seems on the face of it an additional reason supporting Maimonides who develops his ideas from the starting point that animal sacrifice was common to all ancient peoples and it pleased the Almighty not to order them to break away from it in one stage.

We now come to a section in which Arama puts forward his view on the place and purpose of the non-sin offering and to do so he first of all refers to Judah Halevi who compares sacrifice and its purpose with food and its effect upon the soul. The body needs food and when it is thus satisfied, the soul cleaves to it. In a similar way the sacrifices are the physical substratum needful to Israel's spiritual life and when they are performed the Divine presence cleaves to Israel. This analogy, according to Arama, has certain difficulties. In the first place, it must not be supposed that Israel needs the sacrifices in the same way as the body needs food, for while food is essential to maintain physical life, Israel can live in the physical sense without sacrifice. Again the Divine presence cannot be thought of as abiding with Israel by means of the sacrifice, as this implies God's need for some kind of material form to connect him with Israel. The figure of speech, however, is useful and we can, by its help, show the real purpose of sacrifice. A man has in addition to his animal soul, which depends for its life upon food, a spiritual soul which needs spiritual food to maintain it in health. While sacrifices cannot be thought of as supplying material food for the body, or for its effect on the animal soul which clings to the body, the sacrifices if carried out with sincerity and full religious devotion can provide the spiritual nourishment which the spiritual soul needs. When the spiritual desire is filled, God's presence can be said to abide with Israel. This then is, in general, the purpose of that class of sacrifice not brought for sin. Its purpose is to inculcate religious feeling in the heart of the worshipper and through its symbolism it impresses important spiritual lessons. By sincerity and devotion to these religious aspects of sacrifice the spiritual soul of man is satisfied and God is said to be with him in his state of spiritual completeness.

The purpose of the non-sin offering is underlined at some length in order to bring out the spiritual and deep religious purpose of this important class of sacrifice. Arama expounds the sacrifices of the twelve princes (Num. 7) homiletically and in an original fashion in order to show how the sacrifices in their detailed ritual correspond with the component parts of man, the Universe and his place in the Universe. All creation is thus brought to God with perfect and absolute submission to his will. וזה מה שממחוייב כל בעל שכל להעלות על לבו ולחשוב בו מחשבות נוספות יום יום לא יסורו ממנו והוא שידע וישוב אל לבו שכל העולם כלו המונו ושאונו אינו כדאי לעצמיותו ושהאדם בגאונו וזדונו להבל דמה רק במה שיכוון מעשיו לשמים להשלים את עצמו בהכיר כל מעשיו ועבודותיו לעשות רצונו ולבקר בהיכלו ולהשתחוות לפני מזבחו ומתמונת עצמו ובשרו עיניו יחזו תוכן יצירתו... וירים את עצמו תרומה לה׳ בכל לבו ובכל מאודו וכל

עצמותיו ראשי איבריו חושיו וכל כוחותיו קרבו וכרעיו כלם יהללו יה
'This is what every intelligent man should consider in his heart and deeply ponder every day that all the world with its multitude and industry is worth nothing in itself and that man in his pride and arrogance is worthless unless he directs his actions in life towards Heaven, to perfect himself to direct all his actions and his efforts to do his will, to visit his Temple, and to worship before his altar and from the commission of his body and flesh to this service his eyes will behold the purpose of his being ... and he will raise himself as an offering to God with all his heart and soul and might and all his bones, his limbs, his faculties and all his powers, his inward parts and his legs, all of them shall praise God.' [81] Further on the purpose is summarised neatly in one sentence. כפרת עון אשר חטא כאלה מזבחי שלמים נדרים ונדבות ועולות ראיה וכיוצא כי כלם הם לכוונת שיכוון המקריב להקריב את עצמו לפני השם 'This is the purpose of all sacrifices enumerated in the Torah with the exception of those which are brought for the atonement of sin—such as a peace offering, vows, free-will offerings, festival burnt offerings, etc.—all of them are designed with the purpose that the sacrificer offer *himself* before God.'[82]

It is clear by now that Arama divides the sacrifices into two main classes: the first is the expiatory sacrifice brought by the unwitting sinner who seeks atonement and the second class embraces every other kind brought either for a peace or thank offering or as a free will and non-obligatory sacrifice. Of these two classes, Arama submits that the second kind of sacrifice is the one more acceptable since it is the expression of the pure service of God. The ultimate goal for man is complete obedience to God and submission to his will and it is this pure and complete service to God which the laws of sacrifice helped to foster.

# 8 PROPHECY

## I

The subject of prophecy was a constant theme among medieval philosophers of religion and few failed to comment, at times extensively, on the various problems involved. An indication of the importance of the subject for the medieval mind may be found in the fact that Maimonides devotes nearly one-third of the second book of his *Guide* to a formal exposition of this single subject in addition to giving it occasional indirect treatment in other parts of his work.

Before we go further, it is necessary to state that our discussion will not deal with the work of the prophet or his place in the religious life of the community, but will deal almost entirely with the subject of prophetic consciousness. The chapter is thus entitled 'Prophecy' more for convenience than as an accurate description of its contents.

The Bible gives us a clear but unphilosophical account of the phenomenon of prophecy. We read how certain individuals appear to be filled with a Divine word and speak to the people in God's name. We read, too, that God appeared to certain men in a vision or in a dream; that God spoke to selected individuals and that he sent angels to them. Now all this raises questions which have to be answered if the prophets and prophecy are to be understood. Who are these people the prophets? Why do they alone receive the prophecy and how do they receive such a gift? Why do some receive God's message in a dream, while others receive it in a vision while in a wakeful state? Are there different grades of excellence among the prophets? Is prophecy reserved only for the Jew or is it something that can be experienced also by non-Jews? Is prophecy possible only in the Holy Land or is the gift bestowed also outside the Land? The Bible speaks of bad prophets and we ought to know what constitutes the essence of a good prophet as distinct from one described as bad. Furthermore, and this is perhaps the most baffling single question, when the Bible records that an angel appeared to a prophet or that the prophet heard the voice of

God, have these things any objective reality or are they merely manifestations of the prophet's imagination? These are the main questions faced by medieval religious philosophers as part of their comprehensive discussion on prophecy.

In order to understand the attempts made by Jewish writers to answer some of the above questions it would be as well to distinguish immediately two different approaches to the problem of prophecy. There are those who see the phenomenon as a natural capacity and there are others who recognise it entirely as a Divine gift. According to the first view, prophecy is merely an extension of man's own perfection. There are, for example, different degrees among men according to their individual standards of intellectual attainment or moral stature. Now a prophet is one who has all his mental, physical and other qualities developed to an extremely high stage of perfection and the ability to receive the Divine message in one form or another is then the natural activity of the perfect man—perfect that is in his entire mental, physical and spiritual being. Just as it is part of the nature of the magnet to attract steel, so it is part of the nature of such a person to prophesy. He then occasionally lives outside the restricted sphere of the material world around him and aspires to live momentarily in communion with the extra-sensory world of the pure spirit. All authentic prophets were of this class and their prophetic message is thus conceived as a special truth which is comprehended through the innate powers of the perfect being. The second view is diametrically opposed to this and maintains that prophecy is a special gift from God which is given to selected individuals for a purpose known to God. The recipient of such a gift need not necessarily be wise or perfect in any way since God's choice of instruments is a Divine secret. Indeed, logically, prophecy can be given to a fool or to an ignorant person since God's choice of messengers need not be governed by a person's inner capacity or natural ability. Prophecy is really a miracle and the people so chosen as prophets are selected by God for his special purpose.

These are the two opposite views on prophecy. The first natural, the second supernatural; the first explaining the phenomenon in relation to man and psychology, the second explaining it in relation to the will of God and miracle. Jewish philosophers rarely adopted one view entirely to the exclusion of the other. Indeed, there are usually elements of both ideas joined together even among the rationalist Jewish writers. But there is clearly discernible among all of them a tendency to stress one aspect—the natural or the supernatural—more than another and the above brief account of the two schools of thought will provide us with a convenient background in which to set two representative Jewish thinkers in order the more easily to relate Arama's own position to that of his predecessors. For this purpose we shall review the theories of Maimonides and Halevi since each can clearly illustrate a special emphasis —Maimonides on prophecy as a natural capacity and Halevi on prophecy as a special gift from God. It will be useful to ignore chronological order and to deal with Maimonides first since his view more conveniently sets the foundation for further discussion on other writers.

## II

At the beginning of his exposition[1] Maimonides sets out three views of prophecy. The first two of these are the opposing attitudes to which we have already referred, the natural and the supernatural explanations. But the Jewish view, says Maimonides, while it agrees with the philosophical natural approach to prophecy requires that the final choice of prophets is in God's hand. This leads us to the third view which accepts all the requirements of the rational view of the philosophers but which suggests that even if a man be perfect in all his physical, mental, imaginative and moral capacity, he still may not become a prophet unless God chooses him.

This third view is also the view of Maimonides and it is important always to remember the place he assigns to God's own choice of the prophet since so many of his successors who criticised him emphasised only his psychological approach to prophecy, forgetting that the deciding factor as to whether a man was to be a prophet or not was left to the Divine choice.

We may put the position like this: God chooses his prophets and in so far as that is the case prophecy is supernatural or in the nature of a miracle. But God will only choose those who are fully prepared for prophecy by the perfection of all their capacities, physical, mental, imaginative and moral.[2] That God's will is an element in prophecy is clearly the view of Maimonides and it seems that it is an error to fail to see the extent to which Maimonides agreed with traditional Jewish thinking in ascribing prophecy as ultimately a manifestation of God's choice. 'We believe that, even if one has the capacity for prophecy and has duly prepared himself, it may yet happen that he does not actually prophesy. It is in that case the will of God that witholds from him the use of the faculty. According to my opinion, this fact is as exceptional as any other miracle, and acts in the same way. . . . There are numerous passages in the Scripture as well as in the writings of our sages which support the principle that it depends chiefly on the will of God who is to prophesy and at what time; and that he only selects the best and the wisest . . . when these (intellectual and moral preparations) have created the possibility, then it depends upon the will of God whether the possibility is to be turned into reality.'[3] Again, in another passage he states clearly that among those 'who direct their minds towards prophecy, it is possible for the Divine presence to rest upon them, but it is also possible that the Divine presence rest not upon them.'[4]

Wolfson is a dependable guide and it is relevant to note his statement[5] that Maimonides insists that despite the qualifications —which are undoubtedly necessary—prophecy depends on Divine will.[6] It has been necessary to emphasise this particularly as several Jewish thinkers who followed Maimonides appear to have misunderstood Maimonides' real position and while appreciating the master philosopher's naturalistic approach to the phenomenon of prophecy they under-estimated the element of Divine will which Maimonides agrees is the ultimate sanction for the prophet to prophesy.

How does the gift of prophecy act upon a man who is suitably prepared? This is understood by reference to Maimonides' definition of prophecy. Prophecy is, in truth and reality, an emanation sent forth by the Divine Being through the medium of the active intellect, in the first instance to man's rational faculty, and then to his imaginative faculty.'[7] The two faculties within man which are called upon to receive the Divine influence through the active intellect are reason and imagination. In the highest prophets both faculties are developed to a state of perfection. But it is obvious that among all prophets there will be various degrees of perfection. Maimonides thus gives a list of eleven degrees one higher than the other. The first degree is found among the Judges who worked with the spirit of the Lord upon them; the eleventh is that reached by Abraham who beheld angels in a vision.[8] These grades apply to all prophets except to Moses who is in a class on his own because, while for all others prophecy is given either in a dream or in a vision and through angels,⁹ Moses alone heard God directly and so his prophecy was unique.¹⁰ The prophecy of Moses is also unique in another important respect and that is that while all other prophets could prophesy only occasionally or at intervals, Moses was in a continuous state of prophecy so that he could commune with God at any moment when necessary.¹¹

Maimonides is aware of the problem of the false prophets but he dismisses the question by stating that the claims of such people to prophesy cannot be upheld in the light of the requirements of intellectual and moral perfection. In all cases the end of the stories of the false prophets show that they were immoral and perfidious charlatans.¹² The question of prophecy among gentiles is not directly posed by Maimonides, but he seems to assume the existence of a lesser degree of prophecy among gentile teachers. Thus, Shem, Eber, Noah, Methusaleh and Enoch were prophets but none of them was of a kind inspired by God to deliver a special message to mankind.¹³ On the other hand, it is necessary to refer to another work of Maimonides where by citing the example of Job and his friends he concludes that prophecy is not restricted to Jews.¹⁴ Maimonides also warns us that when we read of a person being visited by God at night, that person does not necessarily merit the title of prophet. In fact, a passage in the Bible which is introduced by the phrase 'And Elohim (an angel) came to him in a dream at night' does not introduce a prophecy at all. So in the case of Abimelech or Laban¹⁵ who are visited by Elohim (an angel) in a dream at night, the incident represents no prophecy but the fact that 'the attention of the person was called by God to a certain thing and that at the same time this happened by night.'¹⁶ In this connection, too, we might note the 'prophecies' of lesser people such as Hagar and Manoah¹⁷ since the visions of these people are not to be recognised as real prophecies at all. They were simple, uneducated people, quite unprepared and unqualified for the gift of prophecy. What they heard was therefore a kind of *bat kol* or an echo of prophecy which they grasped by their very imperfect powers. Such echoes may, in fact, be experienced by men without prophetic qualifications.¹⁸ Like the soothsayers and false prophets they have not the fullest intellectual perfection required by a true prophet and the difference between the two types is clear.

But the most important element in Maimonides' theory of prophecy is his view that, with the exception of Moses, all prophets received their prophecy in a dream or a vision. The appearance of God or an angel as well as the voice comes to the prophet in a dream or vision.[19] The starting point of prophecy is the creative imagination at work and it is the prophet's imagination, influenced by God, which produces a psychic fact for the prophet. Such phenomenon, visual or oral, is real and true subjectively but without reality outside the prophet's inner experience.[20] What the prophet experiences, i.e., hears or sees, is not a real event of the outside world comprehended with the senses but an event in the inner subjective world of the prophet, reproduced by his imagination. From one point of view the event which takes place for the prophet is quite true. In itself, it is a fact, although it is quite different from a physical fact which can be established by physical experiment.[21]

In this way, Maimonides understands, for example, the record of the angels appearing to Abraham,[22] the wrestle of Jacob with an angel,[23] the meeting of Balaam with an angel[24] and the meeting of Joshua with an angel.[25] All these things were prophetic visions produced by the creative imagination of the people concerned. 'Wherever Scripture relates that the Lord or an angel spoke to a person this took place in a dream or prophetic vision.'[26] But more than this, he says that it really makes no difference whether the Bible indicates that it was a vision or not: this principle applies in all instances and we should not imagine 'that an angel is seen or his word heard otherwise than in a prophetic vision.'[27] This is the feature of Maimonides' approach to prophecy which must have been startling not only to the Jewish scholars of the day, but also to the medieval church, for both parties held that the literal sense of the Bible is a tenet of true religion.[28] It was to be expected, therefore, that Maimonides' anti-literalist theory would have its staunch opponents, for it seemed to question many basic religious doctrines, including that of biblical truth.

We have perhaps dealt sufficiently with Maimonides to notice the main features of his interpretation of prophecy. They are, first of all, his view that prophecy is to be understood very largely with reference to human psychology. It is an overflow from a state of natural, intellectual, imaginative and moral perfection. Secondly, the element of the miraculous is there in God's choice, but even God's choice is restricted only to those who are by nature equipped to receive the gift of prophecy, since only such as are perfect in intellectual and imaginative capacities as well as in other things could receive the Divine message through a vision or a dream. Thirdly, that all prophetic experiences come to the prophet in a vision or a dream and that the creative imagination of the prophet makes those experiences real enough for him but that the object of his imagination has no real existence in the world outside.

We must now turn to the representative of a view which is very different in these three points and which in addition introduces an emphasis on two matters which are left undecided by Maimonides.

## III

Judah Halevi's theory of prophecy is consistent with his general philosophical standpoint which stresses the element of Divine providence as a direct force in human affairs and which accepts the literalness of the Bible to a much greater extent than is the case with the rationalist thinkers. From these two characteristics of his philosophy we can understand how Halevi would disagree with the conclusions arrived at by Maimonides and the rationalists.

Halevi argues that prophecy is not largely an overflow of a state of perfection, and the strong emphasis which we find in Maimonides on the necessary qualification of intellectual perfection is strongly denied by Halevi. Indeed, Halevi argues the opposite case and claims that intellectual perfection is not necessary for a state of prophecy.[29] If knowledge and intellectual excellence were such an important preparation for the prophet, then we ought to expect many prophets among the philosophers. 'Moreover, one might expect the gift of prophecy to be quite common among the philosophers, considering their deeds, their knowledge, their researches after truth, their researches and their close connection with all things spiritual. . . . Yet we find that true visions are granted to persons who do not devote themselves to study or the purification of their souls. This proves that between the Divine power and the soul there are secret relations which are not identical with those thou mentionedst, O Philosopher!'[30] It must not be thought that Halevi considered no kind of perfection important, but simply that he insisted that intellectual perfection is in fact not a *sine qua non* for prophecy. On the other hand, where he seems to relegate intellectual preparation, he brings forward moral perfection as an important prerequisite for true prophecy. Maimonides also regarded moral perfection as necessary but for him it was secondary in relation to the excellence of the intellect which he regarded as of highest importance.³¹

For Halevi, however, the order of precedence may perhaps be put in reverse.³² This moral perfection for Halevi is, of course, closely bound up with obedience to God's law and is not thought of as adherence to general principles of benevolence. The Torah alone is the guide for the life of a morally perfect man.³³ It is interesting to note that in accordance with his view of the relative unimportance of intellectual perfection, Halevi can conclude that all the Children of Israel directly and clearly experienced the revelation at Sinai. To Maimonides, this was impossible and he therefore maintains that only Moses received all the commandments from God in distinct words. He then transmitted them to the people since they heard only a sound for the first two commandments and not even a sound for the remaining eight commandments.³⁴ For Halevi, there is no obstacle in the way of the entire people receiving the direct revelation of all the commandments from God himself after they had prepared themselves for a few days 'morally as well as physically.'³⁵

Again we note with interest that Halevi makes no mention of intellectual preparation, the absence of which was no bar to any of them 'to actually hear in person the words of God' and to distinctly hear the Ten Commandments.³⁶ This non-intellectual theme which runs through Halevi's arguments can, of course be overstated to the extent where he appears to be set against pursuit of knowledge and all manner of theoretical speculation. Of course, the case is not so, for Halevi recognises without doubt the value of theoretical knowledge. It is only that he insists that it is not of first importance for the moral life and that if it leads to a negation of traditional beliefs then it is a real danger to the religious life. The prophet may not only be free from theoretical knowledge but he actually stands in a class against the philosophers. Comparing the two, Halevi finds greater excellence by far in the prophet for while the philosopher may have knowledge of the cosmic forces and the God of creation, only the prophet recognises the God of history and of individual providence.³⁷

What then, for Halevi, is the real key to prophecy? The answer is clear; it is God's will. Prophecy is a supernatural gift which depends little on prior preparations but entirely on God's will which bestows the gift of prophecy on whomsoever God chooses.[38] Moreover, God acts directly upon such a man without the mediary contact of the intelligences.[39] This, briefly put, is the essence of Halevi's approach and from which we see that everything depends on God's will in the matter of prophecy. The difference between him and Maimonides can be stated thus. For Maimonides, who also admits the element of Divine will, God will not choose a prophet who is not previously prepared with the perfection of his moral, imaginative and particularly with his intellectual faculties. For Halevi, the prior preparation of a potential prophet is of no moment, for God may choose anyone as a prophet, even one who has not risen to intellectual heights. For Maimonides, two conditions are necessary: preparation and Divine choice. For Halevi, one condition alone is necessary and that is Divine choice.

We have already seen that Maimonides regards the experience of the prophet as an experience of his creative imagination which has no relationship with the objective world of reality. This we suggested was his chief original contribution to the theory of prophecy,[40] and one which raised a storm of protest from those who had been accustomed to accept the doctrine of the literalness of the Scriptures. As can be readily understood, Halevi holds that the experience of the prophet at times represents the recognition of reality. He holds that in some miraculous way the prophet is able to perceive spiritual forms such as the pillar of cloud or of fire and the image of God.[41]

Similarly, when the Bible relates that prophets like Isaiah, Ezekiel and Daniel beheld visions of the throne or of a heavenly chariot it means that such objects which were seen could exist. In that case, they were either created as temporary existences or perhaps they are even permanent fixtures in the celestial world.[42] Of course such things are perceived only by the prophet and are not recognised by ordinary men for the prophet is endowed with a special kind of perception[43] so 'it is not strange at all that they saw visions either in imagination, in consequence of their lofty thoughts and pure minds, *or even in reality as did the prophets*.'[44] So too, we may reflect on the reality of the *bat kol* often heard in the time of the Second Temple and which ranks after the prophetic experience of the Divine voice. 'Do not consider strange what R. Ishmael said, "I heard a Divine voice cooing like a dove" or similar passages; for the visions of Moses and Elijah prove that such a thing is possible; when there is a trustworthy tradition, it must be accepted.'[45]

There remains now merely to notice two points which are

not found properly treated in Maimonides. They are the uniqueness of Israel as a prophetic people and the special characteristic of the Holy Land as a land of prophecy. Halevi argues throughout his book that Israel is unique and specially chosen by God for his purpose. It is birth rather than belief that makes the Jew a son of God's covenant. Therefore, 'Any gentile who joins us sincerely shares our good fortune but is not equal to us. If the Torah were binding on us because God created us, the white and the black man would be equal since he created them all but the Torah is binding because he led us out of Egypt and remained attached to us. For we are the pick of mankind.'[46] Here is not the place to examine Halevi's theory of the election of Israel but it has a very definite bearing on his views on prophecy since he holds that the best of mankind alone are the prophets and since we know by tradition that God has given the gift of prophecy to the Jewish prophets it follows from this that they are the pick of men. Just as plant is superior to mineral, animal to plant and human to animal, so Israel is superior to others and has alone merited the gift of true prophecy.[47] Side by side with his concept of Israel as the people of prophecy we must place his attitude to the Holy Land as the land of prophecy. Different lands are suitable for different growths and there is special power in the Land of Israel which gives impetus to the prophet. For this reason, Abraham had to leave Ur of the Chaldees and inherited the Land for his children who were his spiritual heirs.[48] The result of these two points is quite clear in that it must emphasise that true prophecy can be found only among the Jews and in the Promised Land.

We have seen enough of the above two views to understand the scope within which the main discussion takes place and we shall now turn to our own author and see wherein he joins with either of his predecessors and wherein he has something new to say.

## IV

Arama's treatment of the subject of prophecy is formally contained in Sermons 35 and part of 19 while important indications of his views on the subject are also found in Sermons 25, 29, 33, 76, 80, 82 and 96.

Before setting down his own opinions he refers[49] to the view of the philosophers who hold prophecy to be a state of natural perfection and to the assumption of the 'ignorant' that the gift of prophecy can come to anyone by accident or chance. The term 'ignorant' used in connection with this second view is not to be taken as a proper guide to Arama's own attitude since the term is undoubtedly borrowed from Maimonides who said, 'There are some ignorant people who think as follows. . . .'[50] The former view he identifies with the rabbinic statement that 'Prophecy rests only on a person who is wise, strong and rich.'[51]

Arama soon makes it clear that he is against the view of the philosophers who assume that prophecy is entirely to be explained as a higher degree of knowledge so that should a man progress from one rung to the next until he reach the very top of the ladder in the *hokmat Elohim* then he automatically enters into the ranks of the prophets and sees visions of the Divine. For the followers of this extreme view, prophecy invests the prophet with no new gift of knowledge of a kind that he did not have before, but it is a state of clearer perception which only confirms the prophet in the truth he already possessed. It has been compared to the case of a blind person who from constant practice over many years has become conversant with all the alleys and byeways of a city and then he regains his sight to realise that his theoretical knowledge of the streets is now confirmed. Arama rejects this analogy and conclusion outright relegating it to the anti-religious opinion of those who attempt to explain everything with reference to natural law forgetting to take account of Divine providence in the affairs of man. This view of prophecy he castigates in the strongest language. באמת דעת זה הוא נצר משורש נחש הקדמוני וענף עץ הדעת טוב ורע כל אוכליו יאשמו מבלתי תת שום מציאות אל הרצון האלהי על מציאות העולם והנהגתו זולתי ע"י הטבע 'Indeed, this view is a shoot from the root of the primeval serpent and a branch from the tree of knowledge of good and evil: all who eat of it are guilty in that they place no reality in the Divine will governing the existence of the world or its direction since (they hold) everything follows natural law.'[52]

For Arama, prophecy is in the nature of a miracle and it depends entirely on God's will who is to prophesy, while who is chosen need not have any necessary relation to his intellectual qualification. האמת הברור היא שהנבואה היא למעלה מהשכל האנושי כמו שהשכל הוא למעלה מהחושים 'The clear truth is that prophecy is above human intellect even as the intellect is superior to the senses.'[53] The inference from this is that if God wills it then he can appoint as a prophet anyone whom he wills even though such a person may be intellectually unqualified from the standpoint of human reason. This is clearly in accord with what we saw was the view of Judah Halevi and with which Maimonides is in absolute opposition because he believed that God would choose only such people as were fully perfect in every mental, intellectual and other capacity. In an interesting passage[54] Arama examines Maimonides' statement about the three views of prophecy which are somehow related by Maimonides to the three views on creation.[55] Maimonides commences the chapter with the following statement: 'There are as many different opinions concerning prophecy as concerning eternity or non-eternity of the Universe. For we have shown that those who assume the existence of God as proved may be divided into three classes, according to the view they take of the question, whether the Universe is eternal or not. Similarly there are three different opinions on prophecy.'

Now we suggest that if Maimonides seriously wanted to use the analogy he would have followed it through to the end of the chapter and explained that the Aristotelian view of eternity corresponds to the philosophical view of prophecy as a natural perfection; the Jewish view of creation *ex nihilo* corresponds to the theory of prophecy as a Divine gift, while the intermediate Platonic theory of eternal matter corresponds to the third view of the prophecy which is a compromise to the extent that it connects the Divine gift only with such as are by nature and ability prepared for it. In point of fact, however, Maimonides does not proceed with the analogy beyond his introductory statement which we have quoted. The reason may be that he used the idea of the three creation theories merely as a convenient opening statement, a stylistic trick, and no more. But whatever the reason for his reference to the three creation theories, it is of great interest and importance to note that Arama understood the comparison seriously and he assumed that Maimonides used the comparison with deliberate intention.

This fact enables us to see two things. First, a further indication of Arama's interpretation of prophecy as belonging entirely to the province of God's will and second, an unfortunate misrepresentation by Arama of Maimonides' view. With reference to the first point, it is already known that Arama resolutely upheld the theory of creation *ex nihilo* as the only view consistent with Jewish teaching.[56] Now this view of creation is that which corresponds to the supernatural theory of prophecy which maintains that it is entirely dependent upon the will of God and no preparatory factors are necessary. אמנם אשר יאמינו

חדוש העולם מהאפס המוחלט אחר שלא היה כלל לפי מה שעלה ברצונו ית׳ יאמינו שהנבואה ג״כ היא תלויה ברצון האלהים ישפיענה על מי שירצה מהאנשים בין שיקדימוהו הסיבות ההנה המחוייבות או לא ' However, they who believe in creation out of absolute nothing in accordance with God's will also believe of prophecy that it too depends upon the Divine will and that God can send his influence on whomsoever he wills whether the preparatory causal conditions exist or not.'[57]

He then goes on to a rather uncertain criticism of Maimonides. The latter rejects the Platonic theory of creation, complains Arama, yet he adopts the corresponding view on prophecy—a view which admits the element of God's will but only after the preparatory conditions have been fulfilled! Had Arama left his criticism at that he may have been justified, since he has room for assuming that Maimonides meant the comparison between creation and prophecy to hold good throughout his entire exposition. But Arama does not stop there. He goes on to imply that Maimonides had leanings towards the view of the philosophers. 'Moreover, it already appears that he approached[58] the first view, as he wrote that if anyone be prepared for prophecy in accordance with these pre-requisites and yet does not prophesy, such a case is very exceptional[59] like one who is deprived of the use of his eyes as was the case with the Syrian king's army in the story of Elisha or like the case of Jeroboam who lost the use of his hand.'[60]

Arama reads the relevant passage in Maimonides as though the latter was expressing a view that because he characterises such a case as exceptional, as a miracle, then he believed it to be impossible and that in fact anyone with the qualifications of full preparation must prophesy as part of the inherent law of nature. But as we indicated above this is a misreading of Maimonides who clearly postulated that God's will is the final factor in whether a person prophesy or not. If, however, a person has the capacity for prophecy and has duly prepared himself but still does not prophesy then it must be accounted to the will of God, and Maimonides simply goes on to say that 'this fact is as exceptional as any other miracle, and acts in the same way.'[61] The most that can be implied from this is that Maimonides held such instances to be rare, but not impossible. On the other hand, there is plenty of weighty evidence to prove that he insisted on God's will as the decisive factor which turns potential prophecy into a reality. All this has already been examined and it is referred to here only in our discussion of

Arama's own misreading of Maimonides and as a preliminary to understanding Arama's own position. We have arrived at the position thus far where our author seems to be satisfied with the point of view that prophecy is entirely a matter governed by the will of God and that he can, so to speak, choose anyone to become a prophet even though the potential prophet is completely without qualifications. Is this Arama's final word in the matter?

We have already remarked on the similarity between the views of Arama and those we recognised as belonging to Judah Halevi.[62] The similarity can be carried one stage further, for just as Halevi's attitude to the question of the preparation for prophecy is merely anti-intellectualistic, so is Arama's merely anti-intellectualistic. That is to say, that in his last examination Arama admits that a prophet must have certain qualifications before he can prophesy. The essential difference between him and Maimonides is that while the latter insists that intellectual qualifications are of first importance Arama relegates this to a position of non-importance. What does he substitute for it? Like Halevi before him[63] he stresses the importance of moral qualifications and for him also it is a morality which is characterised by intense devotion to God and loyalty to his laws.

When a person obeys the law of God in every detail and shows throughout his life a passion for following God, then the gift of prophecy which is a miraculous manifestation of God's reward comes to him enabling him thereby to prophesy with the spirit of God. The relevant passage is worth quoting in full:

ונקבל באמונה שהנבואה היא מהענינים היותר מיוחדים אל הפלאים הנעשים מלמעלה ממה שיחייבהו הטבע האנושי ושהיא מושפעת מרצונו ית' על הראוי לה ומוכן אליה לא לפי הכנות הטבעיות אשר זכרום לבד כי אם במה שילוה עליהם טוב הכוונה ועוצם הכוסף התשוקה להתהלך אל האלהים ולקרבה אליו להפיק רצונו ואהבתו לפי הדעות והמעשים התוריים כי בהצמיח האיש השלם בטוב בחירתו ורוב השתדלותו אלו הזכיות והשלמיות משפל ארצו ומצבו הנה באמת אז צדק משמים נשקף עליו בתורת גמול ... והנה הנבואה הוא השכר היותר גדול שאפשר לו לקבל מאת האלהים חלף עבודתיו 'And we accept the belief that prophecy is one of the exceptional miracles belonging to the supernatural and that it is an emanation from God's will on one who is suitably prepared, for it is not in the natural preparations to which alone they (the philosophers) have referred but in the qualifications which become attached to them through good intention and strong devotion and desire to walk with God and to draw near unto him so that he may show his favour in accordance with Divine knowledge and actions. For when the perfect man, by reason of his good choice and strong efforts which are pure and perfect, grows out of the material lowliness of his position then righteousness looks down on him from Heaven in the nature of reward. . . . Thus prophecy is the greatest reward which he can possibly obtain from God for his good works.'[64] We notice here that Arama is even willing to acknowledge the usefulness of natural perfections which were regarded as so important by the philosophers.

His own debate with them is that *alone* natural perfections or even together with intellectual perfections are insufficient qualifications for a prophet לא למען זכות מוחו ומה שהתחכם בכח פילוסופותו לבד 'Not because of the purity of his brain or by reason of his intellectual and philosophical prowess alone.'[65] On the other hand moral and religious qualifications alone would seem to him to be worthy of the Divine reward of prophecy. In a similar vein Arama proceeds to expound the rabbinic statement that 'the Divine Presence rests only on one who is wise, strong and rich.' This means, he says, that the potential prophet must be wise in aspiring to religious faith, strong to withstand the discipline required in such a life and rich to avoid the outside detractions of the flesh which would tend to disturb him from his religious duties.

As a further preparation Arama stresses the importance of the moral qualification of modesty in accordance with the rabbinic dictum 'Modesty leads to the Holy Spirit.'[66] But withal, these good qualities are in the nature of useful preparations only, since in themselves they will not cause the spirit of prophecy to rest on the person unless God wills it. For if these preparations led automatically to prophecy then prophecy would be a natural effect of a state of perfection. But prophecy is the שפע רצון אלוהי למעלה מחטבע האנושי 'emanation of the Divine will which is supernatural'[67] and therefore it may not be assumed that even those who are religiously qualified for the gift of prophecy will, in fact, be so chosen. As a further illustration of this latter fact, Arama instances, in addition to those examples acknowledged by Maimonides,[68] the talmudic statement that the pupils of Hillel merited the gift of prophecy but did not in fact prophesy, simply because the generation they taught were not considered by God worthy enough to be spoken to by prophets.[69]

In this connection it is very relevant to point out that for all Jewish philosophers, true prophecy involved not only a revelation from God but also the definite call to communicate that message for others.[70] If, therefore, the people among whom the prophet worked were unworthy to receive the message from God then it must follow that there could be no real prophetic experience. For Jewish history has produced many examples of worthy men who have been prevented from prophesying, not on account of any deficiency in themselves but because of certain other factors because of which God did not grant them the power of prophecy. שלא כל הראוי לנבואה ינבא אם לא שיסכימו תנאים אחרים הכרחיים 'For not everyone worthy of prophecy can prophesy unless other essential conditions are favourable.'[71] Among these other conditions we have already noted the factor of the suitability of the time or the historic occasion.[72] In this way Arama elaborates upon Maimonides' reference to Baruk ben Neriyah who, although qualified, could not prophesy because the times were unsatisfactory due to the imminent destruction and exile.[73]

All this leads Arama to the statement that Moses was the greatest of all prophets, for in addition to his own unsurpassed qualification in every respect, the generation and the historic moment were the most opportune for the revelation. The supremacy of Moses is a point which finds unanimity among all Jewish writers and we shall just note a few characteristic references in Arama. 'And indeed there can be no doubt that since our Master, Moses, possessed all these qualifications in the most excellent degree ... he was able to ascend to the highest degree of prophecy unattained by any other prophet.'[74] The qualifications referred to in Arama's context are those religious and moral characteristics he expounds from the rabbinic dictum noticed above, that the Divine presence rests only on a person who is wise, strong, rich and modest. The superiority of Moses is as a great master over his pupil. 'The superiority of the prophecy of Moses makes it entirely different (from any other class of prophecy) and the only connection Moses has with the other prophets is in his title—The Master of the Prophets.'[75]

The sin of Moses in striking the rock was of a kind that was unavoidable and was an expression of Moses the man, made of flesh and blood. It is not to be recognised in the same class as any other kind of sin for which a man is culpable and therefore, although Moses 'sinned' he is still the most perfect of the prophets that have existed in the past or who will ever live in the future. Because of this the Torah was given at his hands.[76] The penetrating treatment of Maimonides of this part of our subject is referred to by Arama and we have already noticed how Maimonides regarded the prophecy of Moses on a higher level than the eleventh degree of prophecy.[77] Arama is more particularly interested in his statement[78] that the prophecy of Moses differed in four ways from that of all other prophets, viz., that while others prophesied in a dream or vision Moses prophesied while awake; while others prophesied in a state of physical excitement or violent ecstasy, Moses prophesied in a manner which was quite normal; while others received their message in parable form, or through the intermediary of an angel, Moses spoke to God 'face to face'; and finally, while all others needed preparation before prophesying, Moses was constantly in a state of prophecy.

Arama makes bold to suggest that these differences, enumerated by Maimonides, are in themslves not adequate and in a characteristically brilliant piece of homiletical exegesis he goes on to expound the biblical verses Numbers 12, 6-8. 'If there be a prophet among you, I the Lord will make myself known unto him in a vision *marah* I will speak with him in a dream. My servant Moses is not so; he is faithful in all mine house; with him will I speak mouth to mouth, even manifestly, *mareh* and not in dark speeches; and the similitude of the Lord shall he behold.' These two verses, explains Arama, contain the essential differences between Moses and the prophets and the key is provided in the word *marah*. The translation is 'a vision,' but the word can also mean a mirror.[79] Other prophets, then, receive their prophecy as though through a mirror *marah* while Moses receives it directly *mareh*. Now what are the limitations of vision through a mirror? They are four in number.

1. Only the object directly within range of the glass can be seen but nothing above or below or behind it.

2. The object can only be seen but the mirror does not help the hearing.

3. An object is only imperfectly seen because its depth cannot be comprehended.

4. Through a mirror an object is seen right to left, e.g., by standing in front of the mirror and raising the right hand, the mirror reflects the action on the opposite side.

All these are the imperfections of prophecy through a *marah*. Moses, however, received his prophecy manifestly, *mareh* and these deficiencies cannot apply to him. Thus the Bible explains the matter point by point.

1. 'He is faithful in all Mine house' means that he has detailed knowledge of all existing things, not only those immediately in the prophetic message.

2. 'With him will I speak mouth to mouth' while others will only see.

3. 'Even manifestly and not in dark speeches.' This redeems his prophecy from the obscurities attendant on the imperfect vision of others.

4. 'The similitude of the Lord will he behold.' Since with Moses no 'turning around' for purposes of preparation was necessary because he was able at any moment to receive the immediate message of God and to comprehend it aright.[80]

We must now proceed to a part of our subject which is of great importance and that is the question of the real nature of prophetic experience. We have already noticed that Maimonides maintained that all prophetic experience was in a dream or a vision, that is to say that there was only a subjective reality in what the prophet saw or heard, but that his experience bore no relation to the truth of the outside world. When Abraham saw the angels[81] and spoke with them, all this happened in a vision. Similarly the whole story of Sarah and Abraham preparing the meal and the angels proceeding to Sodom occurred in a vision. In this way the experience of Jacob wrestling with an angel and Joshua speaking with an angel occurred not in the world of fact but in the creative imagination of those people.[82]

Now Arama is not satisfied with this explanation and is inclined to ridicule the philosophers who are unable to reconcile the biblical story with their own advanced theories. The fact of the matter is that while such a theory goes only part of the way to explain certain incidents recorded in the Bible, it can by no means explain every instance of biblical prophecy. For true prophecy as experienced by the great prophets of Israel is, as has been insisted before, in the nature of the supernatural. To say, therefore, as does Maimonides[83] that every instance of recorded prophecy was an experience of the imagination is quite incorrect and God forbid we should think so. חלילה חלילה... אלא עדות ה׳ נאמנה בכל מה שספרה מהם כי אחר שנדע כי אין מעצור לה׳ לצוות ולעשות ברב או במעט מי מעכב מי שיהיה הדבר כן ואסור לשמוע מפיהם דבר מהם רק במה שיעיד במראה שהיא במראה כמ״ש, ותבוא אותי ירושלימה במראות אלהים׳ 'The testimony of the Lord is true in all that it relates about these things. For since we know that there is no obstacle before God to command or perform anything, great or small, then what can prevent the prophecy from having actually taken place? One ought not therefore to hear a word of this kind from them except in so far as Scripture testifies that it was a vision; for then the prophecy was in a vision, e.g., as it is written (Ezekiel 8) 'And it brought me in the visions of God to Jerusalem.'[84]

Here we have an instance of Arama's attitude not alone to the phenomenon of prophecy but also to his acceptance of the literal truth of the scriptural record. With regard to prophetic experience in general he is prepared to maintain that unless otherwise suggested in the Bible all that a true prophet saw or heard was an experience related to the fact of the outside world, i.e., he saw or heard not alone in his imagination but an actual existence. Of course, such an experience is not subject to sensorial proof by the outside world because the experience is not general and only a true prophet with his fine prophetic wisdom and sensitivity could see or hear such things,[85] but that they actually exist cannot be doubted, for we have the testimony of Holy Writ to support this.

The exception is the prophetic experience which is described in the Bible as having actually taken place in a vision. As an example of this Arama refers to the vision of Abraham which was discussed by Maimonides and for which he was strongly criticised by Nahmanides.[86] For Maimonides, the whole experience of the Patriarch was seen in a vision; he saw the angels in a vision and spoke with them, they ate, departed and proceded to Sodom—all happened in a vision and the fact that the word 'vision' is not explicitly stated does not matter since 'it makes no difference whether this is expressly stated or not.'[87] Nahmanides strongly opposes this and castigates them as words 'which should not be heard let alone believed.'[88] He complains, among other things, that if all this took place in a vision then the historicity of the biblical narrative is debased to the level of ordinary dreams and imaginations. What then happens to the account of Sarah, who is said to have been instructed to take fine flour, to knead it and to make cakes? What happens to Abraham's own preparations for the meal? If the whole thing was merely a dream then it was a senseless dream, for why should the Bible give us such useless details? Again what will Maimonides do with the account of Jacob's wrestling with the angel,[89] which is also thrown into this class of dreams, particularly as Jacob is said to have come out of the struggle limping.[90]

Arama agrees that the whole incident from beginning to end is the record of a prophetic vision but he maintains this view not for the same reason as that given by Maimonides but for the effective reason that the Bible itself implies that it all took place in a prophetic vision. Firstly, when the Bible states 'and he saw them and ran to meet them'[91] the verb 'and he saw' is superfluous because the narrative has already stated 'and he saw'[92] therefore the second 'and he saw' can only refer to the fact that what follows is a description of what Abraham saw in a vision. Secondly, this section of the narrative concludes with the words 'And Abraham stood yet before the Lord.'[93] Despite the fact that Abraham had been following the angels to see them off on the next stage of their journey, the narrative can still conclude with those words as if to imply that whatever happened took place from beginning to end in a prophetic vision and at the end of it all Abraham was still standing before the Lord. For these reasons, Arama rejects the interdiction of Nahmanides against the belief that the prophecy of Abraham was experienced in a vision. And what are Nahmanides' real objections to such a view? he asks. First of all, he believes that if all that Abraham experienced was the vision of angels eating and conversing then what is the meaning of the opening phrase of that chapter 'And the Lord appeared unto him'? The rationalist view will have no room whatsoever for the idea of the appearance of the Lord since the chief actors were angels and even they only appeared in a vision. The answer, says Arama, can be grasped with reference to similar biblical narratives. For when Moses beheld the burning bush the Bible states 'And the angel of the Lord appeared unto him'[94] while, in fact, Moses saw not an angel but the bush.

So, too, in the story of Jacob, the Patriarch exclaims 'I have seen the Lord face to face'[95] although all that Jacob saw was a man who wrestled with him. This was an experience which the Bible interprets as a meeting between God and Jacob, although God himself did not appear to Jacob. In the same way the Bible can write that God appeared to Abraham although not God but angels appeared to him—and even then in a vision. But the second criticism of Nahmanides taken up by Arama is given greater prominence. If all was experienced in a vision, why should the Bible give such careful details about Sarah and Abraham hastening to prepare the food for the angels? If the whole narrative is debased into a class of unreal dream then what purpose does the Bible exhibit in the narration of these details?

Arama answers this criticism in several ways. First, and following a rabbinic homily,[96] the story proves how God rewards his pious ones, for Abraham who circumcised himself at God's command, now receives a visit from three angels of God.

Secondly, and here Arama shows himself at his best, the detailed account of the hasty preparation of the meal is significant. Nahmanides complains in case this was not carried out in reality, but Arama finds greater worth in that it takes place only in a vision, for the vision like a dream is an inner picture of a reality which is strongly impressed on the subconscious through constant usage. If a man does anything in the world of reality then it proves that he has done it once only, but if he dreams of having done that thing as a matter of course, then it proves that it is a regular part of his conduct. The vision thus shows the hospitable character of Abraham and Sarah more than the act in reality. יותר יורה ענין המראה הזאת על היות כך מנהגה תמיד ממה שיורה כשיאמר שעשה כן בפועל כי אז לא יעיד הכתוב אלא על פעם אחד ועגור אחד לא יעשה קיץ אבל עכשיו הכתוב הורה אותם בדמותם וצלמם המורגלת אצלם ' The vision can prove more than the reality for it shows that was her (Sarah's) regular custom while had it described the actual deed it would have proved no more than behaviour on a single occasion and one swallow does not make a summer. But now the Bible portrays them in their true shape and character with their regular conduct.'[97]

Although Arama is prepared to grant that where the Bible allows for the interpretation, then prophetic experience took place in a vision, such a vision would be experienced only by the true prophet. And for Arama true prophets are found only among Israel. Like Maimonides he recognises different grades of prophetic experience and in one place he suggests that there are three types of prophetic experience represented by the Hebrew terms *n'vuah, tardemah,* and *halom*[98] or prophecy, deep vision and a dream. The first two are the higher types and are found among Jewish prophets alone while the last is only a weak form of prophecy which is experienced also by non-Jews. Elsewhere he clearly recalls Judah Halevi's treatment of the subject. Man is the noblest of creatures, his spiritual life is the highest part of man, and Israel is the highest type of mankind by virtue of their closer relationship to God and the Divine law which is their heritage. This creates the greater potentiality for prophecy among Jews and they remain distinguished among other nations.[99] It must be emphasised again that with Arama the single source of distinction for Israel is that they are the people of Torah. It is entirely a religious difference which sets them aside—nothing else. From this religious distinctiveness other characteristics develop, one of which is Israel's greater capacity for prophecy. ולזה נמצא זאת המעלה אצל ישראל ולא בזולתום מהאומות

# THE MEDIEVAL JEWISH MIND

כי היא לבדה אשר קבלה דת אלהית  'Consequently, this virtue (prophecy) is found in Israel alone and not among other nations, for Israel alone received the Divine law.'[100]

The greatest of all heathen prophets was Balaam but the term 'prophet' is only applied to him as a homonym, for really he, as well as all other heathen prophets was no more than a magician or soothsayer. Arama explains the rabbinic commentary [101] of the prayer of Moses to God as meaning that Israel be distinguished from other nations of the earth[102] to signify that their distinction shall be in prophetic ability. This is not to be understood, warns Arama, as a piece of exclusive nationalism, but as a natural difference among peoples for just as 'a horse cannot become a philosopher' so other people cannot become prophets although they may be qualified to be magicians and soothsayers.[103]

It is relevant to point out a noteworthy feature of the medieval attitude to diviners, soothsayers, charmers, magicians and such like. For their attitude was so totally different from the approach of the modern mind to such things. The point is that in the Middle Ages the 'black arts' were regarded as nothing impossible or extraordinary; they were accepted as a matter of course and it was understood that there were some people who had the art of performing difficult tricks. If a comparison may be introduced with that of the conjuror to the modern mind we would not be very far off a true appreciation of the commonplace attitude of the medieval mind to this type of lower 'prophet' whose sole ability lay in his skill in performing magic. Maimonides includes such people with statesmen and lawgivers who do things by the power of their imagination alone.[104]

# 9 SUMMARY

## I PHILOSOPHY AND RELIGION

The Bible and rabbinic writings do not present a systematic theology. Not only that but the Bible contains many texts that appear to contradict each other while the Talmud and Midrash abound in aggadic references which, far from being submitted as serious theology, were deliberately intended by their authors as fanciful or poetic homilies containing ethical teaching in parable form: but this is not a religious philosophy.

For many years the lack of a religious philosophy was not seriously felt. Then in the Middle Ages when the Jews came into contact with Christian and Arab theologians, and when they learned for the first time some of the great philosophical teachings of Aristotle and other ancient masters, it became necessary for them to explain their Judaism philosophically and to be able also to defend the traditional beliefs of Judaism against the attacks of the rationalist philosophers. Among Jewish thinkers who undertook this new task there were some who managed a fine reconciliation between the principles of religious faith and Aristotelian philosophy. Others modified their religious beliefs to accommodate the accepted philosophical theories while some remained firm with their traditional beliefs and in case of conflict they ascribed the deficiency to philosophical speculation. Arama praises the theologians of the Christian faith who were loyal to their own traditional beliefs in the face of rationalist philosophy and he directs the full fury of his attack against those Jewish thinkers who compromised with their religious doctrines.

There were many questions of a controversial nature which troubled the religio-philosophical scene in Arama's day. But among all the questions, Arama finds that the most important are those which touch upon God's knowledge, providence, miracles, creation, prophecy, reward and punishment. All these and many other questions are expounded by Arama in his long and comprehensive *Akedat Yitzhak*. In addition to the latter work he wrote the small *Hazut Kashah* which contains an account of his general philosophical principles in his approach to all these subjects.

Arama complains that the philosophers have been over-zealous in their rationalisations. Thus, for example, in their theories about God they have gone as far as to leave God quite impersonal and with no contact at all with the world of men. This is a very serious danger because it can lead to an attitude which is tantamount to atheism. Rather than fall into such an error, it were better, he says, not to philosophise at all and to accept the simple meaning of the scriptural text. This latter attitude, be it said, is not really correct, but he insists that it is better to remain a pious believer with incorrect views about the nature of God than a rationalist whose scientific views lead him to a denial of God's providence.

The all-important thing to remember is that true philosophy must recognise the limitations of the human intellect and will therefore acknowledge the superiority of religion which goes further than reason because it rests on Divine revelation. The legitimate task of philosophy is thus to help us to understand the content of revelation. In this role, as the handmaid of religion, there is great usefulness in philosophy. But should it attempt to usurp the place of religion as the final source of truth, then it becomes a danger which the faithful must resist.

## II THE CONCEPT OF GOD

Throughout Arama's writings there are scattered indications of his concept of God but the whole subject is not formally treated by him in any group of sermons and what he says on the subject contains nothing original.

Arama does not philosophise about the question of God's existence. God exists. This he takes for granted as a logical corollary of the created world, since nothing can create itself. Having stated that God exists, it is necessary to point out, says Arama, that we cannot know much about him. We certainly cannot know anything about the essence of God, while as for his attributes, it is debated whether even these may be ascribed to him since to do so would impair God's simple unity. Maimonides belongs to the non-attributists who would not ascribe to God even those essential attributes such as life, power, wisdom and will. Arama goes far with Maimonides although he is clear that in so far as we must have descriptive expressions of God's work and his relation to man, then it is permissible to ascribe to him all attributes of action and emotion, being careful, of course, not to imply that they are distinguishable elements in God's essence, for that would destroy the idea of his unity. But perhaps the most satisfactory way in which to use the attributes is as negative descriptions of God. In this respect Arama agrees entirely with Maimonides and his other predecessors.

On the question of anthropomorphisms, Arama is against regarding them as legitimate expressions describing God. Yet, for Arama the most important thing about our concept of God is that we should regard him as ever-present in the world and in the affairs of mankind in which he exercises his control. We must avoid a concept of God which makes him a mere philosophical abstraction, far removed from the world in which we live. Arama's opposition to anthropomorphic ideas of God is therefore theoretical like Judah Halevi's; not dogmatic like Maimonides'.

### III THE CREATION OF THE WORLD

Three main theories were current among the thinkers of the Middle Ages. These were the Aristotelian theory of the eternity of the Universe, the Jewish belief in the creation of the Universe *ex nihilo* and the Platonic theory of creation from an eternal basic matter. These three views are all examined and we conclude that with the few known exceptions, all Jewish thinkers held firmly to the belief in creation *ex nihilo*.

Following the lead of Maimonides, Arama also concludes that creation *ex nihilo* is a fundamental dogma of Judaism. The theme recurs again and again throughout his entire work and it is one on which he lays greatest emphasis because he argues that the doctrine of creation *ex nihilo* is the source for other Jewish beliefs such as the belief in miracles and in prophecy. For this reason perhaps, Arama gives a very lengthy exposition of the subject and deals with each aspect of the creation in some detail. His exposition of the order and method of creation is modelled on his close examination of the biblical text.

'In the beginning God created the heavens and the earth.' The word 'heavens' refers to all that is in the spiritual world, i.e., the intelligences or angels as well as the hyle or original matter out of which God made the spheres and the elements of the sublunary world. The word 'earth' connotes here the four elements—fire, air, water, earth which once having been created were then acted upon by the spheres and the chain of sublunary existences was thus set in motion.

The spiritual world of the intelligences and the hyle were created on the evening of the first day of creation. From then and until the evening of the seventh day all else was created in accordance with the ten stages enumerated by the ten creative acts of God and the sequence of created things is in strict accordance with the order as related in the Bible. Arama connects the ten creative acts or 'sayings' of God with the ten categories of Aristotle by which all existences are defined. From the seventh day and onward the acts of creation are continually renewing themselves in their different species in accordance with the laws of nature implanted in each kind by the Divine Creator.

The heavenly spheres have a circular movement, not because they have an intelligent soul as suggested by Maimonides but because this is their nature and the property implanted in them by God. Arama argues that it is probable that the spheres are not even animate beings at all, but he finally agrees with the majority view that the spheres are animate. The intelligences or angels which move the spheres are important as God's intermediaries in the process of volitional emanation. The intelligences move the spheres; the motion of the spheres acts on the four elements of the sublunary world. These same intelligences also act as God's messengers in the affairs of men.

A great deal of discussion seems to have taken place in the Middle Ages as to whether the intelligences are more important than man or man more important than the intelligences. Arama strongly opposes Maimonides' standpoint on this question and he holds that the acme of God's whole creation was the creation of man for whom the entire Universe, including the intelligences, were brought into existence.

Proper time as the measure of motion existed only from the fourth day after the luminaries were finally set in the stations in the heavens. Nevertheless, from the beginning of the first day when the luminaries were created and until they were placed in the heavens on the fourth day there was a kind of time, not dependent on the motion of the spheres. This concept of time or kind of time is of sufficient validity, says Arama, to enable us to conceive of the notions of posterior and anterior.

The Sabbath was instituted as a sign of God's creativity during the preceding six days. It is the seal to the ring of God's creative acts in fashioning the world *ex nihilo*.

## IV THE SOUL

The soul is the first form or entelechy of the body and in this Aristotleian definition which is accepted by Arama the soul cannot exist without the body, no more than the body can exist without the soul. But the subject of this definition applies only to the soul with which a man is endowed at birth. Throughout life, this original soul changes in character and quality to become something quite different.

The soul which the human being receives at birth and which is described as the first form of the human body belongs to the same category of 'souls' which is the substantial form of everything in existence and which makes everything precisely what it is. Thus there is a mineral soul, a plant soul, an animal soul and a human soul. Each kind of soul has its own particular faculty and power—the mineral soul for one thing, the plant for another thing, the animal soul with an additional faculty and the human soul with a unique force of its own. The human soul is the highest of all soul forms for it incorporates the powers of the other soul forms to grow, produce, move and to enjoy the use of all other senses. But in addition to all these things the human soul has a rational faculty which is its distinctiveness over other souls. In writing on the subject of the human soul, Arama is concerned now, only with that part of it which is superior over other soul forms, i.e., its rational or thinking faculty.

This human soul is recognised in three different gradations. First of all, there is in every human soul a potential or passive intellect which is a mere capacity for future development. This potential is often referred to as the hylic or material intellect because it is the basic form from which the subsequently developed soul of man is produced. It does not pre-exist man but joins to his body by a union of inexistence from birth and is the same kind of soul which is given to every human being. This first soul is equated with the biblical term *nefesh*. From this grade it can be developed, as a result of self-discipline and religious exercise, to the second graduation which Arama understands to be the true meaning of the word *ruah*. This higher grade of soul is no longer a mere potential intellect but is the first grade of potential intellect transformed into an actual intellect. To help in the development, the lower soul receives the Divine influence which acts through an emanation of the active intellect—the last of the ten intelligences created by God.

From this second gradation the human soul can rise to even further heights and become a *n'shamah* which is the ultimate state of soul development. It then becomes a separate active soul intelligence of the kind that is seen in the prophets.

The subject of immortality is obviously one which exercised the minds of all thinkers and forms an integral part of their exposition of the doctrines of the soul. The doctrine of soul immortality is important in Judaism and is implicit in the Scriptures. But not every soul survives. When the body dies, says Arama, the sensory soul which depends on the organs of the body will die with it. What survives is the rational soul, by which we must exclude the first grade of soul or the potential intellect, leaving only the developed rational soul of man. This survives in a state of individuality. With regard to the lower soul which has not developed out of its state of mere potentiality, Arama seems to think that this perishes with the body. On the other hand there is room for the view that Arama was himself somewhat doubtful about this and may have believed that the lower soul of the wicked is also indestructible, or at any rate remains in some form of existence in order to suffer punishment.

## V  FREE WILL

Jewish teaching, from earliest times raises the doctrine of the freedom of the will to a doctrine of greatest importance. Insistence on human freedom and responsibility is clear in the Bible and apparent negations of this idea in a few texts can be explained without difficulty. Among the philosophers, Philo was the first post-biblical philosopher to investigate the problem and in opposition to Plato he submitted the theory of man's freedom. At the same time he teaches that God has foreknowledge and he fails to reconcile the belief in man's free will with the belief in God's foreknowledge of events.

In rabbinic writings we notice the same apparent contradiction for the rabbis held fast to both beliefs—man's freedom and God's foreknowledge. There is no serious attempt to come to grips with the problem until the medieval writers, among whom we notice three points of view. Maimonides held both teachings to be true. Man is free and God has foreknowledge. The difficulty was answered by submitting that we cannot know the true character of God's knowledge. It cannot be measured with reference to human knowledge and we cannot have any conception of its real scope. All we can say is that he knows all particulars and contingencies, yet his foreknowledge is not causative. A second approach to the problem is seen in Gersonides who cannot reconcile both views so he sacrifices part of God's knowledge in order to retain man's perfect freedom of will. On the opposite side we find that Crescas concedes some of man's freedom in order to be able to maintain without any difficulty the doctrine of God's foreknowledge of all particulars. Nearly all Jewish thinkers followed the general approach of Maimonides. Among these is Isaac Arama.

On God's knowledge, Arama says that God must know everything, including particulars and contingencies, since if his knowledge did not comprehend all things it would constitute a defect in God who is omniscient and omnipotent. With regard to man's freedom, Arama firmly holds that man's freedom is a necessary corollary of God's perfection. For God would not have made such an imperfect creature as man without freedom. Further, the Divine law has relevance only on the prior supposition that man is free. How to reconcile God's foreknowledge with man's freedom is a problem which Arama answers chiefly by following the agnosticism of Maimonides on this question. These two principles of faith, he says, are too precious to discard and we must therefore hold on to both of them. But we cannot know or understand the nature of God's knowledge and consequently it is impossible for us to understand how man can be free yet do nothing which is not known by God beforehand.

On the question of the sources of man's fate, Arama holds that providence, the stars, free will and chance are all involved. Chance is so rare that it may be ignored. The stars play an important part but their importance should not be overemphasised since the most that the stars can do is to create a tendency in man towards a particular kind of conduct. Against this, man has his freedom to strike out on an independent line of conduct and to reject the tendency indicated by the stars. Therefore, although the stars may indicate a man's fate, this may be confirmed or negated by man's voluntary action. Diligence is required of man to safeguard his position and he should not rely on a fortunate star or on his good voluntary conduct only. Free will and diligence are the most important factors, for through them man can attract Divine providence in his favour if he merits Divine protection, just as providence can turn against him should his conduct deserve it.

So far the system holds good and can be borne out by our

own experience. Nevertheless, we know that there are instances when man's fate does not seem to follow from his conduct. In other words, good conduct does not always result in a good reward any more than bad voluntary actions always result in an evil fate. This touches directly on the problems of Divine retribution, God's justice and the existence of evil.

## VI  REWARD AND PUNISHMENT

The doctrine of reward and punishment is a fundamental belief in Jewish religious teaching. In the main it follows on from the belief in an omnipotent and omniscient God who is not only the Creator of the Universe but who exercises his control over the affairs of individuals, all of whom are known to him. Furthermore, God is just; consequently his dealings with men must necessarily be just so as to conform to this attribute.

The general principle of Divine retribution is that God rewards the righteous for their good deeds and brings punishment to the wicked for their sins. Having established the doctrine, many teachers claim that we cannot know any more and that the details of Divine providence are quite beyond human understanding. We can never know therefore, why some wicked prosper and some righteous men suffer. All we can aspire to is to a faith that God in his justice knows all, and that in the final account of things, somehow and somewhere all matters will be seen to be just.

Nevertheless, Jewish thinkers have attempted to solve many of the problems inherent in the doctrine and their views may be broadly recognised under two chief headings.

1. That there is physical retribution in this world.
2. That retribution exists only in the world of the spirit after death.

Arama holds the clear view that Divine reward and punishment works both in this world and in the next. He agrees, however, together with all other Jewish theologians that the greater reward and punishment is in the next world.

A question of some importance is faced as a result of this exposition. If true reward and punishment exist in life after death then why does not the Bible emphasise this idea of retribution rather than the idea of material retribution in this world. Arama tries to show that the warning of spiritual punishment or punishment in life after death is explicitly stated in the Bible. But this still leaves the question of the comparative silence of the Bible about man's reward for righteousness which will be given him in life after death. Arama answers this in two ways. First, he denies that the Bible is altogether silent about spiritual reward; it is only that the references to it are not explicit. But more important still, is the idea that the Bible approaches the subject of retribution very realistically and speaks clearly only of that kind of reward and punishment which will be readily understood by ordinary people. Material retribution is thus the easier prize or punishment by which to train man. Where the promise of spiritual reward or punishment can have no educative effect on the common man, the promise of material retribution in this world can serve as a powerful instrument to train man along the paths of the Divine law. This is not to say that material retribution has no reality as retribution. To Arama, physical prosperity or suffering are real and are sent by God in direct recompense for good deeds or for sins.

Our author has now to face the obvious problems. What can he say in answer to the suffering of the righteous? Arama will say, in the first place, that it is for some sin, since no one is perfectly righteous; or he will say that it is a manifestation of God's love in accordance with the thought that 'he whom the Lord loveth he chastiseth'; or he might say that an individual righteous man may have to suffer for the good of the community as a whole since the good of the greater number is a greater good than the good of an individual; or he might say, finally, that there is little or no reality in physical suffering or prosperity in any case. This last answer introduces a note of inconsistency while each of the former contains some weakness which destroys the principle of God's justice.

In reply to the question of the prosperity of the wicked, Arama suggests that God sometimes withholds punishment from the wicked to allow him more time to repent; or the wicked person might even enjoy the prosperity which has been decreed for the entire community; or he might say, more or less as a last solution, that there is little or no meaning in physical reward and punishment since the only true retribution is in the other world after death where all things are seen to be just. Each of these answers can be criticised for the same reasons we criticised his answers to the preceding problem.

Arama shows a fair amount of ingenuity in his treatment of this subject. But it would seem, on the final summing up that he has nothing new to add to the solution of the problems involved.

Indeed, as long as he regards physical suffering and prosperity in the nature of real reward and punishment sent by God as a measure of just retribution then these problems are greatly aggravated and appear to be incapable of finding a solution.

## VII THE PURPOSE OF DIVINE LAW

In common with other Jewish teachers, Arama holds that the greatest happiness of man is to be found in spiritual perfection. The general purpose of the Torah is to serve as an instrument leading man towards such a state of perfection and happiness which is his ultimate good. But if the Torah is to serve such an end then it must be practical. It must be applicable to all. It must be easy to grasp. It must not be easy to reject or ignore and it must be readily available for all who wish to live by its teachings. Hence the way of the Torah is to adopt the practical precept and prohibition in a way that can readily enter into the daily life of every man since its laws can govern every aspect of a man's life and thought.

The function of the various commandments, or rather the particular effect they have on man is the subject of a long debate among Jewish philosophers who have discussed the subject from the point of view of the real nature of the ultimate good for man. The great Jewish thinkers do not hold one view to the exclusion of all others but rather emphasise one particular approach more than any other, while holding others to be valid in a secondary capacity.

Among the various opinions which have been held by Jewish philosophers, four are of special interest. These are as follows.

1. That the Torah helps to train a man's character by inculcating virtues.
2. That through the observance of the laws of Torah man can earn God's reward and it is a measure of God's love for man that he gave him the opportunity of meriting such reward.
3. That because the Torah was given by God, then it must be obeyed and it is only through obedience to God's laws that God can properly be served.
4. That the function of the laws of Torah is chiefly educative since they can train man to have correct opinions and beliefs.

As examples of the exposition of the above four views in Jewish philosophy we can turn to Philo, Saadia, Judah Halevi and Maimonides respectively. In each one we can notice how one view is emphasised in a rather special way.

When we turn to Isaac Arama we find that, like his predecessors, he is not really committed to a single view. Indeed, there is room within his long explanation of the different kinds of Torah law and Jewish ceremonial to accommodate for each of the above four functions of the Law. Nevertheless, we can conclude that Arama's exposition can be said to follow chiefly Halevi and Saadia, in that order. His characteristic attitude to the subject is that the laws of the Torah have as their first function the provision of a means by which we can sincerely serve God with love. At the same time, we should hope that as a result of such observance we would merit the grace of God which makes itself manifest in the highest spiritual reward, but which may also be realised in a temporal blessing. Arama insists that these two theories as to the purpose of Divine law are not contradictory.

The subject of the sacrifices has long been regarded as representative of the kind of Torah laws for which there is no apparent reason. An examination of Arama's treatment of the subject shows how Arama's general principles serve as a guide to his approach to the more particular problem of the purpose of the sacrifices.

## VIII PROPHECY

Among Jewish writers, the phenomenon of prophecy can be examined, generally speaking, from two points of view, represented by Maimonides and Judah Halevi respectively. For the former, prophecy is first of all a faculty recognised in perfect natural, intellectual and imaginative capacities. The intellect and the imagination are of greatest importance. When these perfections are joined to a moral character then God may choose such a person for the gift of prophecy. God will not choose anyone as a prophet whose capacities in these respects are not perfect. On the other hand a person whose faculties are altogether perfect need not necessarily prophesy since the final choice is with God. Although, it would be exceptional if God did not give the gift of prophecy to such a perfect man. Prophecy, then, is an emanation from God which turns the potential prophetic gift into a reality. The Divine emanation influences the prophet through the active intellect, the last of the intelligences. This in turn acts on the perfect human capacity, on the intellectual level, and through that to the imagination. Among all the prophets there are different degrees, but the highest degree—

excluding that realised by Moses—still means that prophetic experience is realised only in a dream or in a vision. What the prophet experiences is a subjective fact only and not related to the world of objective reality. Moses, however, is a prophet entirely different from all others, since he alone had real and direct communication with God.

Judah Halevi shows an entirely different attitude to prophecy. For him, the important thing is God's choice of his prophets. Although it is unlikely that he would choose anyone of imperfect moral character yet it is a matter which depends entirely on God's choice since prophecy is not a natural perfection but a supernatural intervention of God. It is in the class of miracles; and such things as intellectual perfection are relatively unimportant. It is justifiable to emphasise moral excellence as a requirement of the prophetic character and this moral excellence has connection with the prophet's observance of the laws of the Torah. For this reason prophecy is found only among the Jews who are the heart of mankind, since they alone are the people chosen by God to receive the Torah. Further, true prophecy is found only in the Holy Land. Again, against Maimonides' view of prophecy as a subjective experience without relation to the objective world, Halevi maintains that prophecy is a real experience and records the events of the material and objective world.

Arama's own exposition follows rather closely that outlined as representing the view of Judah Halevi. For Arama also, intellectual perfection is not necessary as a preparation for the prophet and while moral excellence is assumed in one whom God would choose to be a prophet, Arama nevertheless emphasises that everything depends on God's will in the matter and in his wisdom alone is a man chosen or rejected as a prophet. There are several factors involved which are fully known only by God and that is why sometimes a perfect saint will not prophesy. Like all other Jewish thinkers, Arama recognises the clear supremacy of Moses who is the greatest of all prophets who have ever lived or ever will exist in the future.

The question about the nature of prophecy and which drew much criticism against Maimonides finds Arama in part agreement with the conclusion of Maimonides that prophecy is sometimes experienced in a dream or in a vision. But he holds this to be so only when the Bible implies that this was the case. Of such a kind was the experience of Abraham who saw the three angels in a vision. Where, however, the Bible does not expressly say or imply that the recorded incident took place in a dream or a vision then we must understand the narrative to be an exact account of the sensorial experience of the prophet. Our faith in the literal truth of the Bible requires that this be so. In addition to his view that the Holy Land is the land of true prophecy, Arama, following Halevi, makes much of the idea that since moral excellence is arrived at only by following the laws of the Torah, then although other peoples may reach the lower states of prophecy belonging to divination or magic, the power of true prophecy is realised only by the people of Israel who are the people of the Torah.

# EPILOGUE

## *DOES MEDIEVAL JEWISH THEOLOGY HAVE ANY RELEVANCE TODAY?*

We have spent some time investigating Arama's teachings under the various headings of the medieval Jewish theology of his day. The modern reader is entitled to ask what meaning, if any, has all this for our time?

First of all, it is conceded that there is a great deal in Arama's presentation which is completely outdated and which no longer appears on the agenda of modern theological discussion. In this respect theology is not very different from any scientific or intellectual discipline whose concepts change in the course of time. It is true, of course, that we cannot altogether compare theology to any scientific subject. The distinction is often made that while the latter necessarily will be treated differently from age to age with man's expanding knowledge of the subject, theological premises are established on the permanent rock of faith and are therefore unchangeable. This distinction, however, is too simple. There is a substantial area in theological investigation which is based on our scientific knowledge of the Universe in which we live. Concepts of the creation, our attitudes to miracles and the supernatural, teachings about the soul and even our concept of God were all partially based on what the ancients believed to be the nature of the world around them. To that extent their theological teachings were conditioned by their medieval science. Consequently much of what they have to say to us under those headings will appear completely out of date.

Historians tell us that one of the great theological controversies between the Pharisees and the Sadducees in the first century dealt with the nature of life after death. According to most authorities the Pharisees believed in physical resurrection while the Sadducees maintained the doctrine of soul immortality alone. Echoes of this controversy are heard throughout the Middle Ages. But is the problem of concern today? Has not our scientific attitude almost wiped out the first idea of physical resurrection, so that the question is no longer debated?

In the Middle Ages theological discussion, so it was said,

could concern itself with a question like 'How many angels can stand on the head of a pin?' It is highly conceivable that disputants in such a curious debate could have been serious about their theories which related to the character of angels and the ability of supernatural existences to perform the seemingly impossible. Today such a question would immediately excite ridicule. A medieval Cabbalistic work could investigate the length of God's 'outstretched arm.' All these and scores of questions of a similar character have been swept away from the arena of serious discussion and few people are today concerned with them. The problems they posed are no problems; the questions they raised are no questions; the difficulties they pointed to are no difficulties. They belong to the 'How many angels can stand on the head of a pin?' class of theology. The fact is that just as there is constant progress in the fields of science and technology so there is a measure of progress in theological thinking and a shifting of emphasis in the kind of questions that concern us.

If this observation is valid then it follows that a good part of Arama's treatment is of little contemporary concern. For example, the entire section dealing with the creation story, as expounded by Arama, is based on medieval astronomy. No one today can take Arama's exposition seriously. The same could be said about his examination of the concept of the soul, his arguments about the influence of the stars on man's fate, and his position on the validity of animal sacrifices. They are chiefly of historical interest.

Of course, to say this, is not to deny the above subjects all relevance. Items of historical interest are not wholly unimportant since we are able to discover through them the process in the development of our thinking in those subjects. The history of ideas is important for its own sake, and in Arama we find a fair representative of the medieval Jewish theologian who spoke to his age within the framework of the knowledge of his time. His expositions thus have an intrinsic interest since we can use even his outmoded concepts as part of our measuring line indicating the development of philosophical notions.

But not everything becomes old fashioned, and there are many teachings and insights found in Arama's work which are as relevant and meaningful today as they ever were before. First of all, there is his general approach which accepts the legitimacy of reason as a proper tool in theological discussion. We learn this best of all from Maimonides, but it is significant to notice a similar attitude in the lesser ranks as represented by Arama. This does not mean that reason is primary in Arama's system, no more than it is with other medieval Jewish thinkers. Faith is still the first pillar on which he bases his theological system. But reason is employed with it to make it a reasonable faith. With many other medieval Jewish philosophers, he holds that philosophy is merely the handmaid of religion and not its mistress. Arama used philosophy to test the content of faith. Philosophy did not replace faith. Faith is first; and from there he proceeds to hold up to examination some components within the Jewish faith. Thus, he has faith in God and then he goes on to question what kind of God. He believes in the Divine authority of the Torah and then he proceeds to examine the reason for the commandments as given by God. He is firm in his conviction that there is life after death; only then can he approach the secondary question, what is the nature of that life?

It is clear that whether the Jewish philosopher did or did not reach a satisfactory answer to his searchings, his faith in the fundamental theological concepts of God, Torah and immortality—to name just a few—were firm and unbreakable. Arama recognised the limitations of the human intellect and realised that final answers to these ultimate questions are not to be reached. As a later teacher put it, there are some things which are above reason just as there are notions which are against reason. It is to the everlasting credit of most medieval Jewish philosophers that they were strong and progressive enough to reject those things which are against reason as no part of Judaism and not necessary to religious faith. On the other hand there are many things which are incapable of comprehension by the created and finite mind of man. These supra-rational concepts depend for their acceptance only on faith and it is faith which takes precedence here over reason. Faith alone is strong enough to enable us to grasp the mystery. Five hundred years have passed since Arama's day, yet this general approach to religion is still valid. Indeed, perhaps we have especial need to gain guidance from it. It can help us to distinguish between the two categories of the anti-rational and supra-rational: to reject the first with its superstitions which have frequently become the stock-in-trade 'religion' of the ignorant, and to be prepared, on the other hand, to approach the fundamental and real questions of religion with a faith which is strengthened by humility.

But it is not only Arama's general approach which is helpful to the modern religionist. In some of the detailed examination of individual subjects he can also offer guidance to the modern student.

Today there is a theological furore around the concept of God, and the naturalists are pushing aside the supernaturalists. Much of the current 'God is dead' debate however, is old fashioned from the standpoint of Judaism. What the new theologians of the Church are doing today—if it goes no further than purifying the God concept from naïve anthropomorphisms—was done by the Jewish philosophers from the time of Maimonides in the twelfth century. Thus far, the Jew of our day can consider the debate as one which belongs entirely to the Church and which has been long ago satisfactorily solved by the Synagogue, thanks to the influence of the rule of reason and common sense in the ranks of Jewish thinkers. On the other hand, however, the current debate offers some evidence that liberal theologians frequently carry their revolutionary concepts beyond anything which is found in classical Jewish theology. These left-wing theologians have gone very far in their depersonalisation of God. They have reduced him to an essence which can have little power or even relevance to life. In a way, the debate is a repetition of an old medieval discussion. We find Arama frequently referring to 'The God of the Philosophers.' This is the impersonal God of the Greek thinkers, the eternal impersonal first cause.

Undoubtedly, Jewish theologians as well as Arabs were at times influenced by these concepts of God in which the Divine power is seen as the impersonal natural ground of all existence but without any contact with man. According to this view there is no providential power in God because God is not a superman who knows all or who intervenes in human affairs. Arama is a representative spokesman of the traditional Jewish view of God in which the concept of the Deity is purified of anthropomorphism, yet God remains personal. He is the all-powerful Creator and source of all things in existence, but he is also the arbiter of our fate because he is the all-knowing Being who exists in a position of control over the affairs of man. God acts in history. He cannot be less than man, but is immeasurably more than man: therefore God is *at least* personal. In this quality he acts in relation to the individual and his power is in evidence in the historical process of nations. The vibrant, life-giving concept of the living God here comes to the forefront and Arama is a strong defender of this normative Jewish concept.

In this respect, it is remarkable how Jews referred to the

outcome of the Six-Day battle between Israel and the Arab nations as a 'miracle.' An objective examination of the situation before June, 1967, would have indicated a very different result of the battle. That Israel was victorious could be explained by them only in terms of the working of God in history. God who delivered Israel from Egyptian bondage is the same God whose providence is active in 1967. God does not walk out of history. Of course, such a theological position not only provides answers; it raises questions as well—the tragedy of the holocaust is one of them. But the classic Jewish approach is not to claim knowledge of all the answers to the problems of life. It is sufficient to hold the faith that God is omniscient. Everything that happens takes place within the framework of God's knowledge and ultimate justice. If this is true then it is sufficient reason for an optimistic view of life. In the present state of theological discussions it is maintained that the teaching of an Arama is still a necessary and valuable guide not only to the standpoint of Judaism but also for the strengthening of a vital faith in a troubled age.

In other areas, too, Arama can be a safe guide since he represents a long line of Jewish theologians whose work sifted and clarified the mass of Jewish doctrines. The average Jew of our day will learn the normative standpoint of Judaism on many questions, from the concept of *creatio ex nihilo* to the immortality of the soul; from the Divine authority of the Torah and the phenomenon of prophecy to the theory of Divine foreknowledge and God's providence. Clearly, many details in these concepts will be debated or even rejected by the modern mind, but in all essentials, the basic doctrines are firm. To this extent, Arama's writings provide the careful student of our time with a guide to classical Jewish theology.

## NOTES FOR CHAPTER I

1 Deut. 11, 26-28; 30, 19.
2 Ex. 7, 3; Deut. 2, 30; I Kings 22, 20.
3 *Moreh Nevukim*, II, 26, 30.
4 *Studies in Judaism*, First Series, p. 147.
5 The following is relevant and worth quoting from Louis Ginzberg's essay The Significance of the Halacha for Jewish History in his book *On Jewish Law and Lore* p. 95: 'When a practical question came before the scholars, even though they differed, they were forced by the pressure of the immediate need to give a clear answer to the enquirer, to vote and fix the enactment according to the will of the majority. On the other hand, in the case of theoretical differences, not only was there no pressure to vote and decide the issue, but indeed there was a fear that by such procedure academic freedom would be decreased, whereas "The Lord was pleased to make the Teaching great and glorious" (Isa. 42, 21).' Dr. Ginzberg's thesis attempted to show that fundamentally the controversies between the disciples of Hillel and Shammai were theoretical and because there was no authoritative norm in such matters controversies increased.
6 *The Theology of Aristotle*, which was a popular work among medieval scholars, has been shown to owe its authorship to Plotinus, the head of the neo-Platonic school of philosophy. See note 17, chapter III.
7 Friedlander's translation, p. xxxix.
8 Quoted by Gilson, *The Spirit of Medieval Philosophy*, p. 19.
9 Weiss, *Dor Dor Vedorshav*, V, 233; Berenfeld, *Daath Elohim*, II, 514.
10 Ser. 7, 59b; 27, 209a; 79, 71a.
11 'While believing where he could not prove, he (Arama) never failed to sift all the available evidence both for and against any theological doctrine he urged upon others to accept. Even the truth of these premises which men of faith have always found indispensable to their thinking, Arama sought to demonstrate, not alone with appeals to authority but with rational proof as well.' Bettan, *Studies in Jewish Preaching*, p. 175.
12 This little work may be considered as a summary of the main elements of Arama's religious philosophy as expounded in greater detail in the *Akedath Yitzhak* and it must be assumed that it was finished after the larger work. Ginzberg believes that the *Hazuth Kashah* was written first (*Jewish Encyclopedia*). So, too, Israel Bettan relying on Arama's preface to the *Akedah* believes that the smaller work was written first although it was published last. The style of the preface and its contents, however, leave the matter in some doubt. Further, it is difficult to maintain antecedence for the *Hazuth Kashah*, especially as there are about a dozen references in this smaller work to what the author had already written in the *Akedah*. Pollack is nearer the truth, it seems, when he suggests that Arama compiled the *Hazuth Kashah* as a small summary of his religio-philosophical views expounded fully in the *Akedah*. This was useful since the *Hazuth* could be more easily read by the masses than the bulky

## NOTES

*Akedah*. In this same connection, Pollack rightly and tellingly points out that Arama refers in his seventy-eighth sermon to the time he was writing, i.e., the fifteenth century *shivatayim mimeot hashanah*. Copying the passage in identical words in the *Hazuth*, section 12, Arama significantly adds the word *ve'od*. The inference is clear, i.e., that while deliberately copying the passage from the *Akedah* into his later work the author felt it to be necessary to add the word *ve'od* in order to mark more accurately the later period in which he then wrote. It is possible, of course, that Arama began and completed the *Hazuth Kashah* before the *Akedah* was actually finished. This is reasonable, particularly in view of the fact that the *Akedah* is extremely lengthy and it must have taken a very great number of years to complete. There is no doubt, in any case, that Arama kept the material of the *Akedah* in a state of incompleteness for a long time and that between his rabbinic labours and his movements from one community to another he took what opportunity he could find to revise and polish his magnum opus. As he himself remarks to this effect in the introduction to the *Akedah*, *u-v'kerev shanim hazarti v'tikanti garati v'hosafti*. 'In the course of the years I revised and corrected, took away and added.' A reasonable conclusion, it would seem, is that Arama wrote his *Akedath Yitzhak* over many years and before completing it in its present form he wrote and finished a smaller work, *Hazuth Kashah*, which was, however, published after the larger work and which contains a summary of his main theological position.

¹³ לעורר קנאה חדשה וגם ישנה על עלבון התורה עם המתפלספים מבני בריתה

¹⁴ The metaphor seems to have been a favourite one in the Middle Ages. Joseph Ibn Akin wrote to his master Maimonides complaining that the woman (philosophy) whom he had married became faithless to him. So, too, Maimonides refers to various branches of philosophy as 'strange women' while the Torah is called his loving bride. The Arab philosopher, Averroes, described philosophy as 'the companion or wife of the Koran and its foster sister.'

An early source for this expression may be found in Philo. For a discussion on the origin and development of the expression that philosophy is the handmaid of religion see Wolfson's *Philo* Vol. 1, 145ff.

¹⁵ Prologue to *Hazuth Kashah* and XI, 28a ; Ser. 46, 120f.
¹⁶ *Hazuth Kashah*, II, 5a.
¹⁷ Ibid.
¹⁸ Ibid. III, 6b. The biblical story of the binding of Isaac was often made the illustration of the absolute sovereignty of faith over reason to the extent that reason and even ethics are at times suspended in the face of the higher demand of faith. See I. Epstein *The Faith of Judaism*, p. 88f. The faith of Abraham as illustrated in the biblical story is made the theme of his book, *Fear and Trembling*, by Kierkegaard.
¹⁹ Ibid. VIII, 16a.
²⁰ Earlier (at the end of VII), Arama criticises the Mutakalimun school of Arab theology for devising a false philosophy to agree with their religious beliefs. Cf. M.N. I, 73ff. Arama seems to imply that it would have been better for them at least to remain honest and deny the validity of any beliefs that could not be established by true reason.
²¹ *Hazuth Kashah*, beginning of VIII, 16b. Arama does not mention here the names of the Jewish rationalists against whose views he maintains his criticism. From his sermons, however, we have no doubt that the chief of

## NOTES

the rationalists were Moses ben Joshua of Narbonne and Levi Ben Gerson, both of whom preceded Arama by one hundred years. Ser. 13, 19, 54, 57, 73.
[22] H.K., end of VII.
[23] Ibid. VIII, 18a.
[24] Ibid. V, 9b.
[25] Ibid. VIII, 16a.
[26] Author's Introduction to the *Akedath Yitzhak*, 2a.
[27] H.K. VIII, 17a.
[28] Ibid: ; Ser. 9, 74b.
[29] Ibid. 18a.
[30] *Hilkoth Teshuvah*, III, 7 and the note of Rabad: 'How many greater and better people than him (Maimonides) have conceived of God in such a manner. . . .'
[31] H.K., XI ; Ser. 7, 45aff ; 25, 73, 97.
Cf. Bahya Ibn Pakuda 'All are agreed that necessity forced us to ascribe corporeal attributes to God and to describe him by attributes properly belonging to his creatures so as to obtain some conception by which the thought of God's existence should be fixed in the minds of men.' (*Hovoth Halevavoth*, I, 10). So, too, Judah Halevi (*Kuzari*, IV, 3) who finds some useful purpose for the simple folk in the anthropomorphic expressions of the *Shiur Komah*.

## NOTES FOR CHAPTER 2

[1] *Behinath Olam*, XIII. Quoted also by Albo, *Ikkarim*, II, 30. The quotation in Arama is in Ser. 54, 185b.
[2] Ser. 54, 189a.
[3] Ibid., 185b.
[4] *Ikkarim*, II, 30.
[5] Ecc. VII, 16.
[6] Ser. 39, 54a.
[7] *Berakoth*, 10a and Midrash *Soher Tov*, Ps. 103.
[8] Ser. 68, 130a-b.
[9] Cf. M.N. I, 54.
[10] M.N. I, 50
[11] Ibid. I, 51.
[12] Ibid. I, 57 ; cf. Albo's *Ikkarim*, II i.
[13] M.N. I, 58.
[14] Ibid, I, 53, 56. Such, too, was the view of Saadia, *Emunoth V'Deoth*, 80-90 (Landauer). Saadia expounds the attribute of unity, existence, omnipotence, wisdom and uncomparability emphasising the most essential attributes which are life, omnipotence and omniscience. They are all involved in the concept of a Creator and they do not imply any plurality in God since we must use such expressions because of the limitations of language. So, too, Bahya (*Hovoth Halevavoth*, X) believed that there are three essential attributes, existence, unity and eternity. They are really one in idea but limitations of language compel us to use these terms. Of importance in Bahya's system is that the essential attributes are to be understood as denying their opposites, i.e., as being negative rather than

## NOTES

positive in their implication. He was the first to stress this idea and anticipated Maimonides by almost a century.

[15] Ibid. I, 57.
[16] The comparison is to the criticism of Averroes who criticised the views of Ibn Sina in his *Tahafut al Tahafut*, Sect. XI-XII.
[17] Ser. 54, 184a. The attributes derived from will such as anger, kindness, etc., are not attributes of action in Maimonides. With him they are attributes of quality. M.N. I, 52 (third definition, C). These attributes of quality are quite inapplicable to God. Arama may have known that Judah Halevi divides all attributes into three classes—active, relative and negative—and places into the category of active attributes such concepts as mercy, compassion, jealousy and vengeance.
[18] *Hovoth Halevavoth* X. See, too, Husik, *History of Medieval Jewish Philosophy* 93ff.
[19] *Kuzari*, II, 2-4. See note 17.
[20] M.N. I. 52.
[21] Ser. 54, 184a.
[22] M.N. I, 57-58.
[23] Ibid. I. 58.
[24] Ser. 54, 184b.
[25] Ser. 68,131a.
[26] Ser.63, 58a-b. Cf. Ser. 90, 25a.
[27] *The Shiur Komah* is the most startling example of mystical esoteric literature which attempts to describe the measurements of God's body and its several parts.
[28] Saadia (*Emunoth*, Landauer, 92, 10ff.) argues that all anthropomorphic expressions have 'a symbolic and figurative meaning.' He recognises ten anthropomorphic expressions in the Bible and suggests a meaning to each one. Thus, God's *head* denotes his sublimity, His *eye* stands for providence, etc. It seems to have escaped Saadia that such a treatment will not easily be consistent with his view on the Divine attributes. Judah Halevi, while opposed to the idea of corporeality of God in any philosophic form, is nevertheless indulgent towards the use of anthropomorphisms on the plea that it can fill the soul with feelings of awe and reverence. See *Kuzari*, IV, 3.
[29] See *Hilkoth Teshuvah* III, 7.
[30] Comment of Abraham ben David of Posquieres.
[31] Ser. 48, 136a.
[32] Deut. 4, 15.
[33] Num. II, 17.
[34] Ser. 48, 137a.
[35] Ser. 48, 137b. Cf. Ser. 39, 54b.
[36] Ser. 89, 18aff.
[37] Ser. 90, 24b.

## NOTES FOR CHAPTER 3

[1] The phrase 'ex nihilo' occurs first in II Maccabees, VII, 28. 'God made them of things that were not.' Ex nihilo fecit illa Deus (Vulgate).

## NOTES

2 'To the Greeks there will be no omnipotent God. Matter and form are alike eternal.' M. S. Foster, *The Doctrine of Creation and Modern Science*.
3 M.N. II, 13.
4 Cf. M.N. III, 15. The belief that God could not perform the impossible was really accepted by most thinkers and certainly by Maimonides. The discussion, however, often revolved around the metaphysical problem as to what does actually belong to the category of the impossible.
5 M.N. II, 13.
6 With the possible exception of Isaac Albalag. See Gutmann's essay in Ginzberg's Jubilee Volume 1946, 75-83.
7 *Emunoth*, 1,2 (third view).
8 M.N. II, 22.
9 *Fons Vitae*, I, 7.
10 The popularity of the medieval philosophies of emanation arose from the difficult problem 'How does multiplicity emerge from the One?' See Tjitze de Boer, *The Moslem Doctrine of Creation*.
11 *Physics II*, 3, 194b, 23; Cf. Arama's Introduction to Esther and Lamentations.
12 This is paraphrased from Aristotle's *Physics*, II.
13 That Arama does not obtain his knowledge of Aristotle from Jewish sources is clear, for he points out that in the *Guide*, II, 20, Maimonides touches upon part of Aristotle's arguments. In fact Maimonides refers only to the first argument.
14 Ser. 1, 14b.
15 Ser. 1, 9a. 'To Aristotle, God is the first mover, but otherwise bereft of any power. Neither matter nor any form depends on him. He is not their efficient cause but their final cause.' M. Foster, op. cit.
16 M.N. II, 20-23.
17 Ibid. 11, 21, cf. 11, 22 and *Kuzari* I, i; IV, 25 'With regard to this Aristotelian theory, it may be observed that both Halevi and Maimonides are followers of the early Arabic Aristotelians, like Alfarabi and (Ibn Sina) Avicenna, who understood Aristotle's conception of the eternity of the world, not in the sense of the world which *existed* from eternity by the side of God, but rather in the sense of the world which *emanated* from God eternally.' Strictly speaking, this conception of the world is more correctly described as the eternal generation of the world. H. Wolfson, '*The Platonic, Stoic and Aristotelian theories of Creation in Halevi and Maidonides.*' During the Middle Ages, much that was neo-Platonic passed for Aristotle's teaching. *The Theology of Aristotle*, was an abridged form of the *Enneads* of Plotinus and circulated among the Arabs as the genuine work of Aristotle. The names of Plotinus and Plato were confused, while the philosophies of Aristotle and Plato were regarded as the same. See O'Leary, *Arabic Thought in History*, p.188. Also Husik, op. cit., XXXVII.
18 'Thou art wise and from thy wisdom thou didst emanate thy creative will, This is really an illustration of Gabirol's theory of volitional emanation. See Schmiedl *Studien uber judische insonders judisch-arabische Religions-philosophie*, p.104. First there is God, then he emanates his will, then the will emanates the 'materia universalis' from which all else was subsequently formed.
19 Cf. M.N. III, 13, to which Arama refers his reader in this connection,

## NOTES

'The ultimate purpose (according to Aristotle) of the species is the propagation of this form by the repeated succession of genesis and destruction. . . . We (who believe in creation) assume that God created all parts of the Universe by his will.'

[20] 'Just as we do not ask what is the purpose of God's existence, so we do not ask what was the object of his will.' M.N. III. 18.

[21] M.N. II, 18. There are several possible explanations offered by Maimonides. God is incorporeal and 'that which is without substance does not include anything which is merely possible; everything it contains is always in existence. . . .' This seems to imply an eternal will, something which calls to mind Albo's later reference to the *ratzon kadum (Ikkarim, II, 2)* Further, Maimonides states that the essence of will is that it should act at one particular time. 'The true essence of the will of a being is simply the faculty of conceiving a desire at one time and not conceiving it in another.' Finally, he points out that the term 'will' as employed of God is not analogous to the term as ordinarily understood of men. 'It is now agreed that the term 'will' is homonymously used of man's will and of the will of God, there being no comparison whatever between God's will and that of man.'

[22] Ser. 1, 10a.
[23] M.N. I, 69.
[24] Ibid. II, 2.
[25] Ser. 5, 43b. See also A. Altmann, 'Essence and Existence in Maimonides' *Journal of John Rylands Library*, II, 35.
[26] Cf. Arama's treatment of the story of the Flood, Ser. 13.
[27] The view of the rabbinic commentators is well known for they often remark on the thought that the various names of God signify different aspects of his power or attributes. Cf. *Bereshith Rabah*, 12.
[28] An identical point is made by Judah Halevi (*Kuzari*, IV). The term Elohim is the term which describes God as the sum of all forces in the Universe, the God of creation, the God recognised by the power of reason. Elohim denotes the God of the philosophers. The term YHWH (the Tetragrammaton) denotes, however, the God of prophetic vision who is understood through revelation and the Divine intervention in human affairs. For an interesting note on the contemporary discussion of the names of God in relation to higher criticism, see I. Epstein, 'The Faith of Judaism,' p.112.
[29] Gen. 14,22.
[30] M.N. II, 25.
[31] Ibid.
[32] Ser. 4, 36a. Arama does not mention the names of the followers of the theory of eternity. Abrabanel (*Mifaloth Elohim*, II, i) cites the following, Ibn Caspi, Falquira, Abner, Narboni and Albalag.
[33] M.N. II, 13.
[34] Ibid. II, 15.
[35] Ibid. II, 16.
[36] Ibid.
[37] Ibid. II, 25.
[38] Ibid. II, 13, second theory.
[39] Among these, Gersonides was the most outstanding representative. His great philosophical work, *Milhamoth Adonai*, contains a searching re-examination of the origin of the world. While he agrees with much of Maimonides' criticism of Aristotle he finally comes to a conclusion

different from the great Jewish philosopher which is, that although the world had a beginning in time, it was not created *ex nihilo*, but from an eternal formless matter which God endowed with form. This is the Platonic view. Gersonides argued that the world originated either from something or from nothing. The former case is impossible since this 'something' would be in itself matter and form and there must have been some motion to bring that into existence. The latter is also impossible since matter cannot come from 'nothing' because *ex nihilo nihil fit*. Besides, it presupposes a vacuum in place of the pre-created world, which is impossible. The only possibility then, is to adopt an intermediate theory by supposing an uncreated formless matter which was eternal.

[40] Ser. 4, 36a.

[41] *m'shutafim* is here translated 'continuous,' in the sense of something quite indefinite, shapeless, amorphous. Wolfson, in his *Crescas' Critique of Aristotle*, p. 420, quotes the word from Saadia's Commentary on the *Sefer Yetzirah*. He equates it with the word *mitdabek* 'continuous,' a term used in relation to one kind of quantity.

[42] *Hyle* from the Greek meaning original matter.

[43] Ser. 4, 37a.

[44] It may be of interest to note further that Nahmanides appears to be indebted to Abraham Bar Hiyya for his ideas about the hyle of the upper world and the hyle of the lower world. Schmiedl, in his *Studien*, p. 124, points out that Nahmanides has taken several ideas from Abraham Bar Hiyya without mentioning his name. Abraham Bar Hiyya's chief mentor is Aristotle, for he, too, sees the world as matter and form. These two principles are in God's wisdom existing potentially apart until God brings them forth and realises them in actuality. But here he parts from Aristotle by holding that the world of matter and form was not eternal but was created in time. There are two kinds of form and two kinds of matter—pure and impure form and pure and impure matter. The pure form cannot join with matter and so embraces angels, seraphim, souls, and all forms relating to the upper world. This pure form then shone on the impure form which, when joined to pure matter gave rise to the spheres. From these the next stage in the process is effected when the impure form joins with impure matter to provide the sublunary bodies. His theory is not quite neo-Platonic since the series of emanations of Plotinus, intellect, universal soul, nature and matter are wanting in Abraham Bar Hiyya.

[45] M.N. II, 30.

[46] See Husik's Albo, *Ikkarim*, II, p. 67, note i. Cf. also M.N. II, 6, 'This agrees with the opinion of Aristotle; there is only this difference in the name employed—he uses the term "intelligences" and we say "angels."' Schmiedl op. cit., 72, quotes Abraham Ibn Daud's *Emunah Ramah-Nikra b'hatkamatam sekel u-vil'shon ha-Torah malak*.

[47] De Caelo ii, 2, 12, 292a, 18.

[48] M.N. II, 5. The Aristotelian view does not entirely coincide with that propounded by Maimonides. The latter regards the spheres as composed of matter and form possessing souls of their own which are the efficient causes of their motion, while the intelligences or *sekalim* are the final causes. According to Aristotle the spheres have no soul of their own in addition to the intelligences. The intelligences are the soul cause of their motion and are called the souls of the spheres in a loose sense. See Wolfson's *Crescas' Critique*, pp. 605-8, 265-7.

## NOTES

⁴⁹ Ser. 2, 17a. The same discussion is reflected in the Church Fathers. Tatian, Jerome and Origen believe that the heavenly spheres are living and rational beings; others deny this, while St. Augustine leaves the matter in some doubt. Among Jewish philosophers who shared Arama's opinion are Saadia, Judah Halevi and Crescas. cf. Wolfson's *Crescas' Critique*, pp. 535-8 and his *Philo*, pp. 417-8.

⁵⁰ Arama states that he found support for his own theory only in the *Shaar Hashamayim* by Isaac Ibn Latif. H. Wolfson, in his *Crescas' Critique*, p. 538, remarks that Arama was criticised by Judah Moscato for failing to notice this view in Judah Halevi. Moscato, however, fails to notice the view in Saadia and Crescas.

⁵¹ Ser. 6, 46a ff. The main argument calls to mind Albo's treatment of the subject, *Ikkarim*, III, 4. See Husik's edition, III, 37, with a note on the Aristotelian theory which is entirely different to the ideas of Albo and Arama.

⁵² *Bereshith Rabah*, I, 3.

⁵³ Two main views are propounded by medieval philosophers in answer to this problem. The first is that God created the first intelligence which was the cause of the second. The second was the cause of the third, and so on until the tenth and last intelligence which emanated from its predecessor. There is thus a difference of cause and effect which provides the basis for plurality and individual character among the intelligences. The second view is that God created all intelligences at one time and created them in different degrees of importance and function. The first view is that of Avicenna, ascribed to Aristotle and followed by Maimonides (M.N. II, 4). The second view is the Averronian view followed by, among others, Albo *(Ikkarim,* II, 12) and Gersonides. See Wolfson's *Crescas,* etc., pp. 108-9; 666-7 and Schmiedl op. cit., p. 86.

⁵⁴ Ser. 2, 18a.

⁵⁵ See Pollack's note *Hara t'hilah ha-malakim b'madregot shonot, zeh l'maalah mizeh, v'zeh ahare zeh, b'ofan shekol chad sibah la-havero.* If we take the last clause as the operative one then it is clear that Arama follows Maimonides' system of the emanation of the intelligences. But even Maimonides is not very explicit in *Yesodei Hatorah,* II, 5-6. The only thing we find in that text is that each intelligence is *different* from the other and they have different functions, but we do not know whether this is the result of a series of emanations from the first intelligence to the next, or whether they were thus created. Indeed, Gersonides and Albo regard this source in Maimonides as a support for the view that God created all the intelligences at once with their respective differences. *V'hakol nimtzaim mikoho shel ha-kadosh baruk hu.* ' And they all exist (in their differences) through the power of the Holy One blessed be he.'

⁵⁶ Ser. 2, 19b.

⁵⁷ Ser. 2, 19b.

⁵⁸ Through the influence of Aristotle the theory was accepted throughout the Middle Ages that these four elements were the first materials out of which all else was brought forth.

⁵⁹ ' Matter for the Platonist is not ponderable stuff, but the all-but-nothing which remains when we have stripped phenomena of all that the mind brings to their interpretation. The elementary blunder of supposing that Plato's hyle is material is responsible for much misleading talk about " dualism " in the Platonists. It will be easier to understand the neo-

# NOTES

Platonic view of matter if we realise that it is a relative term. Matter is matter only as a passive recipient of the form from above it. The same thing may be form in relation to what is below it, and matter to what is above it.' Inge, 'Platonic Matter' in Church Quarterly Review, Jan., 1939. For a clear statement of this view see Stace, *A Critical History of Greek Philosophy*, p. 207 ff.

[60] Ser. 5, 43a. Cf. *De Caelo* 1, 3, 270b, 17-25. Against this Saadia and Bahya argue that even the heavenly bodies are made of the same four elements as the earth.

[61] Phys. IV ff., *De Caelo* I, 9, 279a, 14.

[62] M.N. II, 13. Cf. I, 73.

[63] Ibid. II, 30.

[64] Ser. 3, 24b.

[65] *Or Adonai*, I, iii, 3. Proposition XV, pt. II. See Wolfson, ad loc.

[66] *Emunoth*, I, 4; II, 2.

[67] *Hegyon Hanefesh*, I.

[68] M.N. II, 13. 'Non enim si mundus nullus erat saecula non erant . . . sed fuit quaedam ab infinito temporae aeternitas' (de Nat. deor. I. 18, Cicero).

[69] *Ikkarim*, II, 18.

[70] See Wolfson, p. 654 ff.

[71] See *Encyclopedia of Biblical Interpretation*, I. M. M. Kasher, p. 198.

[72] Ser. 3, 24b.

[73] Ibid. 24b-25a.

[74] M.N. II, 30.

[75] Ibid.

[76] *Ikkarim* II, 18.

[77] Ser. 3, 25a.

[78] 'All things were created together but were separated from each other successfully.' M.N. II, 30.

[79] Hullin, 60a.

[80] Arama makes the interesting observation that the talmudic text proves that the fruit came before the seed, and the chicken before the egg!

[81] Isa. 48, 13.

[82] Ethics of the Fathers, V.

[83] Verses, 3, 6, 9, 11, 14, 20, 24, 26, 28 and 29.

[84] All the objects of our thought, says Aristotle, fall under one or other of the following concepts or categories: substance, quantity, quality, relation, place, time, situation, possession, action, passivity. The medieval Jewish term for category is *ma'amar lit.*, 'a saying.' The ten categories of Aristotle influenced practically all philosophers, directly or indirectly.

[85] Ser. 3, 24a.

[86] Ser. 3, 27a.

[87] Ser. 3, 27b.

[88] Bereshith Rabah, IV.

[89] Ser. 3, 27b.

[90] Gen. I, 12.

[91] Ibid. I, 20.

[92] Ibid. I, 24.

[93] Ibid. I, 21.

[94] Ibid. I, 29.

[95] See below on the sixth category.

## NOTES

**96** Ser. 3, 29b.
**97** Ser. 3, 30b.
**98** Gen. I, 21.
**99** Arama follows Aristotle in his definition of the concept of quantity as either a plurality or a magnitude. Aristotle wrote, 'A quantity is a plurality if it is numberable; magnitude if it is measurable. Plurality means that which is divisible into non-continuous parts; magnitude that which is divisible into continuous parts.' (*Metaphysics*, V, 13, 1020a, 8-11). The continuous quantity or the magnitude Arama calls *mitdabek* and the non-continuous is the *mitpared*. In the intermediate categories, II, 2, Aristotle designates these two classes of quantity as continuous and discreet, terms which again refer to magnitude or plurality. Arama ingeniously interprets the 'great sea monsters' as indicating a quantity in magnitude and the 'multitude of every living thing that moveth' as an illustration of quantity in plurality.
**100** Gen. 2, 7.
**101** Ibid.
**102** Gen. I, 34.
**103** Bereshith Rabah, XIX.
**104** Cf. Ser. 15.
**105** Gen. I, 26.
**106** Cf. Ser. 18.
**107** See Schmiedl, *Studien*. p. 83, for several talmudic texts.
**108** *Emunoth*, IV.
**109** For a similar standpoint among the Arab philosophers the following may be noted: 'In accordance with Islamic tradition, Ghazali regards man's composition from body and soul as more perfect than the pure spiritual state of the angels. Angels were commanded to bow before Adam and the human prophet stands above the highest of created spirits.' Tjitze De Boer, The Moslem Doctrine of Creation, in *Proceedings of the Sixth International Congress of Philosophy*, 1926.

### NOTES FOR CHAPTER 4

**1** *De Anima* II, 412a, 27-8; 412b, 4-5.
**2** Ibid. II, 2, 414a, 19.
**3** *De Anima*, II, 2, 415b, 8.
**4** Ibid. III, 6, 430a, 10-25.
**5** Ibid. II, i, 413a, 9; II, 4, 415b, 18 ff. Cf. II, I, 412a, 19-21.
**6** Ser. 7, 64, 68, 70, 76 and a few others deal also with the nature and immortality of the soul. Sermon 6, however, is our chief source since this contains Arama's comprehensive exposition of the subject.
**7** Ser. 6, 47a. The term *kesher m'tziut* is translated 'union of inexistence.' For a similar translation see Wolfson, *Crescas' Critique*, 251. Inexistence here means existing inwardly. See also op. cit., 560.
**8** This was a keenly debated problem. Some thinkers held that the soul, coming from without, straight away has a distinct and separate individuality. Others believed that the soul on entering the body is not a distinct individual entity but part of the active intellect or universal soul and it is only as man's soul acquires knowledge that it achieves individuality. A similar approach revolved around the question of the soul's immortality.

## NOTES

Will it be an individual immortality of separate souls or will it be merely that the individual soul is absorbed in the active intellect ? Cf. Wolfson, *Philo*, pp. 416-7.

⁹ Ser. 6, 48b. This is a charming feature of Arama to acknowledge that he says nothing new but recasts the views of others. See 55b. The honesty of Arama is all the more noteworthy in view of the plagiarism of Abrabanel who took extracts of Arama's commentary and incorporated them into his own commentary without the slightest acknowledgment of their source. This, of course, was a common feature in medieval writings.

¹⁰ *Ha-tzurah ha-rishonah.*
¹¹ *Ha-tzurah ha-ilaniyut.*
¹² *Shivui mizgo.*
¹³ *Avicenna's Psychology*, Rahman, p. 34.
¹⁴ See Husik, *History of Medieval Jewish Philosophy*, XX, XXI, XXXIX, XLVI, also p. 175, where reference is made to the way in which Halevi's exposition of Aristotle's psychology is taken bodily from a youthful work of Avicenna.

¹⁵ 'The existence of the soul presupposes a mixture or blending of the elements in a certain proportion. But Avicenna adds that the physical functions are over and above this mixture. The soul then is not merely the harmony of the elements but something distinct from it.' *Avicenna*, Rahman, 70.

¹⁶ The whole argument is found in Albo's *Ikkarim*, III, 1. 'That the matter always moves from a less perfect to a more perfect form of existence, as the character of the composition rises in quality, is proved by the coral, which is intermediate, so to speak, between mineral and plant; by the marine sponge which has only the sense of touch, and is intermediate, as it were, between plant and animal; and by the ape, which stands midway between the animal species and man where the process stops. It follows, necessarily therefore, that man, who is the end of all the lower creatures, is nobler and more perfect than all since in him are combined all the earlier forms which stand to him in the relation of matter.'

¹⁷ Ser. 7, 56a. Cf. Ser. 8, 10, 76.
¹⁸ Ser. 17, 127b.
¹⁹ See Rahman, op. cit.
²⁰ Ser. 6, 49a. The remainder of the sentence tends to obstruct the meaning of this statement, but I do not think that the author intended to qualify it.
²¹ Niddah, 30b.
²² Ser. 68, 129b-130a.
²³ Ser. 68, 131a.
²⁴ Ibid. 131b.
²⁵ Ser. 70, 144b ff.
²⁶ Ser. 7, 57b ff.
²⁷ 'The active intellect in Jewish philosophy is unanimously held to be the last of the angelic substances, the proximate inspirer of the prophet.' Husik, *History*, p. 323.
²⁸ M.N. II, 4 and 12. One may also assume Maimonides to to be Arama's guide in the rest of his theory, viz., in the distinction between the two faculties in the rational soul, on the mortality of the lower and the immortality of the higher souls. M.N. 1, 32, 41, 68, 70, 72, III, 22; also *Hilkoth Teshuvah*, VIII, 8.

## NOTES

[29] Ser. 6, 49a. Arama states that the theory of the immortality of the higher rational soul of man is found in Aristotle's *Physics*. The actual source is *De Anima*, III, 6, 430a, 10-25.

[30] *Studien*, pp. 148-9.

[31] Ser. 6, 50a.

[32] Arama was well acquainted with Ibn Daud's work. See 1, 14a. Isaac Israeli also divides the human intellect into three classes, the potential intellect, the actual intellect and an intermediate stage. *Definitions*, 135. 'Israeli introduces an intermediate stage in his classifications of the intelligences. True it is there is a potential and actual intelligence, but there is an intermediary stage, namely, a process of realisation of the potential (or passive) intellect through the sense stimuli on the one hand and the influence of the active intellect on the other.' Bookstaber, *Development of the Soul in Medieval Jewish Philosophy*, p. 22.

[33] Rahman, *Avicenna*, 87-88. The last part of this quotation is a further illustration of the way in which Avicenna and Arama harmonise the views of Alexander and Themistius.

[34] Ser. 6, 48b.

[35] Ibid. 50a.

[36] *Ikkarim*, III, 35.

[37] Ibid. IV, 28.

[38] *Hilkoth Teshuvah*, VIII, 3.

[39] Ser. 6, 51b.

[40] Among the texts referred to by Arama are, Num. 23, 10; Sam. I, 25, 29; Isa. 45, 17; 64, 3; Job 33, 29-30; Ps. 16, 10; 25, 13; 26, 9; 27, 13; 31, 20; 49, 16; 56, 14; 61, 5; 116, 9; 142, 8.

[41] Lev. 23, 29-30; Num. 15, 30.

[42] Ser. 6, 50b.

[43] *Hilkoth Teshuvah*, VIII, 3.

[44] Ibid. VIII, 1.

[45] Ser. 6, 52a. The discussion on the corruptability of the lower soul goes back to Greek philosophy. Plato recognises the existence of an irrational and a rational soul which were also distinguished in their ultimate fate after the death of the body. While the rational soul went back to its Divine source, the irrational soul must first go through a series of reincarnations. The important thing, however, is that by its very nature it is indestructible. Timmaeus, 42b ff., 91d ff., Phaedrus, 249b, 610a.

In Judaism, despite the passionate belief in the retribution of the wicked there is room in classical sources to support the doctrine that the punishment of the wicked lies precisely in the destruction of their souls, i.e., the souls of the wicked are not kept alive for retribution but the very extinction of these souls is their punishment. In this way, several Jewish thinkers, including Maimonides, have interpreted the biblical warning of *karet*. Cf. *Wisdom of Solomon*, 3, 11; 4, 19; *Psalms of Solomon*, 15, 11 (10).

[46] M.N. II, 27. In this chapter, Maimonides argues that belief in the creation of the world need not imply belief in its inevitable destruction, for everything is according to the will of God—both that which is created and that which is destroyed. He holds that 'the souls of the pious have been created, but at the same time they are immortal.' Crescas submits the same view in his criticism of Aristotle, *Or Adonai*, III, 1, 5.

# NOTES
## NOTES FOR CHAPTER 5

1 Deut. 2, 26-28.
2 Jeremiah's parable of the potter and the clay, 18, 1-17, illustrates the power of God to make a new man out of original material. Isaiah 6, 10 illustrates the law of habit in human action. So does the apparently deterministic text 4, 21 (cf. Deut. 2, 30).
3 Deut. 30, 15, 19.
4 Gen. 4, 7.
5 *Immut*, 10, 47.
6 Bereshit Rabah, 8.
7 See Wolfson, *Philo*, Vol. I, 455 ff.
8 Abot. III, 15.
9 Josephus says of the Pharisees that they 'attribute everything to fate and God. To do the right or the contrary lies chiefly in man's power, but fate is auxiliary in each particular case.' (*Wars* II, 8, 1.) This was the intermediate view between the Sadducees who were absolute 'free-willists' and the Essenes who were complete fatalists denying that man is given any choice at all. See Finkelstein's *The Pharisees* I, 195 ff.
10 Among the Arab thinkers the orthodox Jabariya and Ashariya hold that God's foreknowledge determines every detail of man's life. Thus they deny the teaching of free will.
11 M.N. III, 17.
12 Ibid.
13 Ibid. It would seem that the last view of Maimonides which he says is the view of the Torah differs from the theories of the Mutazillah in the following points: Maimonides believes that man's freedom is complete; the Mutazillah hold that it is limited. Maimonides holds that God's providence and justice extends only over human beings while the Mutazillah hold that it governs also the irrational animals, even the flea, the louse and the mouse. Maimonides agrees with the Mutazillites that all things happening to man are in accord with God's justice but while he simply says that we are ignorant of the working of that judgment the Mutazillites answer all difficult points with reference to what they believe will happen in the world to come.
14 M.N. III, 19.
15 Ibid. III, 20.
16 'From the standpoint of eternity, every moment of time, past, present or future, is absolutely *now*.' Alan W. Watts, *The Supreme Identity*, quoted by Isidore Epstein in *The Faith of Judaism*.
17 *Hilkoth Teshuvah*, V, 1, 2.
18 *Commentary on the Mishnah*, Shemonah Perakim, VIII.
19 M.N. III, 30; *Commentary on the Mishnah*, Shemonah Perakim, VIII; *Hilkoth Teshuvah*, V, 5.
20 See comment of Rabad ad. loc.
21 See I. Epstein, loc. cit. 224, n. 5a.
22 *Emunoth*, IV, 3; *Kuzari*, V, 20.
23 *Ikkarim*, IV, 1; IV, 3; I, 3.
24 Ser. 21, 148b.
25 Ibid. See also Ser. 54, 183b; 79, 71a.
26 Albo refers to the same view, *Ikkarim*, IV, 1. 'Some of the moderns solve this difficulty by saying that a thing may be necessary if we consider

NOTES

it in relation to its causes and possible if we consider it by itself. Take, for example, the question of rain tomorrow. Considered by itself it is possible; considered in relation to its causes, namely, the rise of vapours, the great quantity of moisture and similar things already in existence, it is necessary. God therefore knows that it will rain tomorrow, because considered in relation to its causes, it is necessary, though considered by itself it is possible.' The 'moderns' referred to by Albo and whom Arama also doubtless had in mind is Hasdai Crescas, who in Or Adonai II, 5, 3, says *teva ha-efshari nimtza bid'varim biv'hinat atzmam, lo biv'hinat sibotam.* 'The nature of the possible is found in relation to themselves but not in relation to their causes.' In this sense it would seem that Crescas introduces a distinct limit to man's freedom since while theoretically the particular action may be free, nevertheless it is the natural effect of a cause which itself is determined. The following summary of Crescas' view is given by Husik, 'The only solution (to the problem of God's foreknowledge and man's freedom) is that the act of will is in a sense contingent, in a sense determined. It is contingent in respect to itself, it is determined by its cause, i.e., the act is not fated to take place, cause or no cause. If it were possible to remove the cause, the act would not be; but given the cause the effect is then necessary. Effort is not in vain, for effort itself is a cause and determines an effect. Commandments and prohibitions are not useless for the same reason.' *History of Medieval Jewish Philosophy*, p. 397. Cf. also the view of Gersonides in his commentary on Genesis 18, 21 where he suggests that God who knows the universal fixed order of the stars will consequently know thereby the fate of individuals. *Hu yodea ma'ase ha-anasim l'fi mah shehukan lahem mip'at ha-g'ramim ha-shamamiyim.* Another view was held by Abraham Ibn Ezra, 'God does not know the particular individual as such, but he knows him only as implied in the whole and his destiny is determined accordingly.' Husik's *History*, p. 193. Arama gives Ibn Ezra some cautious support. The source for Arama is Ibn Ezra's comment on Genesis 18, 21 *Ki ha-emet shehakol yodea kol helek al derek kol.* The implication of this view of God's knowledge is that God does really know individuals and contingencies even before the events take place, only he knows them out of the knowledge he has of the universal of which the individual is a part. This, of course, is quite different from the view of Gersonides who thought that God has no knowledge of contingencies until they happen. On the view of Ibn Ezra, Arama writes: *V'im l'kak kiven hu da'at nakon v'yishaer ha-Ralbag l'vado* (Sermon 19, 141a). This, despite Arama's own insistence that God has complete and constant knowledge of particulars, can be explained perhaps only with reference to the last three words quoted above. Arama is so outspoken an opponent of Gersonides' theory that God has no knowledge of particulars till they happen, that he would seem to be anxious to remove Ibn Ezra from the proximity of Gersonides' totally heretical views. See Friedlaender's *Essays on the Writings of Abraham Ibn Ezra.* . . . 'God's knowledge of all individual creatures is absolute and complete because it is generaliter *derek k'lali* that is, it reaches them from one common source through its various ramifications, divisions and sub-divisions,' p. 23. Cf. Rosin. Die Religionsphilosophie Abraham Ibn Ezra's *Monatsschrift*, 1898, 62 ff.

[27] Ser. 103, 124b.
[28] Ibid. 131a.
[29] Ser. 121, 150a.

## NOTES

[30] Ser. 103, 129a.
[31] Ibid. 131a.
[32] Ibid. 129a.
[33] Ibid. See also Ser. 21, 150b.
[34] Ser. 21, 151a. See also Ser. 103, 131b.
[35] *Hazuth Kashah* IV.
[36] Some people during World War II refused to take shelter during enemy air raids on the strength of the same argument that if God wills the death of the individual then no shelter would prevail, while if he wills man's safety, then the shelter is not necessary. The attitude was central in the thought of the Arab fatalists of the Middle Ages.
[37] Ser. 26, 198b.
[38] Ser. 1, 8b.
[39] Ser. 56, 205a ; Cf. Ser. 78, 15a f.
[40] Ser. 54, 187a-188b.
[41] Gen. 6.
[42] Ibid. 11.
[43] Ibid. 18.
[44] Lev. 20, 26 ; Deut. 6, 31 ; Isa. 63.
[45] See article by Kohler in *Jewish Encyclopedia*, II, 243-5.
[46] *Commentary on Mishnah*, Eight Chapters, VIII.
[47] Ser. 22, 158a.
[48] Ibid.
[49] Ibid.
[50] Ser. 28, 214b.
[51] In the final chapter of *Hazuth Kashah*, Arama writes a powerful polemic against those who credit the duration of the exile and other national disasters to the influence of the stars rather than to their own sins.
[52] For an almost identical treatment of this subject compare Albo's *Ikkarim*, Book IV, and particularly chapters I-VI.
[53] For a very brief but lucid account of the outlines of the modern discussion see Mackenzie, *Manual of Ethics* (6th edition), pp. 74 ff.
[54] Ser. 29, 138b.
[55] Ser. 28, 214b.
[56] Ibid. 215a.
[57] Ibid. 221a.

## NOTES FOR CHAPTER 6

[1] Joseph Albo states at the outset of his exposition that the doctrine is the purpose of the Torah as a whole *ha-taklit hamagia mikol ha-Torah, Ikkarim*, Book IV. See also Bahya, *Hovath Halevavoth*, Portal IV, *Shaar Habitahon*.
[2] M.N. III, 17.
[3] Ibid.
[4] Sayings of the Fathers, IV, 19. An alternative translation is given by Chief Rabbi Hertz in his Commentary, ad loc, and also by Schechter *Studies in Judaism*, Vol. I, p. 226.
[5] The Jewish Religion, 8th ed., 151.
[6] *Faith of Judaism*, 330.
[7] Berakoth 7a ; Sanhedrin 104a.

## NOTES

⁸ Deut. 8, 5 ; Prov. 3, 12. The rabbis very vividly suggest that God tests and tries only the righteous, just as a potter will only bother to test sound vessels, or a flax worker will beat flax of good quality in order to make it glisten more brilliantly. Gen. Rab. 32, 3.

⁹ Deut. 5, 16, 26 ; 11, 13 ff. ; 22 ; Amos 5, 5 ; 6, 7, 15, 13 ; Jer. 31, 12.

¹⁰ Num. 11, 33 ; 14, 37 ; 17, 12 ; Josh. 7, 5 ; II Sam. 21, 1. Significant also in the close relationship between sin and punishment is the fact that the same word is often used to express both the sin as well as the punishment. See Gen. 4, 13 ; 15, 16 ; Ez. 14, 10 ; Zech. 14, 19.

¹¹ Sabbath, 55a.

¹² Ethics of the Fathers V, 11.

¹³ Taanith 21a. See Schechter *Studies in Judaism*, Vol. I, 214 f.

¹⁴ Berakoth, 5a.

¹⁵ Ser. 70, 148b.

¹⁶ The doctrine of creation was the source for the medieval view of Divine providence. 'Jahve never ceases to remind the world of his authorship and it always is upon this right that the Bible founds his claim to dispose of human affairs at his good pleasure.' Gilson, *The Spirit of Medieval Philosophy*, p. 148 ff.

¹⁷ Ser. 93, 46b. Cf. Ser. 26, 201b ; 103, 131b.

¹⁸ *Emunah Ramah* (Weil) 93 f. M.N. III, 10.

The root of this belief seems to be in the Plotinian doctrine that matter is the source of evil. Since being is good, what is non-being is evil. In a Platonic sense matter is a non-being and hence evil. The evil in matter is due to its negative or privative aspects as the formless, which makes it the root of defect and evil. See Husik, *History of Medieval Jewish Philosophy*, p. 288 ; Gilson, *Spirit of Medieval Philosophy*, p. 110 ff. Maimonides, of course, could not hold that matter as such is evil, but rather that in its defective state, i.e., without the positive element of good, matter is evil. God produced matter and in so far as it is the source of evil, it is true that evil can be attributed to him. But this only in a special and indirect sense cannot be bracketed with the creation of a real evil. 'It cannot be said that God directly creates evil or that he has the direct intention to produce evil ; this is impossible. His works are all perfectly good' (M.N. III, 10). Maimonides does not deny the reality of evil; he denies only that God produces it. Evil, for Maimonides, is the necessary growing pain in an imperfect world still learning to make good its deficiencies (III, 11). Maimonides thus shows faith in the 'process of growth and development' inherent in the Universe (Epstein, *Faith of Judaism*, 379), and holds up the optimistic belief that there is greater good than evil in God's creation (III, 12). He denounces the pessimists and attempts to show that instances of suffering are due to 'the defects existing in the persons themselves.' Maimonides gives an explanation of the existence of evil by submitting that it is part of the constitution of the world of matter to contain defects (reason 1) but he still leaves the problems of theodicy untouched. Granted that man, made of flesh and blood, lives in the path of illness and decay, the question still remains why one man should be the subject of great physical pain while another lives in a state of perfect health throughout his life. Even when he submits (reason 2) that illness and pain are often brought on by man's self-indulgence it is an explanation of the existence only of *some* physical evil; it does not touch on the problem of the prosperity of the wicked or the suffering of the truly good and wise.

## NOTES

[19] Cf. 'The righteous who fares badly is one who is not perfect in his righteousness.' On the same basis 'The wicked who fares well is one who is not wicked throughout.' Berakoth, 7a.
[20] Taanith, 11a ; Kiddushin, 39b-40b.
[21] Ethics, I, 4.
[22] Ser. 69, 138a.
[23] Aboth, III, 21.
[24] Ser. 69, 138a.
[25] Ecc. 7, 18.
[26] Ser. 70, 150a-b.
[27] Ser. 70, 145a.
[28] See Husik's *Albo*, IV, pt. 2, 281, n. 2.
[29] Cf. Sifre on Deut. 11, 21.
[30] Ser. 70, 144b.
[31] Ibid.
[32] Ps. 27, 14.
[33] Ibid. 16, 10.
[34] Ser. 70, 148a.
[35] Cf. p. 98, above.
[36] *Commentary to the Mishnah*. Introduction to Helek. Bahya Ibn Pakudah uses a similar illustration. *Duties of Heart*, IV, 4.
[37] Cf. Albo, *Ikkarim*, IV, 7, for the suggestion that the suffering of the righteous is less of a problem than the prosperity of the wicked.
[38] Ser. 67, 121a.
[39] Ibid. 118a-121b.
[40] Ser. 69, 137b ff.
[41] Ser. 78, 15a f. At one point Arama suggests that since God exercises little or no providence over the gentile nations, He allows them to do more or less as they please because they will be without any reward in the world to come. Israel, however, will enjoy the true spiritual reward in the world to come and their long exile and suffering is intended to expiate them for their sins.
[42] Ser. 13, 100a.
[43] Ibid.
[44] See Aboth,V, 2.
[45] Ser. 13, 100b.
[46] Gen. 18, 25.
[47] Jonah 4, 11.
[48] Ser. 13, 100b.
[49] The problem is very modern. Many criminals, having been sentenced to terms of imprisonment leave behind an innocent wife and children who may languish in penury and bear the stigma of social disapproval. The argument given by Arama can be taken further, as is done by Albo, *Ikkarim*, IV, 12, where he suggests that a wicked man may prosper while he enjoys the general state of happiness decreed by providence for the entire community.
[50] Gen. 50, 20.
[51] Ser. 33, 268a.
[52] See H. Wheeler Robinson, *Religious Ideas of the Old Testament*, 87.
[53] II Kings 5, 27 ; Daniel 6, 24.
Of course the *fact* of communal suffering for the crime is real enough and needs no illustration. There is, however, something to be said in explaining

NOTES

the teaching that the community *should* share the moral guilt for the sin of the individual. In ancient Hebrew society, the family had a personality of its own and each member of it acted as part of the family. As no limb has life except in the body, so no individual had meaning or separate existence outside his family. 'Israel of the Old Testament never abandoned this fundamental view of the relation between the individual and his family.' (Pederson, *Israel*, I, 14, 278.) Consequently, the sin of the individual was the sin of the entire family which bears the responsibility for the conduct of each of its constituent members. In the same way the individual will often be involved in the happiness or the suffering of the whole community, although he himself may not merit such a particular fate. Albo makes much of this suggestion as one explanation for the prosperity of the wicked and the suffering of the righteous. . . . 'And therefore the evils came upon them whether they deserve them or not, as Daniel and his companions were exiled in the captivity of King Jehoiachin and Jeremiah went into exile in the captivity of Zedekiah. They did not deserve to be exiled personally, but were involved in the decree which was made concerning Jerusalem or the Nation.' *Ikkarim*, IV, 13.
54 Ser. 3, 22a.


## NOTES FOR CHAPTER 7

1 92b.
2 Ps. 68, 21.
3 Ser. 44, 95b.
4 Ibid. 93b. Arama adapts the analogy from the *Behinath Olam* of Jedaiah Penini (Bederasi) called in Arama's writings Ha-melitz.
5 94b-96a.
6 Ser. 44, 97b-98a.
7 Ibid. 99b.
8 Ibid. It is interesting to note that this defence of the laws of the Torah is still popular among the most modern exponents of Judaism.
9 See Arama's Introduction to *Akedath Yitzhak*; *Hazuth Kashah*, IV, VIII, XII; Ser. 70, 146b.
10 Cf. above, p. 98 and 146.
11 Ex. 23, 7.
12 Exodus Rabah, 27.
13 A Palestinian teacher, c. 70-110 c.e., of heretical views.
14 Ser. 68, 131a.
15 Ser. 33, 262a, f.
16 See, for example, Sanhedrin 21b, ' Why were the reasons of the Mitzvoth not revealed ? Because in the two cases where reasons were given the leader of the people himslf committed an error.' This refers to the explicit instructions given in the Torah prohibiting the king from having many wives and many horses. Solomon, however, thought that he could indulge while avoiding the evils that the Torah warns would ensue. See, too, the clear statement in *Shulhan Aruk*, Yoreh Deah, 181, ' We have no need to seek out the reasons for the commandments. We are obliged to perform the King's decrees although we do not understand their reasons.'
17 Wolfson's *Philo* II, 200 ff.
18 *Laws* III, 688a, f.

## NOTES

[19] *Repub.* X, 612b.
[20] *Ethics* X, vi.
[21] *Diogenes* viii, 8a, 127.
[22] The popular religion with the prominent place of the wrath of the gods was only for the ignorant masses. The philosophers did not really believe in the gods of Greek mythology or in a supreme ruler. Their view was that wisdom and virtue alone bring happiness and these things need no Divine sanction. See Kathleen Freeman's *The Greek Concept of God, Law and State* and Wolfson, loc. cit. pp. 284-5; cf. also on this point I. Heinemann, *Taamei Hamitzvoth*, pp. 30-38.
[23] Leg. All, III, 57, 167.
[24] Congr. 14, 80. See Wolfson p. 296 f.
[25] Ibid. 223.
[26] Aboth I, 3. It is perhaps significant that this first apparent stoicism has as its author one who lived in the Hellenistic period of Judaism, when Jewish teaching was subject to greatest influence. In the same category one might include R. Jose's statement 'let all thy deeds be done for the sake of Heaven.' (Aboth 3, 17.) So, too, numerous other rabbinic aphorisms. See, for example, Ber. 17a; Yer. Peah. 1; Ned. 62a; Sanhed. 99b; Sifri Ekev. 41. It is, of course, possible to interpret these and similar statements to mean that man is to do good not for the sake of virtue in itself, but rather out of pure disinterested love of God. This, in fact, is the immediate and literal meaning of the statements referred to above. In this case they belong to group 3 in our exposition, i.e., that the purpose of the commandments is to enable man to serve God with love.
[27] *Emmunoth*, 113, 13 (Landauer), Altman's translation.
[28] Ibid. 118, 11.
[29] For an excellent summary see I. Heinemann, *Taamei Hamitzvoth* pp. 42-3.
[30] *Emmunoth*, end of chapter I.
[31] Ibid. 113, 12.
[32] *Kuzari* I, 115; II, 26; III, 11.
[33] See Epstein, Judah Halevi as Philosopher, in *J.Q.R.* XXV, pp. 223.
[34] *Kuzari*, II, 56.
[35] Ibid.
[36] *Teshuvah*, X, 1-3. See also 4-5.
In this connection we might point to the remarks of Maimonides, M.N. III, 26, where he implies that the details of the laws may have to be observed merely as a test of our obedience to God who commanded them.
[37] The phrase *ad sheyishgeh* is not very clear. See comment of Rabad ad. loc.
[38] *Teshuvah*, X, 6.
[39] M.N. III, 27.
[40] Husik is probably justified in his criticism of Maimonides' intellectualistic attitude to the commandments, *History of Medieval Jewish Philosophy*, 300 pp. ff. There is, of course, a very great difference between Greek and Hebrew ethics since the latter are essentially practical. In his attempt to find an educative and rational purpose in the commandments, Maimonides was led into some strange difficulties. The institution of sacrifices, for example, was rationalised and its purpose was to be understood as a means of weaning the Israelites away from some of the idolatrous practices of the heathens. Since this could be done only gradually, the sacrifices could not be taken away altogether since they

were too well established as a part of the people's life. What God did therefore, was to allow the sacrifices to continue, but in a highly different form, purified from immorality and sanctified with religious direction. On the face of this, the sacrifices are a relic of an earlier period in Israelitish history, a stage in the development of its religious life. But here the question clearly arises. If this is true of the sacrifices could not something similar be said of so many other laws of the Torah? Further, to be consistent and logical within the intellectual view of Maimonides would lead to the conclusion that the earlier laws, representative of an early stage in the people's religious development, could be annuled by a more highly developed generation. The fact is, it must be admitted, that Maimonides nowhere gives room for any suspicion that he was prepared to follow his theoretical arguments to such a drastic conclusion. On the contrary, he makes it clear enough that the sacrifices, whatever their origin, are Divine laws and unless God were to indicate that this particular part of Torah was no longer valid then the sacrifices are to be regarded as an essential part of the constitution of the messianic state and are to be restored as soon as conditions allow. To this end he wrote two whole books out of the fourteen in his *Mishneh Torah* which were devoted to the sacrificial system (VIII, Sefer Ha'avodah and IX Sefer Korbanot). However, this is to recognise the gap between the two aspects of Maimonides and even to find in them an element of inconsistency.

[41] See I. Epstein's essay, Maimonides' Conception of the Law, etc., in the VIIIth *Centenary Volume*, 60 pp. ff., where the author claims that the intellectualistic purpose of the Torah was, for Maimonides, only a means to the final purpose which was his moral perfection in imitating the ways of God. With this final aim, of course, none would disagree. The point which is really at issue is how best to find such moral perfection. There are many paths to the same goal; but for Maimonides, apparently, the broadest path is that of knowledge and true opinions which can be gained by reflection on the meaning and the purpose of the laws of Torah.

[42] Mention could be made of what might perhaps be expounded as a fifth view of the purpose of the commandments. According to this, the laws of the Torah are recognised as a means of transforming society. Torah thus has a far wider purpose than the perfection of the individual and observance is seen as a social act of great importance since it can ultimately lead to the perfection of society as a whole.
See I. Epstein, The Conception of the Commandments of the Torah in Aaron Halevi's Sefer ha-Hinnuk, in *Essays Presented to J. H. Hertz*, 145-158.

[43] Cf. Ser. 81, 94b ff.
[44] Ser. 44, 100b.
[45] Ibid.
[46] Aboth, I, 3.
[47] Ibid. IV, 2.
[48] See *Teshuvah*, X, 4-5.
[49] Ser. 44, 101b.
[50] Ser. 42, 47a, ff.
[51] Ser. 44, 101b.
[52] Ethics X, 6.
[53] Ser. 44, 101b.
[54] Ibid. 102b. The explanation of this Mishna is different from that given

# NOTES

by Maimonides in his commentary ad loc.
<sup>55</sup> Ps. 19.
<sup>56</sup> Ser. 44, 102b.
<sup>57</sup> Cf. Ser. 15, and *Hazuth Kashah*, II, where reference is made to Midrash Tan. Tazria in support of this view. Arama states conclusively 'God created his world only so that his creatures should hearken to his voice and keep his covenant without any scruple or complaint.'
<sup>58</sup> The student of the text notices from time to time certain apparent inconsistencies in Arama's exposition. Some of them are important but many are of a minor character and it is suggested here that in his characteristically fulsome literary style with its many repetitions and variations on the same theme, Arama inadvertently allowed a word or a phrase to creep in here and there which could, if taken seriously, upset the main thesis. Thus, at the foot of Sermon 44, 102b, after pointing to the two purposes of the commandment as amply set forth and explained, he says: *tahlit rishon hashlamat ha-m'tzuveh v'ha-yirah v'ha-aharon hagaat hatzlahotav.* 'The first purpose is the perfection of the person commanded and the fear (of the Lord); the other is the attainment of his success.' The second purpose fits in with what has been explained; the first implies that there is another purpose in Torah which is 'perfection of man,' i.e., the Torah is primarily educative. Now Arama has not touched on this hitherto and one is surprised to find the idea referred to in his conclusion in this definite way. One is surprised, too, at finding perfection of man joined with fear of the Lord in the same primary purpose. It is therefore presumed that the phrase may be one of those injudicious slips of the pen of which Arama must occasionally plead guilty. The trouble lies in his over lengthy style since a writer or speaker who repeats the same arguments again and again must be tempted to vary his phrases and admits into them words which are misleading or inaccurate and which would not be allowed by one who was sparing with the words he used.
<sup>59</sup> *De Victimis.*
<sup>60</sup> Commentary on Lev. 1, 9.
<sup>61</sup> *Kuzari*, II, 25 ff.
<sup>62</sup> Commentary on Lev. 1, 1, 4. The point established by Ibn Ezra is that sacrifice may be regarded as a fine or ransom paid by the sinner as a punishment.
<sup>63</sup> Commentary on Lev. 1, 2.
<sup>64</sup> M.N. III, 32.
<sup>65</sup> Introduction to Commentary on Lev.
<sup>66</sup> M.N. III, 4; Issurei Hamizbeach, VII, 2.
<sup>67</sup> Meillah, VIII, 8.
<sup>68</sup> Probably for the detailed rules. Cf. M.N. III, 26.
<sup>69</sup> Commentary on Lev. 1, 9.
<sup>70</sup> See Rashi on Lev. 3, 1. Shelamim. *Sheyesh bahem shalom la-mizbeah v'la-kohanim v'la-b'alim.*
<sup>71</sup> For a parallel treatment by a modern English Old Testament scholar cf. T. H. Rowley, The Meaning of Sacrifice in the Old Testament in the *Bulletin of John Rylands Library*, Vol. 33. No. 1.
<sup>72</sup> Arama's argument seems rather weak here. It is true that sin cannot be evaluated in terms of hurt done to God but it is conceivable that a fine might be imposed upon one who breaks the law, not so much because he offends against a person but purely because he offends against the *law*.

A better argument might have made use of the fact that many kinds of sacrifice were not brought at all to expiate sin.

[73] There seems to be an interesting connection between the biblical offering for inadvertant sin and the Greek idea that virtue is knowledge and sin is ignorance. The Greek philosophers took it for granted that the right knowledge led to right action and incorrect understanding of a situation was at the basis of sin. Hence, all sin is essentially sin through ignorance. It is further possible to draw a connecting line between the emphasis placed on unwitting sin by the biblical law and the recent theories of psychoanalysis to the effect that it is largely due to the outworkings of the sub-conscious. We often sin, that is, because of our state of immaturity and sin is an expression of the mass of tangled unconscious forces in the hidden nature of the soul. If this is so, it is not impossible to see the psychiatric effect of the offering brought for unwilful sin.

[74] Ser. 57, 3a.

[75] M.N. II, 32. It is not always recognised that Maimonides' rationalisation of the sacrifices was directed not against all kinds of sacrifice but only on the non-obligatory or free-will offering. Arama clearly understood the limited direction of Maimonides' criticism. So, too, the prophetic criticism, as represented, say by Jer. 22, 23, is related not to obligatory and sin offerings but to the variety of free-will offerings. Maimonides as well as Arama seem to place this prophetic criticism in this more limited area. In this connection, see the interesting Introduction to Zevahim (Soncino Talmud, English Translation) by Epstein, where the author makes it clear that the prophets in denouncing sacrifice had in mind only one kind, the non-obligatory—but not the part of the statutory service of the Temple. So, indeed, when Maimonides rationalises the purpose of the sacrifice and holds forth the view that they are not binding as a regular form of worship, what Maimonides has in mind again is the non-obligatory sacrifice.

[76] Commentary on Lev. Nahmanides opposes Maimonides on two main points. First, if the sacrifice of certain animals was ordained because the Egyptians and other heathen nations venerated these animals as gods, then the Jewish use of them as sacrifices might well have the opposite effect to the one desired in so far as the sacrifice of these animals on the sacred altar would tend to place them in a sanctified category. Further, if the sacrifices were instituted to turn Israel away from the idolatrous practices of the nations around them how can we account for the incidence of sacrifices in the time Noah when there was no Egyptian influence?

[77] Ex. 13, 17-18. The shorter route to Canaan would have taken them into the hostile territory of the Philistines and in order to avoid this the Israelites were led in a long roundabout journey. In order to achieve the prime object a long and difficult method had to be adopted. So, too, the object of a sacrificeless spiritual religion could be achieved not by the short way, which was full of difficulties, but by the long method of gradual training.

[78] M.N. III, 46.

[79] Ibid. 32.

[80] Ibid. III, 32. Arama himself remarks on Maimonides' differentiation of sacrifice and prayer.

[81] Ser. 57, 6a.

[82] Ibid. 7a.

# NOTES
## NOTES FOR CHAPTER 8

1 M.N. II, 32.
2 Ibid. II, 36.
3 Ibid. II, 32.
4 Yesodei Hatorah, VII, 5.
5 H. A. Wolfson's *Philo*, Vol. II, 67. His more detailed account of the subject is in his essay, Halevi and Maimonides on Prophecy, in *J.Q.R.*, Vols. 32-33.
6 A brief but lucid summary is given by A. Cohen in his *Teachings of Maimonides*, 129. 'Maimonides maintained that prophecy was not in *essence* an endowment bestowed by God upon a few select individuals, but a degree of mental and moral perfection to which all may aspire. Man, by his own will and effort, created the *potential* gift of prophecy which God converted into an *actuality*.' (My italics.) See also Husik's *Albo*, III, 70, note 1 and other references cited there.
7 M.N. II, 38.
8 Ibid. II, 45.
9 Ibid. II, 33, 34, 44.
10 Ibid. II, 45.
11 Ibid. II, 35.
12 Ibid. II, 40.
13 Ibid. II, 39.
14 *Iggereth Teman*, II, 4a.
15 Gen. 20, 3; 21, 24.
16 M.N. II, 41.
17 Gen. 16; Judges, 13.
18 M.N. II, 42.
19 Ibid.
20 Cf. Wheeler Robinson, *Record and Revelation*, p. 315. 'Men may believe or may disbelieve that God of old time spoke unto the fathers . . . in diverse manners, but what we cannot do is to establish the claim of the prophets on something wholly external to their own activity, whether on a psychical event within or a physical event without.'
21 Cf. Jung, *Answer to Job*, XI-XIII:
'The fact that religious statements frequently conflict with the observed physical phenomena proves that in contrast to physical perception the spirit is autonomous, and that psychic experience is, to a certain extent, independent of physical data.' Jung makes the point that physical facts need not be appealed to in order to establish or refute psychical facts since each may be independent of the other to the extent that a psychic fact cannot be contested and needs no physical proof.
22 Gen. 18.
23 Ibid. 32, 25.
24 Num. 10.
25 Josh. 5, 13.
26 M.N. II, 41.
27 Ibid. II, 42.
28 See J. L. Teicher, Christian Theology and Jewish Opposition to Maimonides, in *Journal of Theological Studies*, Vol. 43.
It is true, of course, as the author points out, that the defence of miracles is far more important for the New Testament than for the Old Testament

because, if miracles are denied then the whole structure of New Testament teaching would all too easily topple to the ground. However, the Old Testament maintains an attitude towards prophetic teaching which seems to be equally important. For the validity of any prophetic teaching is that it is not the prophet's message but the message of God. The psychic event during which the prophet receives the direct message of God is therefor of greatest importance to Judaism.

²⁹ *Kuzari*, I, 79-98 ; II, 49 ; III, 23.

³⁰ Ibid. I, 4, 99. The argument seems to have been popular among medieval Jewish writers and is found represented in Albo, among others. 'We never find the gift of prophecy in any of the philosophers, though they were wise men in theoretical speculation. . . . This shows that it is not a natural phenomenon associated with theoretical speculation. For if it were so, why should this gift have been kept from the other nations, so that their wise men, despite their perfection of intellect and imagination, are devoid of the prophetic inspiration ? '

³¹ M.N. III, 27.

³² *Kuzari*, III, 1, 5, 11, 23.

³³ Ibid.

³⁴ M.N. II, 33.

³⁵ *Kuzari*, I, 87. Cf. Philo, *De Dec.* V, 18-19 for a similar treatment.

³⁶ Ibid.

³⁷ Ibid. II, 1 ff ; IV, 1 ff.

³⁸ Ibid. I, 11.

³⁹ Ibid. I, 97 ; IV, 26 ; V, 14-21.

Halevi repudiates the neo-Platonic Aristotelian system of the Universe by which God acts in the world through the mediary of the intelligences. Accordingly, he attributes all sublunary existences to the direct action of God's will.

⁴⁰ The view that prophecy is a natural outflow of human faculties had been taught before Maimonides. Abraham Ibn Daud explained prophecy from a similar standpoint and based his theories on the Aristotelian philosophy of Avicenna. He did not carry his views anywhere near as far as Maimonides but a similar intent in regarding prophecy as a perfected natural and spiritual capacity is there. *Emunah Ramah*—70-75. See Husik's *History*, lxix, 224.

⁴¹ *Kuzari*, IV, 3 ff.

⁴² Ibid.

⁴³ Ibid. I, 43.

⁴⁴ My italics. The meaning is thus clear and Halevi explicitly states the objective reality of prophetic experience.

'The main contention of all religion is that reality is not exhausted by the senses, but that there is another reality behind the sensible, and that this is also revealed to us.' S. H. Bergman, Philosophy and Religion, in *Judaism*, Vol. IV, No. 1, p. 65.

⁴⁵ *Kuzari* III, 73.

⁴⁶ Ibid. I, 27 ; cf. I, 95, 115.

The expression 'pick' denotes here the religious choice of mankind. Halevi believed that the gift for religion is bestowed on one particular group and it cannot be adopted by one not of that group. See I, 1, 4 ; IV, 23.

⁴⁷ See Wolfson's essay, J.Q.R. Vol. 33, p. 61 ff. for the interesting view that in claiming special gifts of prophecy only for the Jews Halevi was borrow-

ing from Christian sources. The Christians argued that the Jews were the people of prophecy; but only at first, since after Jesus the gift was transferred to the Christians. Halevi is therefore only reclaiming for the Jews 'that distinctive position among the religions of the world which later other peoples have arrogated to themselves in their belief of being the rightful successors to the Jews.'

[48] *Kuzari*, II, 10, 12, 14. The fact that Abraham's prophetic gift was manifest in Babylon or that Jeremiah, Ezekiel and Daniel also prophesied outside the land causes Halevi no difficulty for he explains it all by saying, 'Whosoever prophesied, did so either in Palestine or for its sake, viz., Abraham to reach it, Ezekiel and Daniel on account of it. . . .'

[49] Beginning of Sermon 19.

[50] M.N. II, 32.

[51] Nedarim, 38a.

[52] Ser. 19, 134b-135.

[53] Ibid. 137a. I am indebted to Epstein, *Faith of Judaism*, 116, 388, for the reference to the distinction made by Jewish writers to what was *l'maalah min ha-sekel* i.e., what is *above* human reason and that which was *counter* to it. Jewish philosophers never accept the possibility that the Torah could contain anything that contradicts reason. On the other hand there are many things which human reason cannot grasp because of the limitations of human reason. Philosophically then, such things can only be understood with reference to what is *above* human reason. It is here that religion steps in where reason can proceed no further.

[54] Ser. 35, 9b ff.

[55] M.N. II, 32.

[56] See above, chapter II.

[57] Ser. 35, 10a.

[58] *Nireh shesamku al ha-rishon*. The verb should perhaps be in the singular to make sense.

[59] *Pele gadol*.

[60] Ser. 35, 10a.

[61] M.N. II, 32.

[62] There is also a noteworthy similarity between the views arrived at by Arama and those expressed by Philo. Philo recognises that in reality a prophet is found with the qualifications of refinement, wisdom and justice but over and above everything else there is the element of Divine grace and selection. This is a type of prophecy which does not even require any qualification for God may send an angel to whomsoever he wills as is seen in the instance of Lot, Hagar and Baalam. For Philo, there is no possibility that prophecy is simply a manifestation of natural or other perfections since prophecy is supernatural. 'He is a shallow thinker who supposes that in strict truth anything whatever derives its birth from the mind or from himself . . . unless God send the object of sense as rain upon it.' (Leg. All. II, 13, 29, 46.)

[63] *Kuzari*, III, 1, 5, 11, 23.

[64] Ser. 35, 11a.

[65] Ibid.

[66] 'Purity leads to piety, piety leads to modesty, modesty leads to fear of sin, fear of sin leads to holiness, holiness leads to the Holy Spirit.' Avodah Zarah, 20b. Cf. 'The Divine Spirit rests only on one who is strong, rich, wise and modest.' Nedarim, 38a.

## NOTES

[67] Ser. 35, 14a.
[68] M.N. II, 32.
[69] Ser. 35, 11b. Cf. Succah, 28a.
[70] Cf. 'The word of the Lord is made a reproach unto me and a derision all the day. And if I say I will not make mention of it, nor speak any more in his name, then there is in my heart, as it were, a burning fire shut up in my bones and I am weary with forebearing, but I cannot.' Jer. 20, 8-9. The text illustrates the inner drive of the true prophet to proclaim God's message to the people.
[71] Ser. 80, 87b.
[72] Ibid.
[73] Ser. 82, 102a-103a.
[74] Ser. 35, 13a.
[75] Ser. 76, 38b.
[76] Ser. 80, 86b-87a.
[77] M.N. II, 45.
[78] *Yesodei Hatorah*, XII, 6. The order in Maimonides is slightly different.
[79] Cf. 'All other prophets prophesied as though through a blurred image produced by a dim mirror, while Moses received the vision like the reflection from a bright mirror.' Yebamot, 49b.
[80] Ser. 76, 39a-40b.
[81] Gen. 18.
[82] M.N. II, 42.
[83] Ibid.
[84] Ser. 19, 137a.
[85] 'Religious experience and sense experience cannot be held together as belonging to one class of experience whereby the latter can be brought in as proof of the former. Sense experience is a *common* experience. What is seen by one person, is also seen by the other if they find themselves in the same place. Sense-data are intersubjective and, therefore, all the means of criticism and control can be applied to them. But when we are concerned with religious experience such control cannot be carried through on prinicple since religious experience is by its very nature not public, not intersubjective. It is not shared in common. For example, the voice heard by the boy Samuel (I Sam. 3), the call of God, is, according to the Bible itself, not heard by Eli who is present. Thus religious experience is at a disadvantage in comparison with sense-experience as concerns the possibility of objective control.' Hugo Bergman, loc. cit. pp. 65-6.
[86] Commentary on Gen. 18, 2.
[87] M.N. II, 42.
[88] Loc. cit.
[89] Gen. 32, 24-33.
[90] J. L. Teicher (*Journal of Theological Studies*, XLIII, p. 73) quotes an interesting passage written by Hillel of Verona in which the following explanation is given of Jacob's struggle with the angel. 'There is no doubt whatever that the struggle was literally real, i.e., that Jacob fought with, or was moved by, an angelic power. There was sensorial contact and the thrust was not part of the 'form of prophecy' but was literally true. I will never believe though, that the angel was a body with joints and arms, but it happened like this: the angel, by means of a spiritual Divine power, created in the air surrounding Jacob, motions of thrust and pressure,

## NOTES

whence the air particles were violently moved and by their movement compelled the body of Jacob, by pressing and coercing it as in the thrust of wrestling . . . to move to and fro. Through this coercion and pressure the distortion or dislocation was produced either by intention or by accident. The angel himself appeared to him, in truth, only in " a prophetical vision. . . ." Thus the tale of this event is literally true, as the real happenings were combined with the prophetical visions.' This account is interesting not only in itself but as an illustration of a kind of compromise theory which suggests that the details of the events were real while the fact of the appearance of the angel is a prophetic vision. It has been suggested that this may have been Maimonides' true view, but it seems quite clear that it is very far removed from it.

91 *Vayar vayarotz.* Gen. 18, 2.
92 *Vayisa enav vayar.* Ibid.
93 Ibid. 18, 23.
94 Exodus, 3, 2.
95 Gen. 32, 31.
96 Bereshith Rabah, 48.
97 Ser. 19, 137b.
98 Ser. 29, 228a.
99 Ser. 76, 35a-37a.
Cf. the view of Philo that direct prophecy can come only to Israel which has the necessary qualifications. Moses 2, 35, 189; Leg. All. II, 9, 33-4.
100 Ser. 35, 11a.
101 Berakoth, 7a.
102 Ex. 33, 16.
103 Ser. 82, 103a.
104 'To the modern mind it is astonishing that Maimonides should include such dissimilar types as lawgivers and diviners in the same category and that he should assert that the imaginative faculty of the former was in the ascendant to such an extent as to deny them a place with thinkers and also that any place should be found for those who practised the black arts. Apparently neither Jew nor Arab in the Middle Ages had any difficulty in believing that wizards and diviners were able to work wonders and they accepted them and their works as part of the natural order of things—a fact which goes to show that even the strongest and most confirmed monotheists still retained a belief in magic.' Prophecy and Divination, The Bampton Lectures for 1958, p. 188.
We cannot subscribe to the last sentence without the reservation that 'to believe' in magic need imply only that it is possible while maintaining a strong attitude about its immorality.

# ABBREVIATIONS

| | |
|---|---|
| BJRL | Bulletin of the John Ryland Library |
| MN | Moreh Nevukim |
| BR | Bereshit Rabbah |
| AY | Akedath Yitzhak |
| HK | Hazuth Kashah |
| JE | Jewish Encyclopedia |
| HUCA | Hebrew Union College Annual |
| JQR(NS) | Jewish Quarterly Review (New Series) |
| MGWJ | Montasschrift fuer Geschichte und Wissenschaft des Judentums |
| PAAJR | Proceedings of the American Academy for Jewish Research |
| PICP | Proceedings of the International Congress of Philosophy |

The quotations from the Bible follow the translation of the Holy Scriptures by the Jewish Publication Society of America (Philadelphia, 1937). Talmudic and midrashic material are cited from the Soncino translation of the Talmud, edited by I. Epstein (London 1935-48) and the Soncino translation of the Midrash (London).

The following bibliography comprises a list of some of the chief works consulted by the author and referred to in this book. It is not a comprehensive bibliography and omits most of the foreign language works dealing with medieval Jewish philosophy. For a fairly comprehensive bibliography on the subject the student is referred to David W. Silverman's English translation of Julius Guttman's *Philosophies of Judaism*, New York, 1964.

# SELECTED BIBLIOGRAPHY

ABELSON, J., *Jewish Mysticism*. London, 1913.
ABRABANEL, ISAAC, *Sefer Mifalot Elohim*. Venice, 1592.
ABRAHAM, BAR HIYYA, *Hegyon Hanefesh*, Ed., Y. I. Friemann. Leipzig, 1860. *Sefer Megillat Hamegalleh*, Ed., A. Pozanski. Berlin, 1924.
ABRAHAMS, ISRAEL, *Studies in Pharisaism and the Gospels*. Cambridge, 1917.
AGUS, J. B., *The Evolution of Jewish Thought*. New York, 1959.
ALBO, JOSEPH, *Sefer Haikkarim*, Ed., I. Husik, 4 Vols. Philadelphia, 1930.
ALI, SYED AMEER, *The Spirit of Islam*. London, 1952.
ALTMANN, ALEXANDER, *Biblical and Other Studies*. Cambridge, Mass., 1963. *Saadya Studies*. Manchester, 1953. "The Climatological Factor in Judah Halevi's Theory of Prophecy" in *Melilah*, Vol. I. Manchester, 1944. "Saadya's Conception of the Law" in *BJRL.*, Vol. XXVIII.
ARAMA, ISAAC, *Akedath Yitzhak*, Ed., H. J. Pollack. Pressburg, 1846. *Hazuth Kashah*. Ed., H. J. Pollack. Pressburg, 1846. *Babylonian Talmud*, Ed., I. Epstein. 18 Vols. London, 1952.
BAHYA IBN PAKUDA, *Sefer Torat Hovat Halevavot*, Ed., Zifroni. Jerusalem, 1928.
BARON, S. W., *A Social and Religious History of the Jews*. 14 Vols. New York and Philadelphia, 1952-69.
BASS, SHABBTA, *Siftei Yeshenim*. Amsterdam, 1680.
BECKER, J., *Mishnato Hapilosophit Shel Harambam*. Tel Aviv, 1956.
BERNFELD, SIMEON, *Daath Elohim, Toldoth Hapilosophia Hadatith B'Yisrael*. Warsaw, 1897.
BERGMAN, S. H., "Philosophy and Religion," in *Judaism*. Vol. IV No. 1.
BETTAN, ISRAEL, *Studies in Jewish Preaching*. Cincinnati, 1939.
BOER, TJITZE, J. DE., "The Moslem Doctrine of Creation," in *PICP*. 1926.
*The History of Philosophy in Islam*. London, 1933.
BOKSER, BEN ZION, *The Legacy of Maimonides*. New York, 1950.
BOOKSTABER, P. H., *The Development of the Soul in Medieval Jewish Philosophy*. Philadelphia, 1950.
CARO, JOSEPH, *Shulhan Aruk*. 4 Parts. Vilna, 1875.
COHEN, ABRAHAM, *The Teachings of Maimonides*. London, 1927. *Everyman's Talmud*. London, 1932.
CONFORTE, DAVID, *Koreth Hadoroth*, Ed., D. Cassel. Berlin, 1846.
CRESCAS, HASDAI, *Or Adonai*. Johannesburg, 1861.
DAUBE, DAVID, *Studies in Biblical Law*. Cambridge, 1947.
DAVIDSON, A. B., *Theology of the Old Testament*. New York, 1907.
DAVIDSON, ISRAEL, *Sefer Milhamot Adonai*. New York, 1934.
DIESENDRUCK, Z., "Saadia's Formulation of the Time Argument for Creation," in *Jewish Studies in Memory of A. Kohut*. New York, 1935.
EFFROS, ISRAEL, I., *The Problem of Space in Medieval Jewish Philo-*

*sophy.* New York, 1917. *Philosophical Terms in the Moreh Nebukim.* New York, 1924. *Hapilosophia Hayehudit Haatika.* Jerusalem, 1959. *Encyclopedia of Islam.* 5 Vols. London and Leiden, 1913-38. *Encyclopedia of Religions and Ethics.* Ed., Hastings. 12 Vols. New York, 1908-1927.

EPSTEIN, ISIDORE, "Judah Halevi as Philosopher," in *JQR(NS).* Vol. XXV. "The Concept of the Torah in Aaron Halevi," in *Essays Presented to J. H. Hertz.* London, 1954. "Maimonides' Conception of the Law," in *VIIIth Centenary volume.* 1935. *The Faith of Judaism.* London, 1954.

FELDMAN, W. M., *Rabbinical Mathematics and Astronomy.* New York, 1931.

FINKEL, JOSHUA, *Maimonides' Treatise on Resurrection.* Ed., S. W. Baron. New York, 1941.

FINKELSTEIN, LOUIS, *The Pharisees.* 2 Vols. Philadelphia, 1938. *The Jews, Their History, Culture and Religion.* Ed., 2 Vols. New York, 1949.

FRIEDLANDER, M., *Essays on the Writings of Abraham Ibn Ezra.* London, 1895. *The Jewish Religion.* London, 1931.

GANZ, DAVID, *Zemah David.* Prague, 1592.

GEIGER, A., *Was hat Mohammed aus dem Judenthume aufgenommen?* Bonn, 1833. English translation—*Judaism and Islam.* Madras, 1898.

GERSONIDES (LEVI BEN GERSON), *Sefer Milhamot Adonai.* Leipzig, 1866.

GIBB, H. A. R., "Law and Religion in Islam," in *Judaism and Christianity.* Ed., E. I. J. Rosenthal. London, 1938.

GILSON, E., *The Spirit of Medieval Philosophy.* New York, 1940. *History of Christian Philosophy in the Middle Ages.* New York, 1955.

GINZBERG, LOUIS, *On Jewish Law and Lore.* Phildelphia, 1955.

GRUNEBAUM, G. VON., *Medieval Islam.* Chicago, 1946.

GUTTMANN, JULIUS, *Dat Umada.* Jerusalem, 1956. *Philosophies of Judiasm.* Tr., D. W. Silverman. New York, 1964.

HALEVI, JUDAH, *Kitab Al-khazari.* Tr., H. Hirschfeld. London, 1931.

HEILPRIN, YEHIEL, *Seder Hadorot.* Warsaw, 1882.

HEINEMANN, ISAAC, *Taamei Hamitizvot B'safruth Yisrael.* Jerusalem, 1954. *Jehudah Halevi.* Oxford, 1947.

HESCHEL, A. J., "The Quest for Certainty in Saadia's Philosophy," in *JQR(NS)* XXXIII, 1942-43. "Reason and Revelation in Saadia's Philosophy," in *JQR(NS)* XXIV, 1944. "Joseph Albo, the last of the Jewish Medieval Philosophers," in *PAAJR,* 1930.

HUGHES, T. P., *Dictionary of Islam.* London, 1885.

HUSIK, ISAAC, *A History of Medieval Jewish Philosophy.* Philadelphia, 1930. *Philosophical Essays.* Ed., Nahm and Strauss. Oxford, 1952.

IBN DAUD, ABRAHAM, *Emunah Ramah.* Ed., Weil. Frankfurt a.M., 1852.

IBN EZRA, ABRAHAM, *Hegyon Hanefesh.* Ed., Freimann. Leipzig, 1860.

IBN GABIROL, SOLOMON, *Mekor Hayyim.* Tr., Blubstein. Tel Aviv, 1926.

IBN YAHYAH, GEDALIAH, *Shalshelet Hakabalah.* Venice, 1587.

IBN ZADDIK, JOSEPH, *Sefer Haolam Hakatan.* Ed., Horovitz. Breslo, 1903.

INGE, DEAN, "Platonic Matter," in *Church Quarterly Review.* January, 1939.

ISRAELI, ISAAC, *Works.* Ed., Altmann and Stern. Oxford, 1958. *Liber Jesod Olam.* Ed., Goldberg and Rosenkranz. 2 Vols. Berlin, 1846-48. *Jewish Encyclopedia.* 12 Vols. New York and London, 1916.

JOSEPHUS, FLAVIUS, *Works.* Tr., Thackeray and Marcus. London, 1926.
KADUSHIN, MAX, *The Rabbinic Mind.* New York, 1952.
KASHER, M. M., *Torah Shlemah.* 21 Vols. Jerusalem, 1926-64.
KATSH, ABRAHAM I., *Judaism in Islam.* New York, 1954.
KAUFMANN, YEHEZKEL, *Toledoth Haemunah Hayisraelith miyemei Kedem ad sof bayit sheni.* 8 Vols. Tel Aviv, 1937-58.
KLIBANSKY, R., *The Continuity of the Platonic Tradition During the Middle Ages.* London, 1950.
LAZARUS, M., *The Ethics of Judaism.* 2 Vols. Philadelphia, 1901.
LEWY, HANS, *Philo.* Oxford, 1946.
MACDONALD, D. B., *Aspects of Islam.* New York, 1911.
MACKENZIE, J. C., *Manual of Ethics.* London, 1929.
MAIMONIDES, MOSES, *Guide to the Perplexed.* Tr., M. Friedlander. London, 1942. *Mishneh Torah.* 4 Vols. Vilna, 1900. *Maamar Tehiyyat Hametim.* Ed., Finkel. New York, 1938.
MALTER, H., *Saadia Gaon, His Life and Works.* Philadelphia, 1921. " Saadiah Studies," in *JQR(NS)* III, 1912-13.
MARMORSTEIN, A., " Philo and the Names of God," in *JQR(NS)* XXII, 1931-32. *The Doctrine of Merits in Old Rabbinic Literature.* London, 1920. *The Old Rabbinic Doctrine of God.* London, 1927.
MEKILTA DE-RABBI ISHMAEL, Ed., M. Friedman. Vienna, 1870.
MIDRASH RABBAH, Ed., H. Freedman and M. Simon. 10 Vols. London, 1939.
MONTEFIORE, C. G. and LOEWE, H., *A Rabbinic Anthology.* London, 1938.
MOORE, G. F., *Judaism.* 3 Vols. Cambridge, Mass., 1927-30.
NEUMAN, ABRAHAM A., *The Jews in Spain.* 2 Vols. Philadelphia, 1942.
NEUMARK, DAVID, *Jehuda Halevi's Philosophy in its Principles.* Cincinnati, 1908. *Toldoth Hapilosophia B'yisrael.* 2 Vols. Warsaw and Philadelphia, 1921-25. " Essence and Existence in Maimonides," *JRL* II, 1935.
NORTH, *The Thought of the Old Testament.* London, 1948.
O'LEARY, DE LACY, *Arabic Thought and its Place in History.* London, 1939.
PEARL, CHAIM, *An Examination of the Concept of Sin in the Old Testament.* Unpublished MA thesis, the University of Birmingham, England, 1954.
PEDERSON, JOSHUA, *Israel.* London and Copenhagen, 1926.
PHILO, *Works.* Tr., F. H. Colson and J. E. Whittaker. 9 Vols. London, 1929-41.
PORTER, F. C., *The Yetser Hara, A Study in the Jewish Doctrine of Sin.* New York, 1901.
RAHMAN, F., *Avicenna's Psychology.* London, 1952.
ROBINSON, H. W., *Religious Ideas of the Old Testament.* New York, 1913.
ROSENTHAL, E. I. J., *Record and Revelation.* Oxford, 1938. *Judaism and Islam.* London, 1961.
ROSIN, DAVID, " Die Religions Philosophie Abraham Ibn Ezra's," in *MGWJ,* 1898.
ROWLEY, T. H., " The Meaning of Sacrifice in the Old Testament," in *BJRL* Vol. XXXIII(1), Manchester.

SAADIA BEN JOSEPH, *The Book of Beliefs and Opinions.* Tr., S. Rosenblatt. New Haven, 1948. *The Book of Doctrines and Beliefs.* Ed., A. Altmann. Oxford, 1946.
SARACHEK, J., *Faith and Reason: The Conflict Over the Rationalism of Maimonides.* Williamsport, 1935.
SCHMIEDL, A., *Studien uber Juedische Insonders Juedisch-Arabische Religions Philosophie.* Wien, 1869.
SCHECHTER, SOLOMON, *Studies in Judaism.* Philadelphia, 1938. *Some Aspects of Rabbinic Theology.* London, 1909.
STACE, W. T., *A Critical History of Greek Philosophy.* London, 1934.
SWEETMAN, J. W., *Islam and Christian Theology.* 3 Vols. London, 1945-55.
SCHOLEM, G., *Major Trends in Jewish Mysticism.* New York, 1946. *Talmud Babylonian.* Ed., I. Epstein. 18 Vols. London, 1952.
TEICHER, J. L. "Christian Theology and Jewish Opposition to Maimonides," in *Journal Jewish Theological Studies,* Vol. XIII.
WALZER, R., "Arabic Transmission of Greek Thought to Medieval Europe," in *BJRL* XXIX, 1945-46.
WAXMAN, M., *The Philosophy of Don Hasdai Crescas.* New York, 1920.
WEISS, I. H., *Dor Dor Vedorshav.* 5 Vols. New York, 1924.
WILENSKY, SARAH, *R. Yitzhak Arama Umishnato.* Jerusalem, 1956.
WOLFSON, H. A., *Crescas' Critique of Aristotle.* Cambridge, Mass., 1929. *Philo.* 2 Vols. Cambridge, Mass., 1947. "Halevi and Maimonides on Prophecy," in *JQL.* Vols. XXXII-XXXIII. "The Platonic, Stoic and Aristotelian Theories of Creation in Halevi, and Maimonides," in *Essays Presented to J. H. Hertz.* London 1954. "The Meaning of Ex Nihilo in the Church Fathers, Arabic and Hebrew Philosophy," in *Medieval Studies in Honour of J. D. M. Ford,* Cambridge, Mass., 1948. "The Problem of the Origin of Matter in Medieval Philosophy," in *Proceedings of the Sixth International Congress of Philosophy.* 1926. "Maimonides on Negative Attributes," in *Louis Ginzberg Jubilee Volume.* New York, 1945. "Notes of Proofs of the Existence of God in Jewish Philosophy," in *HUCA* Vol. 1. "Note on Crescas' Definition of Time," in *JQR(NS).* 1919. "The Classification of Sciences in Medieval Jewish Philosophy," in *Hebrew Union College Jubilee Volume.* 1925. "Halevi and Maimonides on Design, and Necessity," in *PAAJR* XI. 1941.
ZACUTO, ABRAHAM, *Sefer Yuhasin.* Ed., M. Filipowski. Frankfurt a.M., 1928.

# GENERAL INDEX

Abahu, Rabbi, 45
Abraham, 10ff., 13, 34
Abraham Bar, Hiyyah, 2, 42
Abraham ben David, of Posquieres, 17, 25
Abravanel, 179
Active intellect, 56, 61, 64
Aggada, 7
Akiba, 71, 87
Albo, 2, 179
   existence of God, 19
   God's knowledge, 74
   prophecy, 195
   time, 42, 44
Alfarabi, 29
Algazali, 2
*Anah*. Place in Creation, 49
Angels, 38-40
Animal life, 51
Anthropomorphism, 25, 172
Aquinas, 9
Arama, Isaac,
   eclectic philosopher, 1
   *Hazuth Kashah*, 3, 12
   homiletic source, 1
   honesty of, 179
   Maimonides, 140-141, 147
   Nahmanides, 148-149
   religious philosopher, 1, 3, 11
   *Yad Avshalom*, 3
Arama on
   anthropomorphism, 25
   Arab philosophy, 1
   commandments and their purpose, 105, 115-120
   correct beliefs, 106
   creation, 29ff.
   determinism and freedom, 86, 157
   Divine compassion, 99
   Divine law, 103-104
   Divine will, 139-143, 152-153, 167
   faith, 166
   free will, 75, 78-79, 83
   God's attributes, 21-23
   God and man, 91
   God's knowledge, 77
   heavenly spheres, 154
   life after death, 166
   Moses, 144-145
   natural law, 35
   prophecy, 138, 143, 145, 147
   reward and punishment, 98, 101, 158
   sabbatical year, 99
   sacrifices, 127-128
   sin offering, 123
   soul, 59, 62-81, 155
   suffering, 91ff.
   time, 154
Aristotle
   commentators of, 2
   categories, 154, 174
   creation, 28, 30ff.
   eternity, 35
   free will, 73
   God, 173
   the good, 94
   intelligences, 54
   quantity, 178
   soul, 56, 62, 68, 155
   time, 41
Ashariyah, 73
Averroes, 2
Avicenna (Ibn Sina), 2, 38, 173
   on the soul, 60

Bahyah Ibn Pakudah, 22
Bass, Shabbtai (*Siftei Yeshenim*), 4
Bedaresi, 19

Bettan, Israel (*Studies in Jewish Preaching*), 4
Bibago, 2
Bible, concepts of,
 language of man, 16
 literal truth, 135, 147
 philosophy and theology, 6, 151
 prophecy, 129
 reward and punishment, 159

Cause and agens, 32ff.
 in creation, 46
Christianity
 sermons preached to Jews, 1
 theology, 13ff.
Classical exegetes, 2
Commandments
 as Divine law, 105
 and Christianity, 106
 function of, 109-110, 113-116, 118
 purpose of, 116-117
 reward for observance, 118
Communal suffering, 185-186
Conforte, David (*Koreh Hadoroth*) 4
Crescas, Hasdai, 2, 42-43, 157, 182

Day and night, 41-47
Divine compassion, 100
Divine justice,
 central doctrine, 88
 community involved, 101
 human understanding, 89
 Maimonides on, 88
Divine law, 160
 as commandments, 105
 practicality of, 105
 purpose of, 103, 105, 113
 result of, 106
 spiritual perfection, 104
Divine providence
 and individual, 101
 and man's actions, 86-87
 and suffering, 91
 Arama's views on, 81ff.
Divine retribution, 88
Divine spirit, 52
Diviners
 and medieval philosophers, 150
 belief in magic, 195

Earth
 creation of, 40
 elements of, 40-41
 *eretz* (dry land), 49ff.
*Ech* Quality in Creation, 52
*Elohim* of natural law, 34
Emanation theories of creation, 29
Epicurus, 73
*Etzem* Substance in Creation, 48
Evil partial and greater good, 102
Exegetes, 2
Existence, causes of, 52
Ezra, 23

Faith
 concept of Arama, 166
 pillar of theology, 166
Firmament, 48-49
Free will, 3
 and astrology, 83
 and fate, 82, 84
 and God's foreknowledge, 15, 71-72, 78-79
 and God's omniscience, 71
 and perfect knowledge, 78
 and providence, 71-73
 Arama on, 76ff.
 human, 156
 Jewish doctrine of, 70
 Maimonides on, 72, 156, 174
 man's approach to, 52
 man's limit of, 182
 medieval discussions on, 72
 Philo on, 156
 rabbis' views on, 71

Gabirol, 173
Ganz, David (*Zemah David*), 4
Genesis, book of,
 on creation, 47ff.
 on time, 46-47
Gersonides, 157
 and creation of world, 29, 174-175
 and man's freedom, 182
 on luminaries, 50-51
 on the spheres, 54
God
 and free will, 71,79-80
 and individual, 74
 and natural law, 103
 anthropomorphism, 23ff., 153
 as Creator, 7, 32, 158,171
 as Divine spirit in man, 52
 attributes of, 7, 20ff., 22
 Avicenna on, 176

choice of prophet, 130-131
Christian concept of, 80
comprehensibility of, 19
corporeality of, 16-17, 24
creative power of, 33ff.
death of, 167
essence of, 20ff.
existence of, 42
fear of, 33
foreknowledge of, 3
grace of, 80
*Hamakom* (Omnipresent), 25
Maimonides on, 176ff.
*Memra* (Divine Word), 24
names of, 174
nature of, 3
nearness of, 26
perfection of, 77
personal, 167
role in history, 167
questions about, 15ff.
submission to, 128
Grammatical works, 2
Greek philosophy, 16

Halevi, Judah, 2
attributes of emotion, 22
concept of prophecy, 131, 135-142, 161-162, 192-193
concept of reason, 9-11
concept of revelation, 136
inconsistencies in, 24
opposition to Maimonides, 135-137
purpose of the commandments, 116
purpose of Divine law, 113
purpose of sacrifices, 121
*Hamakom* (see under God)
*Hazuth kashah* (see under Arama)
Heilprin, Yehie (*Seder Hadoroth*), 4
Hillel and Shammai, 169
Holocaust, 168
Human existence, purpose of, 68
Human freedom
and determinism, 85-86
Arama's view of, 77
as contingency of God's perfection, 77
Torah as indication of, 78
Hyle
earth, 40-41
matter, 48-49

Ibn Daud, 65
Ibn Ezra, 182
classical exegesis, 2
on spheres, 54
purpose of sacrifices, 122
Ibn Gabirol, 31
*Kether Malchuth*, 29, 31
theory of creation, 29
Ibn Janah, 2
Ibn Sina (see Avicenna)
Ibn Yahyah (*Shalsheleth Hakabalah*), 4
Imagination, 132
creative, 135
prophetic experience as opposed to, 146
relation to prophecy, 161
Interpretation allegorical, 17
Israel
distinction of, 150
uniqueness as prophetic people, 162-163
Israeli, Isaac, 2, 48, 180

Jeremiah, 181
Jews
Christian relations with, 138
prophecy limited to, 162-163
spiritual superiority, 138
Jost, 4
Judah ben Simon, 43

*Kamah* Quantity in Creation, 51
*Kether Malchuth* (Ibn Gabirol), 31
Kimhi, David, 2
*Kinyan*, Possession in Creation, 53
*Koreh Hadoroth* (David Conforte), 4

Lessing, 10
Life, classes of, 60
Lo (see Kinyan)
Luminaries, 50-51

Magic, 195
Maimonides, 1
and Aristotle, 73
attributes of action, 22
attributes of essence, 22
concept of creation, 27, 31, 33, 38-39, 46
concept of free will, 73-74, 156, 174
concept of God, 153ff.

concept of the highest good, 114
concept of matter, 184
concept of prophecy, 129, 131-135, 137, 140-141, 146-147, 161
concept of sacrifices, 122, 124-125. 190
concept of time, 41, 43-45
disagreement with astrologers, 83
disagrees with Halevi, 135-137
disagrees with Mutakallimun, 170
on Divine justice, 87
on function of commandments, 113-115
on knowledge, 115
on negative attributes, 22
on spheres, 54
on soul of the wicked, 68
rejected idea of attributes, 20-21, 24
*Yesodei Hatorah*, 40
*Maamar* in Creation, 48
Man
  as highest creature, 60
  character of, 54
  creation of, 52, 54
  differentiation from animals, 52
  dominion over animal world, 53
  faculties of, 132
  fate of, 81-82, 157
  free will of, 83-84
  freedom of, 156-157
  human intellect, 180
  propagation, 53
  soul of, 127
  submission to God, 128
  ultimate goal of, 128
Marine Biology, 179
*Matai*, Time in Creation, 51
*Matzav*, Position in Creation, 49
Matter, 175-176
  Albo on, 181
  Maimonides on, 179
  Plato on, 176-177, 184
Messiah, 3
Midrash
  creation of angels, 39
  on man's creation, 52
  on time, 43
  quoted from, 2
*Mitztaref*, Relationship in Creation, 53
Moses
  different from prophets, 145, 162

qualities of, 144
talks with God, 133
uniqueness of, 133
vision at burning bush, 148
Mutakallimun
  disagreement with Maimonides, 170

Nahmanides, 2, 148, 175
  on creation, 37

Passive Intellect, 61-63
Philo
  and free will, 70-71, 156
  and function of commandments, 110
  and God's knowledge, 71
  and platonic divisions of soul, 66
  and purpose of sacrifice, 121
  and reason of Torah, 110-111
Philosophy
  and Aristotle, 151
  as a science, 9
  Greek, 8
  Jewish lack of, 14
  medieval, 129, 150, 153
  task of, 152
Plato
  classes of soul, 58, 65, 180
  concept of free will, 156
  concept of matter, 176-177, 184
  theory of creation, 28, 35
  theory of eternity, 35
Plotinus, 42
Pollack, H. J., 4
Prophecy
  Arama's view of, 3
  biblical account, 129
  conditions for, 137, 144
  creative imagination, 134-135
  Divine character of, 161
  gift of, 192
  God's will, 139, 143
  Halevi's concept of, 131
  limited to Jews & Israel, 162-163
  Maimonides discussion of, 129, 131-135
  medieval philosophical concept of, 129
  nature of divine gift, 130
  potential for all men, 191
  prophetic experience, 146–149
  revelation and, 162

starting point of, 134
teaching, 192
true, 143, 163
Prophet
chosen by God, 131, 139-143, 162
false, 133
gentile, 133
Maimonides concept of, 133
moral perfection required, 135
nature of Moses, 133, 144, 162
qualities of, 143-145
requirements of, 162
Punishment
corporate personality and, 101
and reward, 158
of soul of wicked, 67

Quantity in Creation, 178
Arama on Aristotelean, 178

*Rakia*
definition of Arama, 37
creation of, 48ff.
Rashi, 2
Revelation, 136, 143
and reason, 6, 10
Aristotelean, 8
Reward
in Bible, 159
material, 95-96, 98, 159
physical retribution, 159
spiritual, 96, 159
Reward and Punishment, 158
and after life, 88
contradictions in Arama's views of, 97
Divine, 94-95
physical well being, 94
prosperity, 93
prosperity of wicked, 98-99
spiritual nature of, 99
views of, 97
and world to come, 102

Saadia
anthropomorphism, 24, 172
creation, 29, 171
man, 54
time, 42
purpose of Torah, 113
Torah as reason, 111
Torah as revealed, 112
view of Torah, 114

Sabbath
concept of, 154
creation of, 53
institution of, 36
Sabbatical year, 99
Sacrifice
Arama's concept of, 127-128, 161
classes of, 128
importance to Israel, 127
Maimonides on, 190
Nahmanides on, 190
non-sin offering, 127
purpose of, 121-125, 128, 187-188
purpose for laws of, 125
and sin, 189-190
Schechter, Solomon, 7
*Sefer Hadoroth*, 4
*Sefer Yuhasin*, 4
*Shalsheleth Hakabalah*, 4
Shammai and Hillel, 169
*Shamayim*
Arama definition of, 37
creation of, 48ff.
*Siftei Yeshenim*, 4
Sin
and death, 89
and evil as absolute, 93
and evil as negative, 93
Greek concept of, 190
material retribution for, 88-89
non-sin offering, 127
and suffering, 91, 100, 159
sacrifice, 189-190
Six-Day War, 168
*Sopherim*, 23
Soul
active intellect and, 56
animal, 127
Aphrodisius and, 57
Arama on, 155
Aristotle on, 56, 155
Avicenna on, 179
composition of, 60
creation of, 58
destruction of, 68
division into faculties, 60
education of, 62
gradations of, 64
highest development of, 64
hylic form, 60, 62
immortality of, 63, 66
individual and universal, 59
indivisibility of, 66

intellectual character of, 61
lower, 180
of man, 127, 155
medieval categories of, 60
passive intellect and, 55
Plato's concept of, 59, 180
potential intellect of, 55
rational concept of, 60
relation to body, 55, 155
spiritual, 127
Themistius and, 57
Spheres, 154, 176
  Arama on, 154
  Aristotle on, 175
  Avicenna on, 176
  concept of, 54, 57, 58, 176
Sublunary elements, 38
Suffering
  for common good, 101
  God's providence, 92
  instrument for improvement, 91
  punishment, 91
  righteous and, 88, 92, 93
  sin and, 91-92, 100, 159

Talmud
  quoted from, 2
  on man, 54
  on time, 45
Terrence, 10
Theologians, 151
Theology
  relevance of Arama, 165-168
  Arama guide to classical Judaism, 168
  faith pillars of, 166
Themistius, 57
Time
  Arama on, 41ff.
  Aristotle on, 41ff.
  completion vs. existence, 46, 47
  Maimonides, 41ff.
Torah
  Arama on, 161
  authority of, 166
  and Christianity, 106
  Divine authorship of, 110
  guide for moral perfection, 136
  purpose of commandments, 187
  reason related to, 111-113
  revelation of, 113, 136
  Saadia on, 113
  theoretical and practical law, 107-108
True value of life, 94

Universe
  completion of, 53
  creation of, 46
  eternal, 35, 44

Vegetation, 50
Vision
  Abraham three angels, 162
  burning bush, 148
  prophetic experience, 147

Woman, 170

*Yad Avshalom*, 3
*Yamim*, 49
*Yifat*, Action in Creation, 50
*Yitpa'al*, Passivity in Creation, 52

Zacuto, 4
Zemah, David, 4